A Clinical Approach to
Children's Rorschachs

A Clinical Approach to Children's Rorschachs

FLORENCE HALPERN, Ph.D.
Assistant Professor of Clinical Psychology, New York University College of Medicine

Grune & Stratton
A Subsidiary of Harcourt Brace Jovanovich, Publishers

New York   San Francisco   London

Grune & Stratton, Inc.
111 Fifth Avenue
New York, New York 10003

Distributed in the United Kingdom by
Academic Press, Inc. (London) Ltd.
24/28 Oval Road, London NW1

Library of Congress Catalog Number 53-11013
International Standard Book Number 0-8089-0170-2

Printed in the United States of America

4-23-90

To

My Children

Introduction

THIS BOOK constitutes an attempt on the part of the author to communicate to advanced students and practicing clinical psychologists her approach to the interpretation of children's Rorschach records and something of the theory underlying that approach. Some of the statements made here are based on the results of controlled investigation. More of them are based on empirical findings. Having taken and interpreted literally thousands of children's Rorschach protocols, it is impossible to remain unaware of the presence or absence of certain patterns of response and the coexistence of such patterns with specific types of problems. The inferences that have been drawn concerning the meaning of certain responses and the significance of certain test factors at various ages have been checked as carefully as possible against case histories, psychiatric findings and therapeutic results. What is offered here is what has "worked," what has proved consistently helpful in understanding why the child acts as he does and in prognosticating future behavior.

The question arises whether it might not be advisable to delay this communication until all the suggestions offered are subjected to rigorous experimental investigation. The answer is that publication would never occur. The amount of time and energy required for such an undertaking would consume more than one individual's lifetime. Furthermore, methods for validating certain aspects of Rorschach procedure and the meaning of many of the test factors are yet to be discovered.

Despite the fact that such validation is not forthcoming, the use of the test goes on apace. In the years to come, studies undoubtedly will appear which will validate or negate some of these formulations. Until such time they should be considered working hypotheses.

In respect to questions of validation and reliability the Rorschach worker is, in many respects, in much the same position that the clinical psychologist occupied at the beginning of World War II. Pressed into service by emergency needs, the clinical psychologist might have insisted on using only those techniques which had been carefully tested, and proved to be valid and reliable. Instead he employed whatever formulations and procedures had proved valuable in clinical experience. The contributions made by the clinical psychologist during the national emergency, in terms of clinical services rendered to the armed forces, establish beyond question the correctness of the course adopted. Similarly, in the battle to understand the disturbed child, to help him become a more effective individual, the experiences of those who have been working with the Rorschach test for years should prove helpful to others.

The discussion in this book deals with children from two and a half to ten years of age. It covers a variety of clinical syndromes and presents records of children manifesting various forms of mental and emotional disturbances. Diagnosis in each case other than those called "well adjusted" was made by a psychiatrist who was responsible for the child's treatment and disposition. The records of well adjusted children were obtained from subjects who, according to their teachers and their parents, manifested no special disturbances and presented no serious problems. Each child had a complete test battery, but only the Rorschachs are reproduced here. The interpretations offered are therefore based exclusively on the Rorschach findings and consequently do not constitute a complete or integrated report, but simply a discussion of what the Rorschach can reveal about the individual's personality development and functioning.

One of the technical problems that arises in any Rorschach study is the matter of scoring. There are at least three forms of scoring in common use now. This diversity need not present any real difficulties. It should always be borne in mind that the scoring is simply a method of indicating in shorthand what the subject has said. Which form of shorthand is employed is relatively unimportant. The essential thing is to understand what the subject is trying to express and how he goes about expressing it. At best, the scoring is a tool and should never be considered an end itself.

It is with the hope that this material may prove helpful to clinical workers and also provide stimulation for continued research in the theory of personality development that this volume has been written.

Acknowledgments

THE AUTHOR wishes to express her appreciation to Dr. S. Bernard Wortis, Chairman of the Department of Psychiatry and Neurology, New York University College of Medicine, for his kindness in granting permission to reproduce the Rorschach protocols obtained from patients seen at the Child Guidance Clinic of University Hospital, New York University-Bellevue Medical Center. She also wishes to thank her many friends and colleagues who discussed the plan of this book with her, and offered invaluable suggestions for its formulation and development. She is particularly indebted to Miss Estelle Shugerman of Queens General Hospital and Mrs. Marilyn Cohen of University Hospital for their patient reading of much of the text and their very constructive suggestions. Finally, she wishes to express her gratitude to her family, especially to her husband, for the patience and understanding manifested during the period when this work absorbed practically all of her time and energy.

Contents

A Clinical Approach to
Children's Rorschachs

CHAPTER I
Theoretical Concepts*

A s EMPLOYED in this text, personality is conceived of as a dynamic force, evolving out of the individual's efforts to fulfill himself, to satisfy his needs and come to terms with his environment. The direction these efforts take lay out the broad, basic foundations of the structure, while innumerable experiences add layer upon layer to it, reinforcing and modifying the overall trend. The development of personality is essentially a learning process, influenced in part by constitutional factors and in part by the impact of the culture and subculture in which the individual operates.

In the early years of life, the "learning process" which underlies personality development is closely tied in with physiological development. There are therefore certain patterns of behavior common to certain ages of childhood. The "shy" phase and the "negative" period are standard experiences. In addition, however, each child goes through his experiences in a way that is unique for him. In assessing his personality growth, it is therefore essential to determine 1) to what extent his reactions accord with those expected at his age; 2) what are his special problems and conflicts, and 3) what methods he is developing for meeting them.

As in the case of adults, the Rorschach test can be of great value in answering these questions. Normative studies of large groups of children and/or repeated tests of individual children afford remarkable evidence of what goes on in the unfolding personality. The time at which the capacity for differentiation and discrimination between the self and the nonself makes its appearance; when external demands begin to be internalized; how frustration is handled at different ages, and so on, can all be determined with considerable accuracy from the test results.

In interpreting the Rorschach records of children, however, adjustments must be made in terms of the differences that exist between the adult and the child. This is not simply a matter of recognizing that the child is likely to have a low good form per cent or many pure color answers. It involves an understanding of what underlies the child's perceptions and his reactions to them. For example, the fact that so much of what the child is experiencing is novel for him, that he has no backlog of associations to bring to these various experiences, makes it unfeasible to interpret his reactions on the same basis as one would interpret similar or nearly similar reactions in the

* The discussion here assumes that the reader has some familiarity with the Rorschach both in its theoretical and practical aspects.

1

adult. His limited time sense, by itself, gives a different coloring to his experiences, to say nothing at all of the other differences between his perceptions and those of grown-ups. For example, the child who at the moment is the victim of his emotions does not envisage, as the adult well might, a future filled with such disorganizing and disturbing experiences; nor do the possible social, moral, economic and other implications of such an experience concern the child. His world is a very different one from the adult, and it is in terms of that world that his reactions must be interpreted and evaluated.

It is important to bear in mind that even when the child's responses appear to be similar to those of the adult and are scored on the test as the adult responses are, they frequently have little in common. For instance, the adult and the child may both give the same good form response to a certain blot. Such a response implies that the subject has studied the situation, and responded to it in an acceptable fashion. Translated into behavioral terms, the response might mean that both the adult and the child recognize and accept society's decree that there shall be no stealing. The very young child gives the acceptable form of response because he knows he will be scolded and possibly punished if he does not conform; a somewhat older child may also be motivated toward conforming behavior because he wishes to avoid punishment, but added to this may be the desire to avoid hurting or offending his parents. Only in the mature adult will the social and ethical significance of such behavior be recognized and play some part in his response. Such differences in motivation can be inferred in part from the nature of the subject's responses throughout the test, the richness of his general understanding, the level of his social and emotional development. Sometimes the way a response is determined, the reasoning that goes into the interpretation and the explanations the subject offers on the inquiry will show whether the conclusions were arrived at in mature, immature, typical or atypical fashion. Such differences in the way a situation is perceived and responded to cannot be quantified, yet they are of the utmost importance in distinguishing one personality from another and certainly play an important part in understanding the nature of the child's reactions and adjustments.

It is essential, therefore, to evaluate the personality factors and behavorial patterns that find expression in the child's test responses against the background of the child's abilities and outlook. This is not simply a matter of age norms, but an interpretation of these norms in terms of developmental factors and dynamic personality functioning. When the Rorschach records are used to define developmental patterns, three stages of growth can be clearly delineated. The first period covers the years from two and a half to four, the second from four and a half to six, the third from six to ten.

In the youngest group, the nature of the child's reactions is such as to point up his inability to exercise discriminatory and objective capacities. It generally marks the beginning efforts in this direction, as well as the establishment of some concept of himself as an entity separate from his surroundings.

In the second period, emphasis is on discrimination and differentiation; on the development of objective concepts of reality and an acceptance of that reality; on the finding of the self and the establishment of consistent attitudes toward that self, primarily through the identification process; on the internalization of concepts which were at first only perceived as part of the external environment. It is during this period that the child's personality takes on definite structure, in contrast to the diffuse, undifferentiated picture he presented earlier. In analytic terms, the ego has been developed and strengthened, and the superego has come into being.

The six to ten year old now possesses the basic ingredients of a structured personality: he has an ego, a superego and a self-concept. With these he may be expected to operate in broader spheres and less sheltered environments than he previously enjoyed. His strengths must be developed by contact with many ideas and many individuals who will react to him in varying fashion.

While the similarity of their problems and the structured nature of their personalities place the six to ten year olds in one group, it is obvious that with each passing year the child's added experiences and increased capacities will make for changes in the adequacy of his adjustment. It is to this end, to the strengthening of his understanding and his capacities that the activities of this period are devoted. At the end of this period, with the onset of prepuberty, the strengths which the child has presumably acquired enable him to face the new problems set up by the changes, physical and emotional, that are now about to take place.

When the specific problems confronting the child at the various age levels are further considered in terms of a theory of dynamic personality functioning, their meaning becomes even more apparent. Any theory of dynamic personality functioning must be based on the following concepts: 1) all the activity of the individual is goal directed, this goal being the achievement of a state of equilibrium. Drive satisfaction and emotional security are the basic factors involved in the attainment of equilibrium. 2) Activity occurs when equilibrium is disturbed. 3) The type of activity the individual exhibits will be the result of all the experiences he has had up to that moment, modified by constitutional factors. 4) The individual's activity is frequently determined by forces of which he himself has no awareness.

It is obvious, for example, that as the child develops a concept of "self," the problem of equilibrium becomes a very different thing from what it was when he perceived no separation between himself and the rest of the environment. Similarly, as his horizons broaden there is the need to reconcile his established concepts and patterns of behavior with new and alien ones, again without disrupting his equilibrium.

The nature of the Rorschach experiment makes it a particularly successful instrument for investigating personality development and functioning. Based on the concepts of perception and projection,[5, 6, 14] it places the subject in a position which compels him to organize his reactions without any guidance or direction, thus forcing him to expose his habitual modes of response. It also leaves entirely to his discretion what he brings to or takes from the experience. It follows that under such pressure much that the individual produces will be concerned with matters which for him are in a state of tension. The things with which one is preoccupied, mainly on an unconscious level, inevitably intrude themselves into whatever experiences the individual is undergoing at the time. It is therefore the problems that have not been resolved, the dreams and hopes that have not been fulfilled, and the fears that assail the subject that will find expression in the test productions. Clinical experience has strongly supported this assumption that it is primarily stress material, and essentially stress material that is being repressed, that is offered by the subject in his test interpretations. If the contents of the responses are viewed as symbolizations or word pictures that reflect or represent the subject's unresolved problems and unfulfilled desires, careful study of them can greatly enrich the value of the record as an exploratory and descriptive instrument.

However, such understanding of the area and nature of the subject's tension is by no means the whole picture. Insight into the nature of an individual's problems and struggles must be supplemented by understanding of what effect such struggles have upon his development, what adjustments he has made to these stresses, how adequate his handling of them is. The quantitative results obtained from formal scoring of the Rorschach test, the ratios that can be established between various personality trends and factors, provide the answer to these questions. Thus, full interpretation requires an understanding of the personality structure integrated with a knowledge of what it is that specifically motivates the subject in question and what it is that he is concerned about and feels he must adjust to and defend himself against.

In a culture as heterogeneous as ours, the goal seeking activities of the various individuals who comprise that culture and the methods they adopt to arrive at their particular goals may take very different form. Equilibrium can be obtained in a variety of ways since the satisfaction and security that constitute such an important aspect of that equilibrium have different content for different people. For one individual security means love, for another security means power, for still a third it means intellectual achievement. One individual attains his goals by exercising strict control over all emotional reactions, another gains his ends by devoting his energy largely to the establishment of social relationships. There is no one form of adjustment that is acceptable in our society with all others being taboo. How then to determine the adequacy of the individual's adjustment? The essential factors in such an evaluation would seem to be the appropriateness of the behavior both for the given individual and for the external circumstances to which he is reacting. Stated differently, good adjustment is a function of internal and external consistency. The subject's reactions must be in keeping with the nature of the outer environment and with the nature of his inner state. The end product, the response or reaction, thus becomes an integration of these two conditions, external and internal. It is obvious that in the child good adjustment will be something different from what it is in the adult, since the internal conditions, the level of intelligence, the extent of his experience, the nature of his needs and drives, are very different from those of the grown up. Such an evaluation of adjustment has the merit of allowing for difference in age, ability, cultural values, on the one hand, and for differences in the nature of the external pressures on the other.

Finally, a word of caution. While the value of the Rorschach as a clinical tool is established beyond doubt, like any tool it has its limitations. It is a screen through which the individual's underlying stresses and motives can be studied. Important as these underlying factors are, they alone can never constitute the whole answer to any question. Over and against these must be placed conscious motives and goals, as well as all the assets and liabilities the individual possesses. To attempt to wring all the answers from one test is pushing an instrument far beyond what it is intended to do. It also shows a gross lack of understanding of what is implied in projective testing. The projective test gives one side of the picture; interview, observation, historical data, and other tests fill in the rest.

CHAPTER II

Test Administration

ORTHODOX ADMINISTRATION of the Rorschach test[8, 51, 59] requires that the blots be presented to the subject one at a time in consecutive order, with instructions to state everything he sees, "everything it might be." After the subject has responded to the ten cards, the inquiry is then instituted. This is the phase of the examination which establishes the areas of the blot that the subject included in his responses, and the qualities of the blot which determined his interpretations. Finally, there are cases where the paucity of responses and the failure to see certain usual figures and/or to employ certain test factors necessitates "testing the limits." This part of the procedure follows the inquiry.

THE PRESCHOOL CHILD

When working with children, and more especially very young children, the test cannot always be administered in prescribed fashion. The nature of the presentation and the place where the inquiry should be introduced depend to a large extent on the examiner's evaluation of the subject, and also on the aspects of the subject's personality most significant for him. Some children, even very young ones, can and do go through the whole test procedure in controlled, formal fashion, much as an adult would. However, for very young children (two and a half to four years) this is likely to be the exception rather than the rule, and in most instances, at this age level, adjustments must be made in terms of the needs of the particular case.

In general it seems best to give the Rorschach to the preschool child after at least one other test—in most cases an intelligence test—has been administered. For the majority of children the intelligence test is less strange and disturbing than the Rorschach. At this age level the intelligence test almost invariably includes the manipulation of toys, and playing with them has led the child to feel happy, relaxed and positively oriented toward the examiner. This makes him more responsive to the examiner's statement that he now has some new materials to show him. Moreover, by the time the examiner has gone through the intelligence test with the child, he has a good idea of the child's attention span, cooperation and general stability. These impressions will help him decide on the best way of presenting the Rorschach material.

The test is best introduced to the very young child (two and a half to

6

four years) with the following remarks: Did you ever see ink spill on a piece of paper? It makes a big spot on the paper, and sometimes when you look at the spot it makes you think of something; it looks like something. Now you look at these inkblots that I have here and tell me what you find in them, what they make you think of, what they might be.

In this youngest age group it is a good idea to invite the child to come and stand next to you and look at the blots with you. In some instances, putting your arm about the child or inviting him to sit on your lap helps the situation considerably. In any event, an atmosphere intended to convey the impression that you are examining these blots together tends to make for greater cooperation and productivity.

In his examination of the card the child should never be hurried, and the whole procedure should have the quality of an interesting experience without tension. If, after the child gives a response, he acts as though he considered the matter finished, he should be told that it is sometimes possible to find more than one thing in the blots. Again he should be given time and encouragement for this continued effort. In very young children, however, second responses are comparatively rare and too much pressure in this connection should not be exercised. Sometimes in response to the suggestion that he find something else, the child begins to enumerate the parts of the object he has already interpreted. He is likely to say, "I see ears, and a mouth, and wings, etc." In such cases the examiner can say, "Yes, that's right. But can you now see something else besides the ——."

Some extremely restless, distractible children barely look at the cards and make interpretations in most impulsive and arbitrary fashion. In such cases it is better to go along with the child at his own pace and in his own fashion, using the results much as one uses any spontaneous production, more as reactions to the total situation than to the test stimuli per se. The responses are actually in the nature of a "sop," tossed off to placate the adult who is bothering him at the moment. However, his fleeting glimpse of the card will have triggered off some association, and its meaning in relation to the particular card and the examiner should be considered.

It is not advisable to have a watch in evidence or to give any indication that time is a factor. The watch almost inevitably will distract the child who generally finds it much more appealing than the inkblots. The result is that either the watch or the relationship between the child and the examiner will be sacrificed. A rough subjective evaluation of time intervals, made by counting to oneself or in any other way the examiner can devise, will serve most purposes. In general, the fewer things standing around to divert the subject's attention, the better.

For most children of two and a half to four years, the Rorschach test is not a particularly interesting or appealing experience. The child's contact with pictorial material up to that time has probably been almost entirely in terms of large, colored pictures which clearly portray a familiar object which is generally named for the child by the adult who is with him at the time. Confronted with the first vague, black Rorschach blot, many children appear quite startled, and show what might be called "initial shock." Their disturbance frequently causes them to look to the examiner for help, or produces attempts at getting away from the situation. It therefore happens that after one look the child says, "I don't know," or "I don't want to do this," or "It's nothing," "It's scribblescrabble," "My mommy didn't tell me." It is then that the atmosphere of "doing this together" helps considerably. The examiner can then say, "It is a little hard, isn't it? Now take your time and let's see what you can find." If the child continues to protest or if he searches and then protests it is well to say, "Well, let's leave that one and see what the next one looks like." In such instances it is apparent that the child is too disorganized by the impact of Card I to do anything with it at that time. After the card is removed and the second one presented, he can generally proceed to interpret, and may even be able to do something with Card I if it is presented to him when the test is over.

Some children latch onto the examiner's statement about looking at the pictures together and demand to know what the examiner sees. If this occurs after the child has interpreted, the examiner can, of course, state that his impressions are just the same as those the child has offered. Such comments as "That's just what I see," or "That's just what it look like to me" are generally sufficient to satisfy the subject. Occasionally, however, the child will insist that the examiner interpret first. This situation has been successfully met in many instances by saying "You are my guest and the guest always goes first," or by pointing out that the game has to be played in a certain way with the child answering first and then the adult responding. Other questions such as "Is that right?" or "Did you make these?" are of course answered in noncommittal fashion.

Up to about the age of four, and in some cases beyond this, the inquiry is probably most meaningful and helpful if it is conducted right after the card has been interpreted rather than waiting until all ten cards have been seen. However, there is no set rule regarding this matter, and in each instance the examiner should act in accordance with his judgment of the case and what he most wants to ascertain from the Rorschach. Sometimes the examiner's major interest may be in the stability of the child's concepts, and he will therefore delay the inquiry until the free association period is completed. By so doing many responses may be lost and new ones are likely to appear, but the strength and consistency of the child's perceptions will be known. On the other hand, if the examiner is particularly concerned with the individual responses—and this is more generally the case—if he wishes to ascertain what determined them and what feelings and ideas the child associates to them, immediate rather than delayed inquiry is advisable.

Certainly in the case of the extremely restless, disorganized child, even the older child, it is best to conduct the inquiry immediately after the response is given if any inquiry is to be obtained. Even when this is done the responses are often so weakly perceived and poorly organized that discussion on the inquiry has little relation to the original responses. Instead, the interpretation is likely to be denied and/or a new one offered. In such instances asking the child if he can possibly find what he saw previously rarely brings forth a positive answer. The best that can be obtained is his new answer which he may be willing to discuss. However, this too may be immediately denied.

If the inquiry is given after all ten cards have been seen by the subject those cards which were refused originally should be presented again and the child urged to make another effort at interpretation. If he gives any responses, they should be recorded as additionals and, if he insists that he still cannot see anything, this fact should also be noted, as well as his general attitude in connection with this failure; that is, whether he appears anxious, depressed, indifferent, defiant, and whether this and all other failures lead to changes in general behavior.

Whether the inquiry be given right after the response or after all ten cards have been interpreted, it needs no special introduction. In fact the fewer verbal directions and explanations that are made to the youngest age group, the better. The examiner can simply place Card I in front of the child and say, "Remember you said this was a bird? Show me the bird." The difficulty with the inquiry begins right here, because what the child almost inevitably does is to put his finger on the blot at any point, and then look hopefully at the examiner. When the examiner says, "Show me the whole bird," the finger is likely to move to a different part of the blot and the hopeful look is followed by a puzzled one. Directions to run the finger around the bird or to point out the different parts of the bird rarely meet with much success. It is therefore frequently impossible to be sure just what area the interpretation covered, and the scoring must be somewhat arbitrary and subjective in this connection (see p. 16). "Tell me more about this bird," or "Did you ever see a bird like that?" sometimes helps to clarify the matter of area as well as determinant. Since the records of these young children are very short and consume very little time, more effort can be spent in this kind of informal conversation which often goes a long way toward elucidating questionable matters. The request to tell more about the bird, or similarly worded questions, sometimes loosens a whole flood of associations and the card becomes a stimulus that produces as much or more than is obtained from a *CAT** picture.

On the other hand, there are children who, despite all efforts to evoke associations, continue to respond with monosyllables which in no way clarify their responses. In such cases more direct questioning can be used. Thus, with the child who says "It's a bird," and can add nothing to that statement other than possibly, "It looks like it," it is helpful to say directly, "Is this bird doing anything?" Any movement elicited by means of this frontal attack cannot be scored as movement, but from the qualitative point of view much can be learned about the child by such tactics. Other questions which do not involve movement are also most important, such as "Tell me about the house? Is it a nice house? Who lives in the house?"

The difficulty in obtaining any inquiry from the child is accentuated by his inability to explain just why he made a particular interpretation. The child who sees apples in the pink area of Card IX generally cannot explain what made him think of apples. His resources are not sufficient for him to be able to expand his perceptions so that others may experience them as he did. Frequent explanations are: "It looks like it," or "I saw one like it," "My mommy has one." To this the examiner should reply by asking, "What makes it look like an apple, what does it have that's like an apple?" Or again, "What does this have that makes it look like the apple your mommy has?" However, too much pushing frequently irritates and tires the child, and cooperation may be completely lost if too persistent an inquiry is conducted with very young children.

Thus, despite the examiner's efforts, it very frequently happens that the responses obtained remain more or less undetermined, both as to area and rationale. While this naturally leaves the results somewhat doubtful, it does not invalidate whatever positive findings do accrue. Again it is important to recognize that the Rorschach sometimes simply serves as a reference point from which to observe the young child's reactions in situations which are completely unfamiliar, uninteresting and possibly disturbing to him. In such circumstances the actual scoring of any one individual response will not be too important. Rather, in cases where the results are meager, and vaguely and arbitrarily formulated, the overall behavior is perhaps the most valuable product of the test experience. Since the child communicates as much through his behavior as he does verbally, the examiner should note all significant reactions, either at the time they occur or, if this is impossible, as soon as the testing session is over. There is a decided difference between the child who is disturbed when first confronted with the cards, and who immediately says, "I want to go to my mommy," and the child who throws the card down and starts to run around the room,

* Children's Apperception Test, Bellak, L. and Bellak, S.

acting in silly fashion. Again, there is the child who does well until he comes to Card IV and then expresses his disturbance by trying to break the card. Sudden recourse to thumb sucking, hair pulling, handling of genitals, all point to an influx of anxiety. There are children who try to distract the examiner and thus escape the situation, but they do this quite maturely, by discussing some object in the room, or some experience they have recently undergone.

It is the writer's opinion that testing the limits should be used as sparingly as possible, and only resorted to when something very definite can be learned about the child which could not be ascertained in any other way. Routine testing of limits seems bad policy both because it tends to invalidate future uses of the test and because it is an additional demand on the child. In the case of the child under five, it is rarely, if ever, advisable to suggest some of the adult populars to him. At best, it would seem helpful to point out one or two of the responses common for his age, such as a "tree" or a "giant" on Card IV, "windows" on Card I. This should only be done when no responses have been forthcoming. Such suggestions from the examiner sometimes help to clarify the situation for the child and with a little urging he will then go ahead and make further associations on his own.

The School Age Child

Administration of the Rorschach to the school age child follows much the same procedure used with adults. The child is told that he is to be shown inkblots and he is to tell the examiner everything they look like to him, everything he sees in them, everything they might be. The wording of the instruction should naturally be such that the child is not left with the impression that he is to interpret the blot as a whole or that only one interpretation is required. The following form has proved most successful with children of five and a half and older: "Do you know what an inkblot is? It is a big spot that you see on paper when ink has been spilled on it. Sometimes when you look at an inkblot it reminds you of different things, you can see different things in it. I have some inkblots here and I want you to tell me all the different things you see in them, everything you can make out of them." The child is then offered the card and, if he does not attempt to hold it, he is asked to do so, so that the examiner may "write down all the things he sees."

Some children launch right into interpretation and there is no further difficulty. Others look at the examiner questioningly and state that it is an inkblot. They are then urged to tell what the inkblot looks like. Sometimes the child picks out from the directions simply the words, "things that you see," and starts out by saying, "I see a line. I see two holes, etc."

At this point the examiner should repeat, "But what does it look like, what could it be?" Occasionally there are children who even then can only describe. These are usually children who cannot interpret, whose personality disturbances make it impossible for them to handle the assignment at any level other than enumeration or description. However, for the majority of children, one restatement with emphasis on "what it looks like" or "what might it be" is sufficient to set them off correctly.

Like younger children, a very large percentage of this school age group also tend to stop after one response. They look at the examiner for approval and are ready to put the card down. The statements used with adults, such as, "Could it be anything else?" or "Sometimes people see more than one thing," will generally elicit additional interpretations if the subject is able to give them. Again, as with the younger child, such prompting may simply lead to further elaboration of the original answer. Thus one little boy interpreted Card I as an "eagle with wings and a tail." Urged to give additional interpretation he said, "and I see a head, and he has white on him, etc." This tendency to elaborate rather than reorganize was directly broken through by saying, "Could you make anything else out of it besides an eagle?" It is important to find out if the child is capable of giving additional responses and has not done so because he has misinterpreted the directions or whether he actually cannot reorganize a stimulus once he has set it up.

Occasionally there is a child who sets up a resistance to the entire test procedure by insisting that he sees nothing. From the very way this is done, with a mixture of defiance and indifference and a superficial scanning of the first card, it is apparent that the child has no intention of cooperating. In such cases accepting the rejection of Card I would be a serious mistake. Rather, the child must be made to understand that he must continue to look at the blot until he finds something. The frustration and anger he feels at this turn of events may provoke tears, but after a short period of weeping, a face saving device offered by the examiner is generally seized on and the testing goes ahead quite normally. The face saving device need only be some concession on the part of the examiner, such as a statement to the effect that it is a hard task, but probably the child has found something by now, or won't it be fun to try this game with his friends when he gets home.

For children of school age, the inquiry can in most instances be given after all ten cards have been interpreted. A good way to introduce the inquiry is to say, "Those were very nice answers; I enjoyed them very much. Now I want you to show me where some of these things are, point them out to me in the blot." The child sometimes looks a little puzzled at this request, but it has been found advisable to go ahead with the inquiry without further explanation. Children on the whole only become confused by long verbal elaborations, while simply presenting the blot and saying, "Show me the eagle you saw" clarifies the whole matter for them in many cases.

The school child can generally give some explanation of responses, although there are some children, expecially the younger ones in the group, who have difficulty communicating what determined their answers. There are also children who tend to deny their responses. Told that they saw a bear on Card I, they are likely to say, "No, I didn't. I never said that. You must have made a mistake." Sometimes pointing out that the answers were written down in the order that they were produced convinces the child that he should make an effort to find the "bear." Others, however, are adamant, insisting that the examiner is in error. When the child persists in this fasion it is advisable to say, "Well, what do you see now?"

As with the younger age group, testing limits should be used sparingly. However, for the school age child there are times when this procedure may have considerable value. There are some children who hold themselves to such high standards that they cannot make allowance for the fact that the blots do not entirely coincide with the associations which occur to them. They therefore hesitate to give any response and sometimes give little or nothing in their protocols. When the examiner suggests certain answers which are apparent to the child he takes courage and proceeds to offer interpretations of his own. In these cases the whole record is sometimes obtained only after such help from the environment.

It is much less frequent and therefore a much more significant deviation for a school age child to be so distractible as to require the instigation of the inquiry immediately after the giving of a response. Most children of five and over can go through the test as the adult does. However, in cases of extremely disturbed subjects the examiner must use his discretion as to how to conduct the examination.

Cards which are refused in the initial presentation should always be presented again in the inquiry. As the examiner places the blot in front of the child he should say, "Now you didn't find anything in this one before. Maybe you can find something now." Very frequently the child can take advantage of this second opportunity, but if he cannot he should not be pressed or made to feel that he is in any way lacking.

A certain number of children at all ages want to known whether the examiner made the blots and how they were made. In some cases it becomes absolutely necessary to demonstrate the process and let the child try his hand at making blots. In fact this is one very helpful way of winning greater interest and responsiveness from recalcitrant subjects.

It goes without saying that all spontaneous remarks, laughter and other reactions should be recorded. Many children begin each card with some sterotyped expression like, "Golly" or "Gee whiz." Sometimes they launch into long accounts of recent experiences, movies they have seen, parties they have attended, and so on. All this should be noted as completely as possible at the place in the testing where it occurred.

Turning of the card should be recorded in usual fashion, that is by means of a caret, with the apex of the figure indicating the position of the top of the card. Some notations on time should also be made. In the case of the very young child, where the use of the watch would be too distracting, the indication of long pauses by the use of dots is sometimes helpful. With older children a watch can be used, though in such cases it may be necessary to point out to the child that the time factor is essentially unimportant, that it is not like a school test, and that he need not rush. When a stop watch is employed it has sometimes been found most helpful to allow the child to explore the workings of the watch for a few minutes. He is then content to go on with the test rather than give his attention to the timepiece.

With the school age child it is also often necessary to convey to him in some fashion that quantity is not necessarily desirable. Some children apparently feel that the more responses they give the better. While in itself this attitude has considerable significance and must be interpreted accordingly, it is well if the examiner can in some way get over to the child the fact that it is not necessary for him to go on searching endlessly for answers. After five or six forced interpretations it is therefore well to say "Now, that's fine," the tone of voice implying that the examiner is more than satisfied. Reaching for the next card while the child continues his search will also sometimes convey to the subject the idea that he has done enough with that particular blot.

Because he is so sensitive to the concepts of right and wrong, so frequently concerned about his marks and his standing in relation to others, such procedures must always be carried out in a manner which in no way discourages the child or makes him feel he has done something that is not correct or desirable. Similarly, when he asks if his answers are "right," and is told that he's "doing fine," he may not always be satisfied. While some children accept this, or similar statements such as, "I find your answers very interesting," or "They're very good answers," others persist in their demand to know if they are "correct." When it is explained to them that there is no right or wrong response, and that anything they see is interesting and acceptable, they become puzzled and possibly disturbed. Among other things, they want to know how the test can be marked if there are no expected answers. The examiner must be careful in these cases not to give the impression that "anything goes" and so open the flood gates of "wild" imagination; yet at the same time he must satisfy the child that what he sees is correct for him. For one thing it can be stated that this test is not marked as others are, that the child will not get an "A" or a "C," that in a sense the word "test" is a misnomer. Rather it is a little experiment which will enable the examiner to understand the child and so help him in school or at home, or wherever he has difficulties.

In general the closer to standard form the test procedure adheres, the more objective the interpretation of the findings is likely to be. On the other hand, production should not be sacrificed to form. It must always be borne in mind that any activity or reaction of a subject is a valid sample of his behavior and should be treated accordingly.

CHAPTER III

Scoring*

SCORING THE RORSCHACH test constitutes a means by which the patient's productions can be quantified, making it possible to set up relationships between various personality factors, and thus deal with the test material in numerical fashion. The scoring is therefore of great value in establishing various norms and, in general, is an important asset in test evaluation. However, it is only a tool, a means toward an end, and should not be considered an end in itself. Similarly, it should by no means be considered the only method by which the patient's productions can be evaluated.

Children's interpretations are scored in the same way that the responses of adults are scored, and any allowance that is made for the child's general immaturity and lack of control and experience is made in the interpretation of the final psychogram, not in leniency of scoring. However, there are a number of special problems that come up in connection with the actual scoring of the individual answers that do not arise in the case of adults. In many instances the child cannot explain why he made a certain interpretation and simply says, "It looks like it," shrugs and points, or gives other indication that he cannot communicate his thinking and feeling in connection with the particular experience. The question then arises as to whether such responses should be scored good or bad form, whether factors other than form should be included in the scoring, if they seem to be implied but are not so designated by the subject.† The answer to such questions must be left to the discretion of the examiner in each case. Certainly, in the case of many children, a response that remains unexplained does not have the same implication of vagueness that it has in the case of an adult. The child may actually have perceived the answer well but be incapable of explaining it. The general level of the child's performance throughout, his productivity and the way he expresses himself on all occasions may indicate whether the immediate failure to express himself is

* Scoring concepts are well covered in the literature, and therefore will only be briefly dealt with in this chapter. For a more complete discussion the reader should consult: Beck, S., *Rorschach's Test*, Vol. I and Klopfer, B. and Kelly, D., *The Rorschach Technique*.

† For example, the interpretation of "flowers" on Card X certainly seems to make use of the color, yet the child may insist that "it just looks like flowers," and no further explanation may be obtainable.

16

the result of vague and inadequate perception or simply a reflection of his limited capacity for communication and explanation.

Scoring concerns itself with three aspects of an interpretation, namely, the subject's mental approach, his emotional approach and his interests and concerns at the time of the testing. The mental approach reflects itself in the area of the blot that is selected for interpretation; the emotional reactions are revealed by the factors that determine the response; and the subject's preoccupations are reflected in the content of his interpretation.

AREA

There are essentially four major location areas. The entire blot (W) can be used in interpretation; the large obvious areas (D) into which the blot naturally divides itself can be selected; small and unusual areas can be chosen (d); and the white background (S) can be dealt with while the blot can be relegated to the background.

Variations occur in the scoring of the whole answer, depending upon the way the whole response is achieved. When the entire configuration is grasped as an entity and so used in interpretation, the response is a whole response and scored W. In some instances the whole response is built up impulsively on the basis of a detail, and it is the perception of this detail that determines the answer, even if the rest of the blot does not coincide with the object or figure interpreted. This is the so-called "confabulated" whole response (DW). The interpretation of Card VI as "a cat because of the whiskers" (the feathery details at the top of the blot) is an example of a DW response.

In contrast to the confabulated whole answer there are whole responses which are built up slowly, in step by step fashion (D → W) with parts perceived and finally organized into a whole. For example, on Card IV, a subject may first see the big feet, then the arms, then add, "And here is something like a head, while that bottom thing might be a tail. I guess it's a gorilla."

Responses which leave out some small aspect of the blot, are scored W̄. Card VII, interpreted as "two women," using all of the blot except the little pawlike extensions on the middle section is an example of a W̄.

Responses which include not only the entire blot but also the white space in or around the blot are scored WS. The response "map" on Card I, using the entire blot plus the inner white spaces, constitutes a WS answer.

The large obvious areas into which the blot divides itself constitute the bulk of the D interpretations.[28, 37, 59] In addition to them, there are certain areas which are so frequently selected for interpretation that, despite the relatively small size of these areas, they are scored D. The two handlike projections on the top center area of Card I and the lower, central areas of

Card VII are examples of such small areas which are scored large detail because of the frequency with which they are dealt with in Rorschach records.

When a large detail response (D) is combined with an adjacent white area the scoring becomes DS. The center area of Card I interpreted as a "face" with the white spaces as "eyes" and "teeth" is scored DS.

Any response which is not a whole or a large detail response becomes a d or rare detail answer. Interpretation of the long, stringlike area of the side red detail on Card III would be scored *d*. The spurlike aspects of the usual boot on Card IV, if interpreted without reference to the rest of the area is scored *d*.

Occasionally a large, but most unusual area of the blot is used in interpretation. It is not a natural, obvious division of the blot, and is not ordinarily responded to by the majority of people. Rather it represents an atypical organization of the stimulus and as such becomes a rare detail. However it is distinguished in scoring from the small rare detail (d) by the use of the symbol *Dr*. The large side figures in Card I are scored D. If these figures are cut in half on the vertical plane, either half would constitute a *Dr* response.

The use of any white area by itself without the inclusion of any of the blot, a white space interpretation, is scored S. The large center space on Card VII is a relatively frequent space interpretation.

DETERMINANTS

Four major types of experience determine Rorschach answers. There are the responses based on the formal aspects of the stimulus (form responses); those which show varying degrees of emotional involvement (color); those where fantasy activity plays a conspicuous part (movement); and those which are concerned with reactions to anxiety (shading).

Form responses are those which concern themselves solely with the outline of the area interpreted. In interpretations scored F, the only factor that determines the answer is the contour of the area involved.

Form responses can be at any one of three levels of accuracy. The form may coincide with the form of the blot with sufficient accuracy to be considered good form, in which case the scoring is simply F+. On the other hand, the interpretation may not bear sufficient resemblance to the blot to warrant such scoring but, rather, being forced, distorted or vaguely perceived must be considered poor form, and so labeled F−. Finally, there are interpretations which the subject states are based on form but where exact form actually plays little part, as in the case of "maps," "clouds," "designs." Such responses are scored F±.

When movement is ascribed to the objects or figures interpreted this is indicated in the scoring as follows: Human figures (including supernatural figures such as ghosts or fairies) are scored M; animal figures in motion are indicated by the score FM; while inanimate motion (leaves falling, wind blowing) are denoted by the score m, or Fm, depending on whether form plays a part in the interpretation or the answer is one dealing with an unstructured force.

Chromatic color is recorded as C, CF, or FC, depending on whether form is used at all in the interpretation, and if it is used, the extent to which it plays a part in determining the response. Thus "the red is blood" would be scored C; while "this is a blood spot" would be scored CF. A "butterfly, probably a tropical one because of the color," would be an FC response.

Achromatic color (black, white and gray) is scored C', $C'F$ or FC', again in terms of whether the form or the color are more important in determining the production.

The shading of the blots is also a factor in the determination of certain responses. A distinction is made between responses based on shading as surface impression (c) and those involving depth and perspective (K). Surface impressions are indicated by the scorings, c, cF and Fc, depending upon the part form plays in the interpretation. A bearskin rug on Card IV where the interpretation stresses the form of the blot but also takes note that the shading gives the impression of fur is scored Fc. Conversely, if the shape is of little importance and the texture is stressed, the same response would be scored cF. The interpretation of "cotton" for the lower third of Card VII, an answer based solely on the impression of texture, would be scored c.

Depth impressions which are of a structured order and employ the concept of perspective or vista are scored FK. The lower center detail of Card VII interpreted as "a house between two mountains" would be scored FK if the inquiry indicated that the shading gave the effect of depth and distance. When the concept of depth is of a diffuse order, the scoring will be either KF, as in the case of "billowy clouds" or possibly simply K, if the question of shape does not enter into the formulation in even a secondary role.

The scoring, k, kF and Fk, is used when a three dimensional concept is projected on a two dimensional plane. Responses like "x-ray" and "topograpical map" and "photograph negative" fall into this category.

A number of responses require scores which combine determinants. For example, the lower red section of Card II interpreted as "an exploding bomb" because it is shooting up, and it is red, and it takes the form associated with an explosion, would be scored mCF. In such cases it is always important to determine whether all the determinants are primary, that is, whether the response would not have been possible for that particular subject unless all the elements were present, or whether only certain aspects are primary and the others simply elaborations. In the example just cited, all three components seem essential to the response, but when Card III is interpreted as "two men bowling," and the subject continues, "They certainly look like men even though they have high-heeled shoes on. I notice that they are wearing white collars," the human activity is basic to the interpretation and the discussion of white collars only an elaboration. The scoring would therefore be M,FC'. The M is the primary determinant, and the FC' included in the psychogram only as an additional determinant. Similarly, responses given during the inquiry are also only included in the psychogram as additionals.

CONTENT

The content of the responses is scored according to generic categories. All animals—birds, mammals, fish, etc.—are scored A, while parts of animals are scored Ad. Humans are scored H, parts of humans Hd and human bones and viscera as At. Inanimate objects are denoted by the symbol Obj; flowers, plants and trees by Pl, and so on.

Responses which occur as frequently as once in every five records or more often, are indicated by the letter P, standing for "popular." Responses which occur only once in every 100 records or even less often are scored O, "original." In scoring the popular answers it should be borne in mind that these responses are "popular" or frequent in the adult, but do not have that significance for the child (see p. 40).

A psychogram is obtained by establishing the number of times each test factor was used. Thus, all whole responses are added together, all large detail answers are totaled, the number of human movement, animal movement, etc., responses are counted. Color responses are weighted in the manner suggested by Rorschach[8, 59] and the color sum thus obtained. Percentages are calculated for the whole, large detail, small detail, form, and animal answers. Also the percentage of form responses which are good form is determined.

As with adults, an experience balance is set up by comparing the number of human movement answers with the color sum.[8, 59] However, in the case of children there is some question as to the significance of this (see p. 33). This matter will be discussed in detail in Chapter IV.

The Significance of the Test Factors

THE COMPLEXITY of the Rorschach procedure is caused in part by the fact that, while each test factor has a certain general significance, this significance is always modified by the nature of the circumstances in which it occurs. Thus, the creative attributes of the human movement answer may take the form of healthy productivity or may be the outpourings of a paranoid schizophrenic. Similarly, an emphasis on large details may reflect the concreteness of an individual of relatively limited endowment or the constriction and detachment of a compulsive neurotic, etc.

In dealing with the Rorschach responses of children, not only must the meaning of each test factor be interpreted in terms of the total configuration, but there must also be understanding of the relationship that exists between each factor and the developmental processes that the child is undergoing. For example, the presence of a number of poor form responses in the protocol of either an adult or a child points to poor intellectual control and judgment. In the adult this is suggestive of serious personality disturbances, whereas in the child, up to a certain age, this is in line with expectancy. Similarly, in the affective area, there are considerable differences in the types of emotional responses the child is required to give at different ages. For this purpose, not only developmental norms,[1, 13] but interpretation of those norms is essential.

In the succeeding pages the general meaning of each test factor will be discussed, followed by an analysis of the developmental course it pursues.

AREA

The Whole Response

The psychological significance of a whole response depends in large measure on the quality of the end product.[2, 8, 37, 59] This can range from a completely undifferentiated, arbitrarily conceived answer to an extremely well organized response of superior quality, in which the essentials have been perceived and welded together to form a successful, integrated resolution of the experience. From the developmental point of view it is the undifferentiated whole answer that appears first. The very young child, that is, the two and a half to four year old, gives predominantly, if not exclusively, these arbitrary whole answers. His emphasis on this type of response stems from his inability to select from his experiences the essential, usual, basic aspects of them. If he does manage to isolate one detail, he is likely to respond impulsively and uncritically, ending up with a confabulation (DW).

Sometimes when pressure is put on him, the child will end up with a W because the examiner's questions have led him to believe something is wrong with what he is doing and that he should not have employed the whole blot. He tries to remedy his error by leaving out some small area; this omission rarely has a truly logical basis. The selectivity on such occasions is therefore an arbitrary gesture, intended to satisfy the immediate demands of the adult with whom the child is working at the moment.

Some selectivity is already present in whole responses of the "crude" but accurate type, such as "bird" on Card I. In giving such an interpretation, the subject has generally recognized the wings and used them for the development of his concept. Such reactions can and, on occasion, do occur at the very earliest ages (two and a half to three and a half), intermingled with less acceptable ones. In other words, when the circumstances are simple and relatively familiar, the reasonably adequate child (average or better) can handle them accordingly.

Responses built up from large details to wholes are not too frequent until school age. It is then that the child is likely to see the usual "boots" on Card IV and suddenly recognize that the entire figure could be a "giant."

Well structured whole responses which require both abstracting and synthesizing for their production occur most infrequently in children before five, and even after five are not numerous. The capacities necessary for giving such an answer are not present much before the seventh or eighth year.

The use of the white space in conjunction with the whole blot is discussed below.

The Large Detail Response

The large detail answers[8, 59] are the most obvious units in the stimulus material. Response to them therefore reflects a certain practical, commonsense approach, a capacity for going along in the usual, commonplace grooves. Despite their obviousness, however, these aspects of an experience, which are so evident to the adult, are not perceived by the child with any frequency until he is somewhere between six and eight years of age. It requires training and experience for him to recognize and respond to them with any consistency. Thus, while the very young child may give one or two large detail responses in his Rorschach record, these are relatively rare until about the fourth to fifth year of life. At six they occur about as often as do the whole responses, and sometime between eight and ten the relationship between the whole and large detail answers is roughly in accord with the W:D ratio found in adults.

Occasionally however there are young children—five to six year olds—

who definitely stress the detail answers, and come up with a high D%. These are children who, given the capacity for such selectivity, exploit it to the limit. This exploitation is motivated by their strong need to find concrete and well delimited experiences which will give structure and security to their world. They employ much of their energy to this end, and so develop a compulsive tendency to handle all their experiences in this detached selective fashion. If the disturbances underlying this drive for concreteness and detachment are not alleviated, these children generally develop into compulsive neurotics (see Record 21, page 174).

The Small Detail Response

The use of the small detail (d) is most rare in the very young child. Before four or five, it almost never occurs. With the development of selective capacities it gradually makes its appearance. However, it is never stressed in the healthy child to any appreciable extent. Its presence is evidence of distractibility or efforts at escape and avoidance.

The Space Response

Space responses are relatively frequent in the records of the preschool child.[1, 13] To a large extent these are space responses in conjunction with all or part of the blot, that is, WS or DS answers. From his discussion of these responses, it is easy to perceive that the child is unduly aware of the open space, the emptiness of the area. His concern about this and the tensions this emptiness appears to evoke in him seem to be a reflection of his own sense of inadequacy. The greater the number of these responses, the greater the child's tension and preoccupation in connection with his sense of insecurity. However, when these space responses come only on the first one or two cards, and then disappear, they may well be expressions of the subject's feelings of inadequacy in the face of the test situation, and give evidence of his negativistic reactions to that situation. When they continue to appear throughout the protocol they reflect a more basic and all-pervasive sense of insufficiency.

Space responses without any adjacent area (S) are less frequent than the WS and DS answers. They are generally considered indicative of oppositional trends in that their production is based on the complete reversal of figure and ground. It is true that children of three and four are described as going through a negative phase. It is questionable, however, if this negativism—if it actually exists—would find expression in the production of space responses. Rather, these very young children are as likely to be attracted by the shiny white surface of the card as by the black area. Thus when large white areas, such as those on Cards II and VII, are selected for interpretation, the reactions need not be indicative of negativism. Rather they suggest unconventional exploration of the environment. It is true that such exploration may give the impression of nonconformity and negativism, but the underlying motivation need not be such.

Approach and Sequence

The "approach" is the term used in Rorschach literature to indicate the way in which an individual handles situations. In the adult there is considerable variability in the approach, some individuals consistently employing a broad, sweeping form of response, others emphasizing practical details, still others escaping into minutiae. In the child there is much less variability. Up until about the age of seven or eight the general tendency is to emphasize the whole response, that is, to deal with experiences in an all-encompassing fashion. To a large extent, as has been indicated (see p. 21), this emphasis on the whole response is essentially a functioning of the child's limited capacity for differentiation and discrimination. These capacities develop, however, from a point where they are practically nonexistent at two and three, to the stage, at about eight or nine, where they are roughly comparable to what is seen in the adult. Only in a small number of children will there be an approach which emphasizes large details rather than whole interpretations. The significance of this atypical form of response has already been covered. For the majority of children there is a gradual development of the capacity to recognize and respond to the commonsense, practical, usual aspects of their experiences and to treat these as the adult would.

In adult records the sequence in which the responses appear and the consistency with which this sequence obtains from card to card is of considerable interpretive value. Again, with children this is less significant, both because of their tendency to emphasize whole answers and their relatively meager productivity. In the case of the preschool child this is particularly true, since the answers are likely to be almost all whole ones. However, any break in this emphasis on whole interpretations, any sudden shift to details, especially as first answers to a card, has significance which should be evaluated in terms of the place where it occurs and the nature of the interpretation given.

Where the records are relatively long and varied, especially in the case of children from seven or eight to ten, some consideration of sequence is indicated. As in the case of the adult, it is important to note what breaks in sequence occur and what underlies these deviations in response.

DETERMINANTS

Form

The form responses are those determined solely by the outlines of the interpreted area. In responding on the basis of form, the individual is drawing on learned experiences, training and memory. The process is therefore a formal one, involving objectivity and control in contrast to reactions which are colored by emotional factors. When the form is acceptable it is assumed that the individual's control and ability have been operating at an effective level. When the form is poor, weakness of understanding and/or loss of control are indicated.

In very young children it is questionable if the form response is the purely intellectual, nonemotional reaction that it is for adults. Rather, there is a fusion of emotional and formal factors which is not clearly reflected in the scoring. The two and three year old child cannot be truly objective, cannot detach feeling from his experiences, nor arrive at the point where the need for such differentiation is recognized as necessary. In consequence his responses have a very subjective coloring, even though orthodox scoring puts them in the form category.

Not only does the fusion of formal and emotional factors make objective evaluation of his experiences impossible for the very young child, but his limited contact with the world, his meager vocabulary, and his general lack of resources prevent him from structuring his world in effective, stable fashion. He has only a weak and fluid grasp of reality, is only beginning to identify, categorize and understand the world about him, and he therefore shifts readily back and forth between realistic and unrealistic formulations. Only with time does he recognize that there is an objective reality by which he must abide. Thus, in the child under four, the number of poor form responses that appear in his Rorschach record is likely to equal or exceed the number of good ones he gives.

Gradually the form percentage improves; generally between four and five years of age it rises to 70 per cent. This improvement plus the appearance and/or increase of other types of responses (movement and color) denote the beginnings of discrimination in the personality structure, the acceptance, even at a weak level, of the distinction between control and objectivity on the one hand, and subjective and emotional reactions on the other. This initial discrimination generally coincides with an increase in the number of large detail responses.

By the time the child reaches school age the form responses have attained an accuracy that compares favorably with that of the adult, that is, his good form percentage will be as high as 80 per cent, if not better. In fact, at about six to seven, the child's rigid concepts of right and wrong, good and bad, often produce very high F+ percentages.

It is at this period of his life that the child feels the weight of responsibility associated with his newly established "self." For him, right and wrong are very definite, clear-cut concepts which cannot be altered by a single jot or tittle; "rules" are emphasized. As the novelty of functioning on his own in the social sense begins to wear off, the exaggerated need for exactness also abates, and the child is more willing to take a chance, to modify his concepts or risk certain experiences. Thus the good form percentage may actually be a little lower at eight or nine than at six and seven.

Movement

Movement answers of all kinds, that is, movement in relation to humans (M), animals (FM), or inanimate forces or objects (Fm), have certain factors in common. To begin with, the fact that there is no movement in the blot, that the subject must bring something to the situation, gives to each movement response the attribute of a creative act. In common with all creative acts, whether these are of a truly artistic order or are in the category of nightmares and daydreams, they reflect the individual's hopes, fears, desires and dreams. Furthermore, since they find their outlet through a creative act rather than through more direct expression, they indicate that the wish, fear or dream, is internalized and, in part at least, experienced on an unconscious level. Such internalization generally takes symbolic form.

That this type of internalization of hopes, desires and dreams rarely occurs in the two and a half to three and a half year old is not surprising. Again, such an approach to desires and wishes can only take place when the individual has some concept of himself as an entity apart from the rest of the world, as well as an awareness that direct release of such emotions into the environment is not desirable or acceptable. When this method of handling emotional experiences on an internalized, symbolic level first occurs, that is, when feelings begin to be internalized, a definite step in the structuring or differentiation of the personality has taken place.

In the early stages of this process, that is at two and a half to three years, any internalization and symbolization that does take place is as likely to be made in terms of inanimate as of animate objects. The child's sense of kinship with the simpler, more primitive forms of life is probably as great as, if not greater than, with the more complex ones. In this sense, the Fm, the FM and the M responses in children up to about four might well be added together to give an indication of the extent to which they can and do internalize their experiences (see p. 34). In this connection, however, there is room for further speculation. Since the child at this age does not yet perceive himself as completely emotionally separated from the world around him, his relatively frequent use of the Fm might well be indicative of the extent to which he still considers himself part of the total universe, the degree to which his sense of "omnipotence" is still operating. In contrast to this is the frequency with which he can actually conceive of himself as a "person," an individual in his own right. In other words, at this period the child is gradually moving away from his undifferentiated sense of oneness with the world to a more discriminating awareness of self, and the ratio between the Fm and the M responses might give some indication of the extent to which this process has been developed.

Between four and six, this process is generally completed and the number of Fm gradually declines. In the latency period the animal responses are the more numerous, and it is largely through the use of the animal interpretation that the child finds the means to express his dreams and conflicts. In the child the animal response is something different from what it is in the adult. For the adult, it may represent unacceptable impulses he cannot ascribe to himself; for the child the activity of the animal is often more meaningful and frequently more truly representative of his feelings than that of the adult. The introduction of the human movement response marks the beginning of the child's identification with adult concepts, outlooks and attitudes. Until prepuberty there is relatively little of this as compared with his more immature perception of himself and his role.

In interpreting the meaning of the movement answers, it is important to feel oneself into the experience, if necessary to adopt the position described and undergo the body tensions the particular activity carries with it. In this way much of what the child is feeling and attempting to express becomes clearer and more fully appreciated. In this connection the question as to whether these experiences are what the child feels and identifies with or what he imputes to others constantly comes up. There can be no doubt that these are what he feels, otherwise he would not produce them. That he imputes them to others is also inevitable, since he can only understand people in terms of what he himself has experienced.

With the coming of prepuberty and early puberty the picture alters radically. At that time, the physical and emotional changes that are taking place necessitate a reevaluation of the self, and at this period this is achieved primarily through human identification. The prepuberty and early puberty records are therefore characterized by many human movement interpretations, and this is the first time that the M answers equal or outweigh the animal movement responses.

Any child who, before the prepuberty or early adolescent period, emphasizes human movement interpretations at the expense of animal movement is manifesting precocity, healthy or unhealthy. The child may be unusually mature, but in most instances such emphasis is likely to be the result of anxiety about the self stemming from difficulties in identification. These difficulties may be due to the child's inability to find himself and integrate his concepts of himself effectively, as in the case of some schizophrenic children. In their anxiety-ridden efforts to stabilize themselves, they take on many roles with much rapidity and fluidity, roles which are frequently out of line with what most children adopt. Unless this role playing is well integrated into all the rest of the child's experiences, unless it makes for mature emotional response and intellectual and emotional control, it is a disruptive rather than a constructive factor in the personality development.

Where many M appear without evidence of gross deviations in control, and the deviations that do occur are not extreme or bizarre, the marked retreat into fantasy that the child is adopting strongly suggests that he has not found security and satisfaction in his contacts with his environment and feels more comfortable when he responds to his inner promptings, to the neglect of external demands. The more such external demands are neglected, the more of a "lone wolf" and nonconformist the child is likely to be.

Human movement responses can and do appear as early as two or two and a half years, but this is not usual. However, from about four years on, one or two human movement and/or animal movement answers are the rule rather than the exception. If such responses are not made by the time the child reaches the age of six or seven, some deviation in personality development is suggested. The nature of this deviation naturally depends upon the rest of the child's reactions. If his intellectual and emotional control are good or even exaggerated, then his failure to internalize his feelings may stem from his fear of his own fantasy activity. In consequence he may be repressing this while developing exaggerated, but pseudoconforming, behavior patterns in his response to his environment. On the other hand, where such control is absent, where the emotional responses are most impulsive and infantile, and judgment and objectivity poor, the lack of internalization is probably part of a general lag in personality development arising either from mental retardation or emotional disturbance of a serious order.

Color

Traditionally color is considered an emotional stimulus, and response to color reflects the capacity for emotional reactions to the environment. In the giving of a color answer, the subject not only reveals his recognition of the emotional pressures from the world about him, but also his ability to react to these in outgoing fashion. His response may stem from a positive orientation to his world, from his need for that world, from his dependency on it and/or desire to dominate, share with it, etc. Whatever the motivating force, the appearance of a color answer denotes an emotional interplay between the individual and the environment. The content and quality of the response will indicate whether such experiences are reassuring or disturbing to the subject.

In order for such an interplay to take place there must be some awareness of the fact that there is a self apart from others, a gap which must be bridged. As long as the child is fused with the environment such responses are unnecessary. The appearance of a color answer is therefore an indication of the fact that some awareness of the self, as apart from the rest of the world, has occurred.

The emotional level at which the child relates to his environment goes through a developmental sequence, as do all his experiences. Initially he can only express his need in highly crude, uncontrolled demanding fashion. The necessity for more contained, objective, socialized reactions is not recognized, and could not be met if recognition were present. The first color answers on the Rorschach given by the two and a half to four year olds are therefore likely to be mainly C and/or CF, often CF— responses. On the whole, at this age the emotional reactions tend to be sporadic and short-lived, as well as definitely unmodulated. Between four and five the pure color answers become fewer and, from that time well into prepuberty, the CF responses are the most numerous. In other words, the emotional reactions of the child are essentially egocentric and demanding, as well as impulsive. Only with the coming of puberty does he develop a real capacity for feeling with and for others. It is then that emotional control and maturity appear and find expression in the increasing appearance of FC interpretations.

In this connection it is important to note that although the educative process prepares the child for the type of emotional reaction society requires, the process cannot be hurried. Most children cannot achieve the mature form of response, that is a predominance of FC over CF and C answers, before ten or eleven, possibly not until even later. Until this preadolescent stage, the child is essentially self-centered and inconsiderate and cannot give the kind of love and understanding that is so often expected of it. As Sullivan[66] puts it:

"Around the age of eight and one-half, nine and one-half to twelve, in this culture, there comes what I once called the quiet miracle of preadolescence. . . . I say 'miracle' of preadolescence because now for the first time from birth, we might say even from conception, there is a movement from what we might, after traditional usage, call egocentricity, toward a fully social state."

He goes on to point out that up to this time no person has the emotional significance for the child that he has for himself.

The child who, prior to nine or ten, has developed strong control of affect comparable to that seen in the adult, has probably been subjected to repressive forms of training by his environment, and/or his own insecurity has made him subject himself to exaggerated efforts at control and compliance. In such cases it is questionable if the maturity reflected in the FC response is a true maturity, that is, if it results from a harmonious resolution of conflicts which has led to a smooth integration of feeling and understanding. Rather it would seem to be forced and precocious. The differentiation can generally be made in terms of the rest of the record as well as the nature of the color answers themselves. If the production of FC responses is the result of real maturity, exaggerated inhibition and repression will not be operative in other areas of the personality; there will be no need for the subject to repress or deny his fantasy or curtail his productivity; there will be no restriction or short-circuiting of mental and emotional energy. The number of whole responses will be adequate for the child's age and ability, human and animal movement interpretations will be made, the content of the record will be sufficiently varied. Moreover, the form-color answers should reflect a true integration of control and emotion. They must not be of the shallow, artificial variety revealed in answers which are scored or tend to be scored F/C, as is the case, for example, when the center blue area on Card X is interpreted as a "blue bird" or the side brown detail on the same card as a "brown frog." Even more indicative of weak efforts at adaptation and basically primitive affect are the responses which use the color without regard to its appropriateness, such as is the case when the side details on Card VIII are seen as "pink bears." Here the inappropriateness of the affect as well as the literal-, concrete-mindedness of the child definitely points away from the maturity ordinarily inferred in the giving of a form-color response. Finally, the achievement of emotional maturity must be paralleled by control and objectivity in all connections. Where the FC responses predominate and poor form answers also occur, the indications are for exaggerated efforts at adaptation because of insecurity and/or environmental pressure, but it can also be readily perceived that these efforts are all out of line with the child's capacity and his understanding of the circumstances to which he is trying to respond acceptably.

On the other hand, if no FC responses appear during the latency period, it can be inferred that the educative process is not making itself felt, that the capacity for emotional maturity is not being evolved. Under these circumstances it is most unlikely that it will suddenly appear in the pre-adolescent or early adolescent period, spring into being, full blown, when no such previous development has occurred. Rather, the adolescent period is likely to be a particularly stormy one.

Where the pure color response continues to be numerically predominant or the only form of affective reaction during the latency period, there is evidence of a lag in affective development. The child who can bring little or no objectivity into his emotional experiences is certainly not developing along the more usual, anticipated lines.

Shading

The diffuse and varied quality which the shading imparts to the blots apparently mobilizes in a large number of subjects a sense of vagueness and uncertainty. It seems as though the uneveness of the stimulus evokes corresponding reactions in the subject, provided he possesses the sensitivity which would enable him to recognize this quality in the stimulus. Shading responses of all kinds have therefore traditionally been considered reflections of the subject's anxiety. The way the subject handles his anxiety, whether he can deal with it in the mature, controlled fashion that makes for good social adjustment or whether he becomes overwhelmed by it, is indicated by the extent of the control he exercises in this connection. Thus the shading responses run the gamut from Fc and FK interpretations to responses which are scored KF−, cF−, K and c.

The anxiety which expresses itself on the Rorschach through the medium of the chiaroscuro answers is the anxiety which comes when the subject's habitual equilibrium is threatened. It therefore presupposes certain established behavioral patterns and a structured personality. In two and a half and three year olds, patterns of acceptable and unacceptable behavior are most simple and only weakly formulated. Disturbances in connection with them are likely to result in a violent emotional outburst, a "hang dog" look, or a denial of the circumstances, rather than in any attempt at more subtle control or defense. At best the child may experience a vague, free floating feeling of disquiet which is likely to reflect itself in a possible K or c answer. Thus the child sometimes talks about "smoke" or "sky," but it is difficult to be sure that shading in any way entered into the interpretation. Similarly, the answer "mud" or "dirt" may have a c quality, but this is open to question.

The older children likewise show few, if any chiaroscuro answers. In fact the sensitivity necessary to perceive and respond to nuances of shading is comparatively rare before prepuberty. While it does occur before that time, it is not the characteristic way in which the child reacts to and expresses his anxiety (see p. 57). The children who do so react are those whose sensitivity has been sharpened by their special needs and problems; in their case the sensitivity often only proves a further disturbance since they do not possess the necessary control or maturity for integrating it constructively into their reactions. These are the children who will give K or KF, c or cF responses, pointing to tension and agitations of a disruptive order.

Occasionally a child can give the mature, controlled form of response to anxiety, that is, he will produce an Fc and/or FK answer. Here again the question as to whether this is real maturity or pseudomaturity must be given serious consideration. A happy combination of control and spontaneity, good judgment and self-expression must accompany such reactions; otherwise they are simply atypical responses, born out of the child's efforts to adapt to a world which he does not understand and with which he is not in harmony. In such cases they represent a guardedness and defensiveness that points to a disturbed, suspicious attitude toward most experiences. Since the shading answers are so rare in the records of children, other ways of establishing the amount of anxiety they experience are utilized. This is discussed in Chapter VI (see p. 57).

Achromatic Color

Interpretations of "black" and "white" as such, that is, a "black bear," "a white cat," are generally considered to be emotional reactions which reflect depression and elation respectively. Klopfer[37] uses the term "burnt child" in connection with this use of black as color, describing the subjects who respond in this fashion as "people who are basically responsive to emotional stimulation from the outside but have experienced a series of traumatic experiences." The efforts of these people at making emotional contact with the environment are always colored by their fear of a repetition of former disasters, and this gives their affect a depressive coloring.

The use of black as color, that is, the production of FC', C'F and C' responses, is frequent from about four and a half to six years of age. It is more likely to appear in the record of the disturbed child than the well adjusted child, but will be found in both. The histories of children giving many "black" responses lead to the conclusion that the "traumatic" experiences which have led to the production of the FC', C'F or C' answer are closely associated with their conflicts with authority figures. The fact that the number of such responses increases markedly during the same period when the child is trying to come to terms with objective reality and internalize authority (the oedipal period) would seem to be further validation of this assumption. It is at this time that the child is overly aware of "good" and "bad," "black" and "white."

If his problems and conflicts with authority are constructively resolved and if the child grows more accustomed to and accepts the standards he is expected to meet and the behavioral patterns he is required to follow, his tensions decrease and the production of responses using black is likely to fall off. On the other hand, the child who continues to use black with frequency well beyond six years of age is the child who is still at odds with authority, still views the world in terms of the frustrations he has experienced in his contacts with authority. Unable to overcome his early feeling of being denied, disappointed and opposed, subsequent disappointments and disturbances are likely to arouse the infantile reactions, the same acting out of problems that accompanied his early brushes with authority.

It is important to note that a reduction in the "black" responses after six or seven does not always mean that the conflict-ridden relationships with the parents or parent surrogates have been resolved. It is possible that these conflicts will manifest themselves in other ways rather than through continued rigid preoccupation with good and bad and an acting out of the tensions associated with these concepts. Explosive outbursts, marked withdrawal, exaggerated repression may also point to unresolved problems with authority figures.

As with the adult, the use of "white" as color is most infrequent. It is difficult therefore to generalize as to its significance. It has been suggested that, since white is the opposite of black, its meaning would be antithetical to whatever implications are present in the giving of a black response, that in contrast to the depression and trauma associated with the production of black responses the white would be indicative of the capacity for or the experiencing of ecstasy. In the records of children this does not seem to follow. The responses using "white" are most frequently associated with "ice" and "snow" and reflect a cold quality. Whereas the child using "black" is in a sense still battling it out with himself and his environment, the use of "white" seems to be associated with a certain remoteness and detachment that constitutes a different way of meeting the unhappiness and rejection experienced in relation to the environment. For children interpreting the white as ice or snow, the environment is perceived as hard, unyielding and ungiving, rather than warm or reassuring, and they either respond in kind or withdraw from it.

Experience Balance

In interpreting a Rorschach record it is customary to compare the emphasis which the subject places on his inner promptings as compared with his responsiveness to external stimuli. This relationship, commonly called the "experience balance," indicates how the individual experiences his life, whether he has capacity for reacting both to emotional stimuli in the environment and to his own fantasies and promptings, and which mode of reaction he favors. The ratio between the human movement (M) and the color sum (obtained by weighing the color answers in the manner described by Rorschach) shows the intensity of the individual's emotional life and the direction it takes.[2, 8, 37, 59]

Another ratio is sometimes used in this connection. It is secondary to the ratio between the human movement and the weighted color answers, being based a) on the less mature fantasies and b) on the more hampered forms of affective response. The immature forms of fantasy are reflected in the FM and Fm interpretations, while the hampered affect finds expression in the texture and achromatic color answers. This ratio attests to the individual's potentiality for fuller and more mature emotional experience, and reveals resources that could be developed. In setting up these ratios it has been found advisable to weight the responses to achromatic color and texture in the same way that Rorschach weighted the color answers. Thus FC' and Fc answers are each weighted a half, C'F and cF responses are weighted one, and C' and c interpretations one and a half. In the cases presented here this formula appears in the following form: FM + Fm: C' + c, C' + c standing for the sum of the achromatic and texture responses, appropriately weighted.

Finally the number of responses given to the last three cards is compared with the total number of responses in the record. This VIII + IX + X per cent constitutes a third ratio which indicates the extent to which an emotionally charged environment can stimulate the individual's productivity.

It is obvious that the child's emotional dependency and general immaturity will find reflection in these ratios, and interpretation of them must be geared accordingly. In the child the potentiality for mature identification and fantasy is almost always outweighed by his more primitive reactions. His FM plus Fm responses will be more numerous than his M's. Whether he will develop more mature forms of response will depend, of course, upon many factors involved both in his past and future experiences. On the other hand, the immature, impulsive nature of his affective responses and his marked dependency on his environment produce a predominance of CF and C responses. In the M:C ratio there is, therefore, bound to be an emphasis on extroversion, and all studies of children agree on this point. To assume therefore, however, that the child is basically extroversive, that he responds primarily to the demands of his environment, is not entirely justified on the basis of such findings. As has already been indicated, the FM responses play much the same part for the child that the M responses do for the adult. When the M and FM responses are considered together there is frequent evidence that the child's inner promptings are as important, if not more important, in determining the way he experiences the circumstances with which he is confronted. In the records presented in the following chapters, the ratios are presented in customary fashion, that is, the M:C relationships are set up separately from the FM + Fm:C' + c relationships. However, they should also be considered in combined form, with the FM's added to the M's and the achromatic color and shading answers added to the chromatic color responses. This would certainly give a clearer indication as to the strength of inner and outer pressures.

Again, the number of responses given to Cards VIII, IX and X cannot be evaluated in the very young child in the same manner that it is in adults. The child of four or less rarely gives more than one response to a card and so it rarely happens that this VIII-IX-X per cent goes higher than 30. This does not necessarily mean that the child is not receptive to the emotional pressures in the environment or that he is not influenced by them. What it does seem to indicate is that he does not have sufficient resources to respond to these stimuli in differentiated fashion, and in consequence his responses will neither be varied nor numerous.

Shock Reactions

There appear to be three types of shock reactions typical for children: initial shock, dark shock and color shock. Initial shock has already been discussed (see p. 8). It is the disturbance the child experiences when he is first presented with the test stimulus, and feels helpless in the face of this strange situation. It is quite common in the child up to about five years of age and can occur even at five and six, though definitely less often. It is suggestive of a lack of self-reliance and resourcefulness which is typical of a large number of very young children. Its occurrence after six is quite significant, showing an inability to face new experiences at a level that can ordinarily be expected of the school child.

Dark shock also occurs in children with some frequency up to the ages of five or six. It finds expression in blocking and delays in time on the concentrated dark cards, particularly IV and V, though it may appear on others. It also is likely to be verbalized directly by the child who may say, "It's all black" or "I don't like it," or by implication with the statement, "I'm not afraid." This dark shock seems tied in with the almost universal fear of the dark, the unknown, that is characteristic of children. Obviously it will be more pronounced in anxious, insecure, guilt-ridden subjects than in happier, better adjusted ones. It also seems connected with their disturbed relations with authority. Again, it is more indicative of lasting conflict when it appears in the school age child than in the child below five.

Color shock is the term used in Rorschach literature to describe the disturbance induced in some subjects by the impact of the colored blots.[28, 37, 59] Inability to deal with these blots effectively manifests itself in a variety of ways, and is taken as evidence that the subject cannot handle his emotional experiences adequately. Application of this concept to the interpretation of children's records requires considerable modification. Very few children can deal adequately with emotional experiences when judged by adult norms, and the child who consistently reacts like the mature adult may well be more disturbed than the child who manifests considerable emotional spontaneity, impulsive and inappropriate though it may be. In the long run the child who feels free to indulge in emotional experiences has the better opportunity for learning about them and how to deal with them than the child who is denied or denies himself such opportunities. It would be wrong therefore to assume that every child who reacted poorly to the color cards, who showed any uncertainty or inadequacy when confronted with them, was manifesting color shock. Furthermore, since emotional demands do not have the same implications for the child that they do for the adult, the ways in which such disturbances express themselves will be different from what they are in the adult. In the child very drastic and prolonged withdrawal from emotional stimuli, in the form of complete inability to deal with the colored cards, or unusually long details in responding to them, can be interpreted as color shock. Children who show this reaction are most probably those who have had emotional experiences of a highly negative order. In consequence, at a period of life when most children are responding to their need for emotional response and support by seeking to make some emotional contact with the environment, these children retreat from such involvements and indicate by their reactions that such involvements are most distressing to them.

CONTENT

The content of the responses reflects the breadth and nature of the individual's interests. When there are few content categories, a constriction of interests resulting either from intellectual limitations or emotional inhibition is generally assumed. Conversely, a large number of content categories points to wide and possibly even scattered interests. As with all personality trends, there appears to be a point midway between stereotypy and scatter that constitutes the optimum for adjustment. However, judgment in this respect must also take into account, age, ability and background.

Despite his boundless energy and the curiosity which leads him into constant explorations of his environment, the very young child actually has only a few concepts to which he can relate present happenings, and which can serve as bases for future operations. These limitations are the result of a number of factors, among them his inability to make fine discriminations, his excessive concreteness and his narrow range of experience. As a result he has comparatively few ways of expressing or symbolizing his problems and desires, other than through motor activity, so not only will his Rorschach records be short, but the content will be most circumscribed. In the protocols of two and a half to four year olds, one or two content categories are the rule, and more than three or four categories most exceptional.

With an increase in discriminatory powers, wider experiences, better reality perception, larger vocabulary, the number of content categories grows. By the time the child has reached school age, the number of content categories may be as large as five, and in the case of very able children and also some distractible ones, the number can go higher.

The nature of the content appears to follow a rather definite pattern. While animal responses are the most numerous at all ages, other responses vary. For the very youngest group, up to about four or four and a half, nature, plant and architectural responses play a most important part. Trees, leaves, flowers, rain, sky, snow, rainbows, houses, bridges occur with great frequency, and this from city children who see trees and flowers relatively infrequently, and rainbows almost not at all. Emphasis on such responses seems indicative of the child's sense of oneness or identification with the simpler and more primitive forms of life.

If the symbolic aspects of the responses are investigated, the child's concern with and dependency on the family becomes instantly apparent. The tree represents the family, and the branches and leaves, as the offshoots of the tree, represent the child himself. The way the tree is described is therefore most important and such descriptions should always be encouraged in the inquiry if they have not come through spontaneously.The trees are sometimes seen as sad, sometimes festive, sometimes dead. In some cases, the response "tree" is perseverated card after card, but in each instance it is described somewhat differently indicating the child's varying perceptions of his family. Similarly, the leaf that is on the tree and growing reveals a greater sense of security than does the interpretation which deals with a leaf that is dropping down from a tree.

Rocks, caves, tunnels, bridges and houses are also frequent in the records of this youngest age group. Such responses seem to symbolize the child's need for security, for the shelter of the house or tunnel, the attachment to something solid that the bridge affords.

At about four and a half the child's better discriminatory capacities, plus his wider horizons and larger vocabulary, make for increased categories in the content of his Rorschach responses. To a considerable extent, the plant, nature and architectural responses so characteristic of the preceding age period drop out, and human and object interpretations take their place. Identification and symbolization now follow more complex life forms.

In particular, the response "tree" which is almost universal as a response to Card IV in the youngest age group now changes to "a man" or something that closely resembles a man, like "a gorilla," "scarecrow," "clown," or "giant." The family is now more specifically symbolized in terms of a father figure and remains so throughout the latency period. Similarly, Card VII, which in the youngest group is often described as a "sky" (by which the child probably means clouds) now becomes an animal or human figure.

Explosions and fires are numerous in the records of the child from four and a half to six or eight. These reveal the pent up aggressive impulses that so strongly beset him at this age, as he experiences many frustrations in his struggles with authority and in his efforts to comply with environmental demands and win the love and approbation of those who are important to him.

Similarly at this age more than at any other, wild animals receive emphasis at the expense of the domestic and/or more passive ones such as birds and insects. In conjunction with what has been said about conflicts with authority as represented in C′ answers, there is much evidence in the Rorschach to suggest that this period from four and a half to six is a stormy one for most children.

From school age on there tends to be a definite increase in human and object responses, and responses involving the more primitive and simple life forms definitely decrease. At this time anatomical responses, which are most rare in the productions of the youngest age group, come into greater prominence and increase with approaching adolescence. They apparently reflect the growing concentration on the body and on sexual tensions. This seems more typical for girls than for boys. When a boy gives an excess of anatomical responses, it is therefore probable that his attitudes and behavior are following an essentially feminine pattern. The same is true where "clothes" and "flowers" are stressed. Such interests are definitely feminine ones and their production by boys at an age when most boys have little use for girls points strongly to a deviating form of development.

Map and geography responses as well as interpretation of the blot as an alphabetical letter are comparatively rare, but they are produced by children who, during this period when school plays such an important part, have a need to display their erudition or use this form of intellectual approach as a means of avoiding emotional and possibly more disturbing involvements.

In evaluating the animal and human responses it is most important to determine the sex of the figure, the nature of the animal and the activity in which these humans and animals are engaged. Everything that has been said about the nature of this activity in the publications dealing with adults[8] applies here also. In one respect, however, the responses of children have different value than do those of the adult. This is in connection with responses which deal with fairies, witches, angels, etc. For the child, identification with these supernatural and fairy folk is natural and part of the developmental process. Through his identification with unreal characters, the child can compensate dramatically and satisfyingly for the feelings of inadequacy, ineffectualness and frustration which he so frequently experiences. As Superman, Batman, witch or prince, the child can exercise infinite power and retaliate for the wrongs he feels have been done him and others in most gratifying fashion. The roles he stresses in this fantasy activity, whether he uses the powers with which he endows himself for constructive or for destructive acts, for social good or for "smashing up the whole world," are revealing of his attitude and feelings toward that world, as well as the intensity of the hostility that his frustrations have produced in him. Only when such identifications continue long past puberty and interfere with the individual's assumption of realistic adult roles can they be considered evidence of immaturity and maladjustment.

One or two aspects of the content deserve special mention. The emphasis placed on aggressive animals and aggressive reactions of any kind must always be evaluated in terms of the child's tendency, particularly from about five to seven or eight, to express considerable aggression and identify with aggressive forces. This expression is probably in part a desire to appear strong and independent, to display power, and it need not necessarily be indicative of strongly destructive impulses. Only where such trends are grossly emphasized and accompanied by a marked lack of control and judgment do they hold such negative implications. In all discussions of aggression, it is important to make the distinction between true aggression where the subject's intent is a destructive one, and aggressive behavior which arises from strivings for self-assertion and independence. Such strivings are part of the child's natural development, and unless they are accompanied by extremely hostile impulses are not unusual.

Occasionally the interpretation "twins" appears in a record. This response, and particularly the response "Siamese twins," seems to symbolize the subject's feelings of being more than one person, and of being unable to integrate these various aspects of the self, yet at the same time being inexorably bound to these various selves in a way that is handicapping. This response is given more frequently by schizophrenic children (and adults) than by any other group.

The "shadow" interpretations carry with them a sense of the eerie, the unreal, the mysterious and the frightening. They are likely to be found in the records of anxious, possibly phobic children, or children whose hold on reality is most precarious. Precarious balance also finds expression in such interpretations as "hanging," "falling" or "standing on the edge."

Emphasis on "two," as when the responses always begin "two men," "two animals," etc. also shows a need for balance. The responses which emphasize "two," and those which show any concern with counting, as "there are three butterflies and four holes," are frequently part of a quasi ritualistic approach to various life experiences. It is true that children are inclined to be ritualistic, but when this is carried to the point where it appears in the Rorschach in this form it generally denotes uncertainty, insecurity and anxiety which are being responded to by a recourse to magic that exceeds what is ordinarily found.

POPULAR AND ORIGINAL ANSWERS

Popular answers are listed in the various texts dealing with the Rorschach method.[2, 8, 37] They are the answers given with great frequency by adults, appearing at least once in every five records. They give evidence of the extent to which the subject shares in the general communality of thought. The word "popular" used in connection with these responses when they are given by children is a definite misnomer, and such interpretation of them is highly misleading. The adult world is not the child's world, and he can understand and partake of the attitudes and reactions of that world only to a limited extent. If his capacity for participating in the common reactions of his own age group is to be evaluated, then popular responses for children at different age levels must be determined. Some efforts in this direction have been made. Vorhaus[69] analyzed the records of 138 superior children from two to six and arrived at the following "populars"* for that group:

Card I:	Bird, bat and butterfly (W) (five and six year olds)
Card II:	Animals (W) (four, five and six year olds)
	Shoe, foot, stocking (top red) (five year olds)
Card III:	People (W) (four and five year olds)
	Birds (W) (four and five year olds)
	Four-legged animals (W) (four, five and six year olds)
	Butterfly (center red) (five and six year olds)
Card IV:	Human figure (W) (five and six year olds)
	Four-legged animal (W) (four, five and six year olds)
Card V:	Bird, bat, butterfly (W) (two, three, four, five and six year olds)
Card VI:	Tree (W) (three and four year olds)
Card VII:	Clouds and smoke (W) (four and six year olds)
Card VIII:	Four-legged animals (side pink) (four, five and six year olds)
	Tree (W) (six year olds)

Ames, Learned, Metraux and Walker[1] find the response "tree" is given once in every six records in the two to three and a half year old groups on

---

* That is, responses given 10 or more times by 20 per cent or more of this group of children.

Cards I, IV and VI. They also report such frequency for the "animals" on Cards II, III, IV, VII and VIII, the "bow" or "ribbon" on Card III, and the "bird" or "butterfly" on Card V. In the four to six year old group the "tree" has dropped out on Card I and the popular responses are the "bird," "butterfly," "bat" (W) and the "face mask pumpkin" (WS). Card II continues to produce the commonly seen "two animals." In addition to the usual "humans" and the "bow" or "ribbon," Card III also produces "two animals" (W) with sufficient frequency for it to be considered a popular in this age group. Again, on Card IV the "tree" has lost frequency and the populars are the "animal" and the "person" or "giant." Card V brings forth the "bird," "butterfly" and "bat" answers in one out of every six protocols. Responses to Card VII continue to emphasize the interpretation of the upper two thirds of the blot as "animals," especially "dogs" or "rabbits." Card VIII continues to evoke the popular responses to the side pink area. There is no popular on Card IX. For Card X, the adult populars, "spider" and "crab" are also popular for this age group. A second popular on this card is a "tree with flowers" and "colored leaves" with color definitely employed.

There is sufficient commonality among these various investigators to demonstrate that the child has his own way of perceiving his experiences and that his participation in usual adult reactions is limited, growing more frequent with age. Interpretation of records below six must take these findings into account and determine to what extent the child is participating in the common reactions of his peers.

In the records presented in this book, the usual adult populars are so scored, but interpretation of them is based on the extent to which they show participation in adult reactions, not as evidence for participation in group responses of children. The child who gives many adult populars may therefore not get along well with his peers, since his reactions would frequently be out of line with those given by other children his age.

When the child gives a popular response that has been so designated because it is given with a high degree of frequency by adults he is simply indicating that there are some situations in which he can share in the common reactions of older subjects. The extent to which he does this will be quite limited in the preschool child and will gradually increase through the school years. The average number of adult populars to be expected at different ages has been statistically determined.[1]

The occasional child who gives many adult popular responses is usually trying to get along by following adult reactions in a highly stereotyped manner. Such reactions are generally not accompanied by emotional spontaneity or much indulgence in fantasy. They stem from great insecurity which necessitates such exaggerated efforts at conformity. They sometimes are found in the records of children who spend most of their time with adults and so have taken on many adult forms of response.

On the other hand, the school age child who shows little or no ability to participate in the usual responses of the adult world is not developing in expected fashion. He is either intellectually incapable of sharing adult experience or deflected from this because of emotional, social and interpersonal difficulties.

Original answers in the records of very young children may occur with some frequency since the child deals with the blots in highly arbitrary fashion. Judged by adult standards, a number of his interpretations might be scored original minus. However, these responses are often found to be common in the child's age group, and on this basis do not warrant being scored original. In general it would seem advisable to ignore the scoring of originals, plus or minus, unless they are most atypical for the child's age.

NUMBER OF RESPONSES

In general children are not nearly as productive on the Rorschach as adults are. The number of responses they give ranges from 0 to 20 with a mean between 10 and 15, depending upon the age of the subject. In the preschool child the number rarely exceeds 10, while in the school age child the average is about 15.

Meager formal vocabulary, limited experiences, concreteness which makes shifting from one concept to another difficult and often impossible, and lack of interest and motivation are the primary reasons for the paucity of answers in the records of the two and a half to six year old. In the school age child, his concreteness and his efforts at exactness, as well as his relatively limited emotional resources account for the short protocol.

Rejections play an important part in connection with the meagerness of the records. They are comparatively frequent up to six years of age, and it is not unusual to get as many as two or three refusals from a relatively well adjusted six year old. Boredom, inattention, fatigue and similar matters are sometimes responsible for the child's failure to respond. As has been indicated, the test experience is not a particularly interesting or stimulating one for the young child. In some cases, however, the refusals are caused by blocking and point to definite emotional disturbance. Observation of the child's behavior during the testing, as well as careful evaluation of the responses he does give, can generally help determine what is responsible for the rejections. The child who is really struggling to meet the situation will only block when the circumstances are too difficult or too disturbing, whereas the child who gives every sign of being indifferent and of giving only superficial cooperation, will easily discard a blot if it presents any difficulty or demands any effort on his part.

The rejections which occur after six are in most cases more closely tied in with specific emotional disturbances and are therefore more revealing of paralyzing conflicts than those which occur in the preschool child. At six and seven, when the child is so concerned with right and wrong, is so rigid and exacting, his fear of being out of line may explain some of his refusals. Again at nine or ten, depending upon when prepuberty occurs, refusals become numerous. Uncertain about himself, his role and his relations to others, the prepuberty child blocks readily in the face of any emotionally charged circumstance.

REACTION TIME

In testing the very young child it is usually better not to have a watch in evidence (see p. 7). Neither initial nor total time are really important in this age group because the child almost always responds in a relatively short time, either making an interpretation or admitting that he cannot. He does not have the capacity for sustained effort and concentration. On those rare occasions when long delays occur, the examiner will be aware of this without the aid of a timepiece. Such delays may be due to emotional disturbance and blocking, but are more likely to be the result of wandering attention and interest in extraneous matters. Time in itself is not too significant or helpful in evaluating the productions of the child below six.

In the school age child, time should be noted. In this age group the time factor has much the same significance as it has in adults, that is, long initial delays denote blocking, shock and conflict, while long total time must be evaluated in terms of its nature and consistency. The child who takes a long time to make each response may be acting in this way because he is a slow thinker, an overly careful, precise person or because he is experiencing some psychomotor retardation. Where the response time is variable, the changes in tempo must be interpreted in relation to the situations in which they occur.

In general the average time per response and the average total time required for completing the test increases steadily from the youngest to the oldest age group. This is not only due to the increased productivity found in the older children, but also to the development of a more critical attitude on the part of the older child, a reduction in impulsivity and also a capacity to elaborate his productions and discuss them in detailed fashion as a result of his increased resources and greater discriminatory powers.

TURNING OF THE CARDS

In the child up to about four, there is likely to be much manipulation of the cards. The child handles the test material just as he handles everything that comes his way, exploring it in his own fashion. Thus, the card is likely to be waved around, slapped down on the desk, spun and even thrown about.

It may also be put in the mouth. In most instances this manipulation is simply part of the general activity of the two and three year old, and has no individual significance. Carried on much beyond four years, it denotes deviant reactions stemming either from a lag in development or from emotional disturbance.

Manipulation of the cards after five years of age becomes very much an individual matter. There are children who never turn the cards, to whom such a possibility never occurs. They accept the situation as given, and have no need and/or initiative as far as altering it is concerned. At the other extreme are the children who turn each card the instant it is handed to them. They refuse to accept the situation as it is presented to them, but must assert themselves in this connection. In many cases they return to the upright position before they begin interpreting, but interpretation cannot take place until they have expressed their resistance to the pattern offered by the authority figure.

Between these extremes are the children who turn each card after they have examined and/or interpreted it in the position it was first offered to them. Having exhausted all the possibilities afforded by this aspect of the blot, their thoroughness, possibly compulsiveness, pushes them into further efforts. In contrast to these children whose orderly turning is habitual, there are children who only turn when the circumstances prove disturbing. These are the children who are likely to turn Card IV or Card VII, or any other blot that has disturbing qualities for them, and who meet such disturbances by trying to alter the nature of the circumstances.

CHAPTER V

The Nature of the Stimulus

THE CARDS

TEN INKBLOTS constitute the stimulus to which the subject is instructed to respond, and which is intended to precipitate samples of his behavioral patterns. The amorphous nature of these blots leaves the structuring and the naming of the end product entirely up to the subject. Nevertheless, each of the inkblots has certain qualities and aspects which tend to evoke specific trains of associations, although in most instances the subject is unaware of this. Thus, each blot has come to have its own meaning and value as a stimulus.

Card I

From the formal point of view, Card I has been considered an "ice breaker," something to set the subject at ease. For adult subjects it is therefore generally an easy card, and only rarely produces "shock" reactions. For children, however, the unexpectedness of the situation frequently arouses considerable disturbance. Initial time on this card is often longer than on many others. Helplessness and bewilderment frequently manifest themselves in the way the child looks at the examiner or in his muttered "It don't look like nothing," or "Gee, is this ink?" Such a reaction is best described as "initial" shock and the relative frequency of it gives evidence of the difference in resourcefulness and ease of adjustment between adults and children.

This card has a number of distinctive features which are significant in the responses of children as well as adults. The card divides roughly into three sections, a center one and two outer ones. In addition, it has four white spaces set roughly around the midpoint of the card.

The very young children tend to respond to this card in a vague, crude all-inclusive fashion or, failing this, become much attracted by the four white spaces. They interpret these as windows, or openings in tunnels, and thus frequently develop the whole interpretation on the basis of these white spaces. Houses, broken-down houses, caves, bridges are frequent answers to this blot. The white spaces appear to arouse tension in the child, probably because they are considered as something "open," something "incomplete." The child's feelings of insecurity, his awareness of his own lacks and gaps, motivate him toward filling in these openings by giving

45

them meaning, and in some way relating them positively to things he can understand and use.

When the child is old enough to recognize and select from the blot the obvious and usual details into which it divides itself (see p. 22), he becomes aware of two similar figures on the sides and a single figure in the center. For most children, from about five years on, such a constellation or composition is sufficient to evoke associations dealing with the parents and himself. The two similar side figures are the parents* while the single figure is himself. The interpretations that are given in this connection vary considerably. "Two animals tearing a man apart," "two witches dragging a girl away," "two angels helping a lady," "two Santa Clauses," and even "a strong man holding up these two men on each side of him." Such answers symbolize the way the child views the parental relationship.

The center figure alone, like all midline figures, is extremely likely to be a reflection of the way the individual sees himself. Thus, the self-concept is not infrequently conveyed by means of such interpretations as "a bad guy ready to grab somebody," or "a guy hollering for help." In the first instance the child accepts himself as aggressive and "bad," in the second he recognizes that something is wrong, but is looking for assistance. Whenever an interpretation of the center figure is given on this or on any card, it is almost always a reflection of the way the subject sees himself.

The center top section alone is sometimes emphasized with responses like "two hands, reaching for something," or "two little birds in a nest with their mouths open looking for food." The need to take or to receive from the environment is clearly indicated, and that this should be so emphasized suggests that the child does not feel he has received sufficient emotional satisfaction. Young children tend to stress oral factors, and seem insatiable in their desire for oral satisfactions as evidence of emotional acceptance. Only when this type of emphasis continues much after eight years is it especially significant of tension in relation to emotional deprivation and affect hunger.

Card II

For the adult subject, the emotional and sexual implication of this blot can be quite disturbing. Relatively few children, however, show serious shock on this card. For many children the appearance of the color is a relief and they rush to it eagerly. These are the children who want to get away from the more formal and serious aspects of their experiences, who want environmental warmth and stimulation at all times. They are also

---

* The fact that the parents are naturally not identical in no way invalidates this symbolism. From the child's point of view at that moment, they have enough in common in their attitude toward him to satisfy his concept of them as identical.

likely to be the children who become easily frightened and tend to develop phobias.

The fact that the card divides itself into two identical figures which can easily be identified as people or animals that are like people, again evokes responses relating to the parents. In this instance however, there is no lone figure in the middle as there was on Card I. Instead the child is likely to associate to these figures in terms of the way he sees them relating to one another. In this connection, the very nature of the figures chosen is significant, as well as the activity in which the figures may be engaging. As a group, children have rather definite attitudes toward animals and toward mythical and fairy-tale folk. The elephant is likely to be considered a strong, overpowering, but relatively benign figure, the tiger as most aggressive and devouring, the rabbit as timid and weak. Also, it certainly makes a difference if these figures are playing or dancing, or if they are fighting or competing with one another. For this reason ambiguous interpretations should always be clarified even if such clarification is not part of the formal scoring. For example, the response "two elephants putting their trunks up together" does not indicate if this is a friendly or an aggressive activity. The child can therefore be asked to tell more about this, to tell "just what this putting trunks together means." Sometimes the child's unwillingness to face the realities of the situation are nicely demonstrated by answers like "they look like they're fighting, but they're only playing." On occasion, such a response may also indicate that the child has witnessed sexual activity. Recently a subject volunteered the information, "they have their trunks up, like on parade. They're always showing off and putting on an act." All manner of humans—witches, clowns, priests, people—and animals serve to express the child's perceptions in this area. Where there is doubt as to how the child may feel about a given figure it is always possible to discuss this with the child at the end of the testing. The child can be asked where he actually saw a bear or an elephant, and what he thinks about the animal.

Sometimes the blot is treated as one figure rather than two separate ones. Again this is more likely to be the case with the very young child, the two and a half to four year old, than with older children. Here the differentiation between the parents is vague and unimportant. Rather, each parent is a "mother" since the difference in their roles is not yet recognized by the child. In these cases the blot, or the black area of the blot, is seen as a house, a cave, a tree. The child is still concerned with his security in its most elemental terms. How he feels about this house can be determined by asking him to tell more about the house. Reactions to such requests indicate that it is an "old, broken-down house," a " house on fire," a "big house with the sun coming in."

Card III

For the child, as for the adult, the reactions to this card are indicative of his perception of people. Some very young children do not perceive the human figures, and this ties in with their general lack of or weakness in human identifications. Rather, he is likely to see the black portions of the blot as rocks or trees, again showing more identification with the primitive and simpler forms of life than with people. After four, the child often interprets the black figures as animals. The nature of these and their activity is again, of course, of primary importance. However, there are some children who, even as young as three, do recognize the human figures and their discussion of them points up their attitude toward and understanding of people.

School age children, as a group, interpret the usual human forms. The descriptions of the figures, the sex of the figures, and the relationship between the figures should always be sought. In the preschool child, the attitudes and understandings reflected in such responses generally apply to their feelings toward and perceptions of the parents. In school age children the horizons have broadened, and the interpretations on this card show the trend of their response to people in general, that is, whether they see them as friendly or unfriendly, competitive or helpful, passive or aggressive. How they view others almost inevitably becomes an exaggeration of their own unconscious awareness of their own trends.

Card IV

This is a dark, heavy blot whose outline suggests a gorilla, a giant, or an ogrelike figure. As such it has been taken to represent "authority." Recent researches[47] tend to support this clinical practice. Interestingly enough the youngest group of children, that is the two and a half to four year olds, almost universally interpret this blot as a tree (see p. 38). Treated symbolically, the tree represents the family, as witness the common usage of such terms as "family tree" or "geneological tree." The child's recourse to such an interpretation at this time seems determined by his tendency to identify with objects of nature, and also by his limited capacity for differentiating between the familial figures. For the child, both parents, and any other adult in constant attendance (grandmother, nurse, etc.) are simply additional "mothers." Their basic differences and the differences that obtain in their relations to him are not yet grasped by the child in this youngest age group.

Sometime between four and five years of age, however, the child apparently does begin to make such a differentiation, and also to differentiate among and identify with the authority figures in his life. At this time the card is almost inevitably interpreted as a "giant," "a big man," "a clown." The way this figure is perceived gives indication of the way the child feels about the authority figures in his life. A child between four and five, whose father is a musician, interpreted the card initially as a dragon shooting fire. Six months later when problems with authority were less acute, it became a "dragon making believe he is shooting fire." The next administration of the test produced a "dragon making music!" "Cut down trees," "stumps of trees," "dead trees" are common interpretations of children who have lost a parent, particularly the father, or whose father plays a negligible or most inadequate role.

It is well to bear in mind that while Card IV tends to be associated with authority as represented by the father figure, there are cases where the mother is really the dominant, masculine figure. In such instances it is possible that the reactions to Card IV may really be reactions to a "phallic" mother.

It is on this card particularly that some children give expression to their interest in excretory activity. The card is seen as a "man making his duty" or "doing a pee." Some children also indicate that the man has a big penis. These are generally children for whom the bathroom activities symbolize their power conflicts with the parents and/or children who have been encouraged to verbalize most freely about sexual and excretory matters. Despite the parents' exaggerated efforts at being "modern," these are often children who have many unresolved problems in this connection.

As with the adult, dark shock can occur on this card. The disturbance thus manifested is generally associated with the child's problems with authority.

Card V

Card V has always been considered an easy card to interpret, a card without disturbing features. Its introduction at this particular point in the series is largely for the sake of affording the subject a "breathing spell," to permit a reduction in tension. It lends itself to an easy whole response and can be broken down into obvious details.

As has already been indicated, the center figure on any card seems to invite identification. The way the center figure is interpreted, therefore, is very likely to reflect the way the individual sees himself, his unconscious concept of himself. Card V, in particular, can be most helpful in this respect. Evaluation of responses to this central figure on Card V over a long period of time, in all kinds of subjects, young and old, sick and well, has substantiated this use of the center area of Card V. Thus, a basically timid individual is likely to see the figure as a "rabbit behind bushes," a more exhibitionistic and dramatic individual as "a woman in a costume on the stage." One woman who felt overburdened by responsibilities from which she could not escape interpreted the card as a "donkey with a heavy pack on each side, and he's so stupid he doesn't have sense enough to slip out."

Children frequently give the "rabbit" answer, and these are usually the more timid ones. "The open mouth of a bird looking for food," or "the horns of two animals fighting," "a fairy," "a goat" are among the ways in which the child symbolizes his feelings about himself.

The side projections on the card are often seen by the child as alligators' heads, with mouth open. The alligator is frequently used as a symbol of the aggressive, devouring parent, and again the fact that it is used in an area which permits the interpretation of *two* alligators, tends to substantiate such a reading of the answers.

Card VI

This card is generally referred to as the "sex card" because of its fairly obvious genitalia. For adults with unresolved sexual problems this blot is likely to be quite disturbing. Children often block on this card, but it is questionable if their shock is caused by the sexual aspects of the stimulus. Actually the card is a difficult one to interpret, and the child's delay is frequently the result of his inability to organize the stimulus, rather than evidence of sexual conflicts. Usual responses to this card in the very young child are: "trees," a "snail with its head poking out," a "caterpillar," a "fire," an "explosion." Very occasionally a child will interpret the lower curves of the card as "buttocks." Older children see the top half of the card as a "butterfly," or "totem pole," and the lower half and/or the entire blot as an "airplane," a "bug," a "map."

Card VII

Again, clinical usage and some research seem to justify the use of Card VII as the "mother" card in contrast to Card IV as the "father" card. In particular the interpretation of the lower center, darker area as a "house" or "church" seems especially significant, since the house is symbolically either the mother's body or one's own body. The use of this area of the blot for such interpretations can give indication as to the way the child feels about the mother. There is a world of difference between "the house that is far away and covered with snow," and "the house that has a chimney with smoke coming out, like someone was cooking dinner." One five year old interpreted the card as "two bunnies playing—and there's a hole here. It's something important, but it frightens them." This child has a schizophrenic mother whose illness makes it impossible for her to give this child the warmth and support she needs. Instead, her behavior frequently upsets the child very much.

Actually, the child's reaction to the whole blot reflects his perception of the mother. There are children who interpret this card as "ice" and those who see it as "two bunnies playing." The nature of the object upon which the two playing figures stand also often has significance. The "bunny that stands in the clouds" is not as secure and down to earth as the "bunny that stands on grass." Rocks, on the other hand, lend a firm foundation, but rocks are not usually considered pleasant things. They are not warm, but rather cold, drab and possibly dangerous.

Phallic mothers are often indicated by the interpretations on this card of elephants, lions and other aggressive animals and figures in contrast to the happier rabbits, children, fairies.

When the two side figures are interpreted as either animals or humans, and are seen in conflict, arguing, fighting, aggressive combative relations with the mother generally prevail. Where the two figures are seen as passing one another, turning and looking back at one another, feelings of maternal rejection are generally strong.

Card VIII

Card VIII, as the first all-colored card, frequently evokes some comment from the child. Questions like, "How many inks do you have?" or "Is this really ink?" are not unusual. Such comments do not necessarily indicate disturbance or "shock" as they might in the adult. The child is still naively interested in concrete experiences and to him the whole idea of playing around with inkblots, and especially a multicolored inkblot, is sufficiently exciting to call for question and comment. A long delay, however, a rejection of the card, a marked change in his general procedure would certainly suggest that the child was disturbed by the emotional demands of the stimulus.

The children in the youngest age group frequently respond to the emotional stimuli in highly undifferentiated fashion. They use the whole blot with the color, without discriminating among the colors or giving any consideration to their appropriateness, calling the blot "flowers" or "rainbow." They proceed to treat all the colored cards in the same way, failing to make use of the differences that are present in cards VIII, IX and X. From about five years on discrimination in responding to the blots is generally evident, and they are no longer treated as if they were all practically identical. Certainly older and more mature children are capable of discrimination, not only within each blot, but between blots VIII, IX and X.

The treatment of the animals on Card VIII is, of course, highly significant. Just as the type of human interpretation given on Card III gives an indication of the way the adult sees people and reacts to them, so the type of animal seen here plays as important a part with children who, until the age of eight at least, identify almost as strongly, if not as strongly, with animals as with people.

Card IX

The diffuse quality of this card, in conjunction with the lush coloring, gives rise to opportunity for considerable fantasy activity of all kinds. Aggressive reactions express themselves in "atomic bomb explosions," "shooting geysers" and the like. "Elves" and "witches" are found in the orange areas; "canals," "water," "caves," are found in the midline area. The fact that fantasy has such free play on this card, and that it is reinforced by emotional pressures proves very disturbing to some children. Explosive and disorganized responses, if they occur, therefore appear on this card almost more than on any other except possibly Card II.

Card X

Investigation of the associations made to the different cards has indicated that Card X also tends to be considered a "mother" card.[47] The frequent interpretation of this card as a sea scene or a flower garden would certainly seem to bear out this idea, and clinical use of this concept has proved fruitful.

As with the adult, the multi-demands which the card makes on the subject and the difficulty of dealing with these in integrated fashion can prove very disturbing to individuals who become upset when pulled at from many directions at once. On the other hand, there are those who find the separateness of the different forms and the fact that they can deal with individual areas one at a time an aid rather than a hindrance. Where the subject has a capacity for selectivity and is not driven to resolve everything with one answer, Card X can prove very enjoyable.

The card lends itself readily to both pleasant and unpleasant experiences. For those who seek for joyful happenings, the colors and the sense of movement convey the impression of gaiety. For those who seek disaster, there are enough threats in the many projecting forms, in the top gray and side brown and in the center open space to enable them to structure the experience in terms of their own feelings.

With children, as with adults, the last response to Card X is likely to have special significance. The note on which the subject is willing to let the matter rest is of great importance, frequently representing a composite picture of his problems and conflicts.

THE EXAMINER

The way the test procedure is set up renders it a highly intimate, interpersonal situation. Thus the examiner is an important factor in the entire procedure, having stimulus value of his own. From the subject's point of view the examiner inevitably holds a position of authority, since he is the person who is directing the situation, and the one who knows what it is all about. Thus from the moment the subject meets the examiner, some of his habitual reactions toward authority figures are mobilized. The importance of this matter cannot be overemphasized, yet it rarely receives recognition in test reports.

How the subject feels about authority figures in general, and the examiner in particular, will certainly help determine how willing he is to communicate his fantasies and feelings to him. It will also affect the nature of these fantasies and feelings, since it will tend to throw emphasis on certain forms of reaction which are typical of the subject's behavior in relation to authority. It is important that the examiner be aware of this, and do what he can to counteract any attitudes that are likely to affect the results too adversely. There should also be recognition of the responses which are determined primarily by the subject's feelings toward authority. In particular, there are those subjects who show their resistance to the whole situation, including the examiner, by giving white space responses on the first one or two cards. However, they do not maintain this oppositional attitude, as the anxiety caused by the novelty of the situation wears off.

In addition to the subject's general attitude toward authority, his specific reaction to the individual examiner will make a difference in his handling of the test situation. Ideally the examiner should establish an air of friendliness and mutual respect, but there are undoubtedly times when his own feelings come through, and his positive or negative reactions to his subject are perceived by the subject. On the whole children seem particularly sensitive to the attitudes of the adults to whom they are relating at the moment. The examiner who understands himself and is aware of his feelings, who can view himself with a high degree of objectivity, will naturally be in a better position to evaluate his attitude toward the subject, as well as the subject's reactions to him and to the test than one who lacks such insight. The same considerations apply in his interpretation of the subject's productions. The aggressive, hostile examiner will be unduly aware of such feelings in his subject. As in the case of the therapist, the better adjusted the examiner, the greater his own insight, the more objective his interpretation of the reactions of others will be.

CHAPTER VI

General Interpretive Problems

THERE HAVE BEEN a number of references in the preceding chapters to self-concept and identification, anxiety, adjustive mechanisms and ego strength. These are the basic ingredients from which the personality is compounded, and the validity and significance of any personality description depend heavily on an understanding of these concepts. They find expression in the Rorschach in a variety of ways, some of them direct, others inferential. Clarity of exposition demands that each of these concepts be discussed separately, although actually they are not independent entities that can be considered apart from one another. The self-concept cannot be treated without an understanding of its relation to anxiety, for example, and anxiety cannot be discussed without repeated reference to the defense mechanisms. The divisions that are made here are, therefore, purely arbitrary ones, created solely for the purpose of expediency.

Self-Concept and Identification

The term self-concept implies, first of all, that the individual regards himself as a "self," as a figure or object apart from the rest of the world. At first this self is undoubtedly only dimly and intermittently perceived and recognized as such, but with increasing experience in living it becomes clearer and stronger, and its aspects more definite.

The self-concept is a product of the experiences the individual has with the world about him. The nature of these contacts determines whether he sees himself as acceptable or rejected, weak or strong, able or inadequate. The child's infantile experiences set the stage for the concepts he will develop about himself. The way he is handled in the earliest days of life, the emotions focusing around his feeding experiences, the amount and nature of the fondling he gets all serve to build up attitudes toward the self. Thus the child comes to feel about himself as he thinks others feel about him. He identifies himself in terms of the appraisals of others.[66] Given a certain set toward the self, the child then tends to select from his experiences those aspects of it which will reinforce his perception of himself.

* Much that is covered in this chapter has already been discussed in Chapter IV. However, the material treated there is reorganized here in connection with the specific entities under consideration.

If he feels he is not loved he will create situations to prove this and manip- ulate his interpersonal relationships accordingly. Again, if he sees himself as intellectually capable he will seek experiences which lend themselves to such a self-concept to the exclusion of contradictory ones.

Once his concept of the self is formulated, the individual must de- velop modes of behavior in keeping with this concept. The way he proceeds to do this, the patterns he evolves for perpetuating his self-concept, will be modeled on the behavior he sees about him, namely the reactions of the parents. The happy child will select from the reactions of the parents those which for him signify cheerfulness, contentment and good will, while the frustrated child adopts response patterns which correspond most nearly to his feelings of anxiety and aggression.

In crystallizing the behavioral patterns that arise from his concept of himself, the child also strives to follow those patterns which he feels are likely to win for him the approval and love of the important figures in his life. To this end he takes on their values and their ways of enforcing those values, but his responses in this connection will be modified and altered by the nature of his feelings for those figures and by his own drives and needs. These various processes—developing a concept of the self, following through on this concept with a given "set" toward the self, and incorporat- ing the parental values—occur concomitantly, meshing with one another to produce the ultimate pattern of the self as seen by the individual.*

In order for the personality to develop constructively, the self-concept must come within the bounds of reality. As such it is a learning process. In the Rorschach responses, therefore, the beginnings of an understanding of reality are the first prerequisite to the development of a self-concept. The child who in no way grasps the objective aspects of the test stimulus (see Record 34, page 237), but simply projects into it what he happens to be concerned with at the moment, is not yet ready to develop a self-con- cept. On the other hand, the child who strives to deal with circumstances realistically is preparing the way for the structuring of his own personality. Thus the presence of even a few good form responses, and a diminution or disappearance of the perseveration characteristic of the very young child (see p. 67) afford evidence that the beginnings of self-awareness have oc- curred.

Meaningful discriminations in perceptions are reflected in the test ma- terial not only in the presence of the good form interpretation, but also in the appearance of some large detail answers. The child who can select out these obvious areas is already differentiating among his impressions, in

* The appearance of anxiety is also evidence of an awareness of self. This is dis- cussed below, on p. 57.

contrast to the child who responds to each blot in crude, unselective fashion. The child who can discriminate in this fashion is on his way toward a differentiated approach to his life experiences. How well he will achieve this depends, of course, on many factors; but the beginnings have been made.

Once given the self, how is it perceived? This concept has already been partially covered in the discussion on the content of the responses and the meaning of the cards (pp. 36–40, 45–52). Important in this connection are the human responses, and especially the human movement interpretations. How the child perceives himself, the roles he assigns to himself, are partly determined through an analysis of the M responses. Since for the child, certainly the child up to seven or eight, the animal is something with which he identifies very closely, the choice of animal and the activities of the animal would have much the same significance. However, the movement responses alone by no means give the full picture. Actually there are many concepts of the self, at different levels of awareness. Thus, all the child's reactions reveal, in one way or another, how the child sees himself, the perception at one level being determined fundamentally by his unconscious needs, at another by what he really feels he is, and at another by what he believes people think he is. All these various self-concepts find reflection in the formal aspects of the test as well as in the content. Thus, the child who employs exaggeratedly conforming modes of adjustment must see himself as inadequate and threatened, regardless of what other concepts he has of himself. Similarly, the child who sees himself as "hanging on" has a picture of himself as precariously balanced in certain relationships.

Since the self is the center of all activity, the core from which all experience radiates, the midline area is of especial importance in an evaluation of the self-concept. Thus the interpretation of midline figures, especially if these are human or animal figures, gives some indication of how the child sees himself (see p. 42).

Since the child's behavioral patterns have been structured both on the basis of how he sees himself and in terms of those aspects of parental behavior which coincide with his concept of himself, the way he interprets human figures on the Rorschach will indicate not only a self-picture, but also his perception of the parents or parent surrogates. His interpretation of Card II as two men fighting not only reveals his own aggression, but also the aggression he recognizes in others.

Once the self-concept and the identifications are initiated, the equilibrium of the individual depends on their maintenance. Anything that threatens to disturb this self-concept, that interferes with the behavioral patterns dictated by the child's identifications, will immediately evoke anxiety. It is in order to avoid this anxiety that defense mechanisms are developed.

Anxiety

The goal of the human organism, as of all biological organisms, is the achievement and maintenance of a state of equilibrium. Ideally, this is possible for man only when all his drives and needs have achieved satisfaction without in any way impairing his status in the social environment where he operates. He seeks simultaneously for maximum satisfaction and maximum security. However, in seeking to satisfy his needs and drives, the individual frequently finds himself at odds with the world that affords him his security. Thus it becomes a matter of altering, deflecting, and denying certain drives or impulses, or foregoing a certain amount of security. Each individual sets up a relationship between these forces. The nature of that relationship, whether it emphasizes security at the expense of drive satisfaction, or vice versa, depends in large measure on which form of behavior proves least conflict-provoking. If the relationship is such that the individual experiences constant doubt, tension and frustration, he does not attain the equilibrium he is seeking. The unsatisfactory nature of the relationship he has set up between inner and outer pressures leaves him in a relatively precarious state of adjustment, constantly threatened by disrupting forces. As a result he readily and frequently experiences anxiety. Anxiety can therefore be defined as the feeling of disturbance or discomfort that the individual experiences when he cannot establish equilibrium between inner and outer pressures, or when there is a threat to the equilibrium he has achieved. Reactions to this threat may take a number of forms.

As with every other force in the functioning personality, anxiety follows a developmental sequence. It is probably first experienced as a generalized sense of discomfort, determined entirely by physical needs. The state of disturbance or tension is purely physiological in nature and does not depend upon the presence of a self-concept. However, when the self has been separated from the rest of experience and becomes an autonomous entity, the need arises for the maintenance of some balance between the individual's drives and the environment's demands and pressures. It is then that a conflict occurs, and anxiety, as the term is here used, first makes itself felt in connection with this conflict. Given the evidence for anxiety of this order, it becomes apparent that some structuring of the personality has taken place. Only when there is an awareness of self, and of the necessity for perpetuating a given concept of self, can it be said that anxiety is present and operating for the maintenance of the individual's habitual relationship between satisfaction and security. Thus anxiety has a definite part in the development of the individual, and in the specific nature of his adjustment.

The presence of anxiety can be determined in two ways, one direct, the other inferential. The direct manifestations of anxiety take the form of multiple shading responses. This anxiety may be well controlled or "bound," as indicated by Fc, FK, Fk interpretations, or may be of a disorganizing order (KF, K, cF, c, kF, k). As against such direct indications of anxiety, its presence can be inferred in a variety of ways. Loss of control, exaggerated recourse to defenses, shock reactions, blocking—all point to anxiety.

Response to the shading qualities of the blots requires a certain sensitivity not commonly found in children. At best, when it does occur, it is likely to be of the vague, free floating variety expressed in KF, K, cF and c answers, indicating that anxiety is producing disorganization and irritability. It is the rare child who can react to his anxiety in mature, controlled fashion (Fc, FK, Fk) before eight or nine and in many instances considerably later. Rather, severe, exaggerated repression of conflict, denial of conflict and of disturbing experiences, extreme retreat into fantasy or repeated, disrupting outbursts with loss of intellectual and emotional control, persistent shock reactions—dark, initial and color—constant and marked indications of unusual feelings of inadequacy, all spell anxiety in the child.

His anxiety in relation to his drives and impulses frequently develops in the child the need to exercise undue control over these or deny them altogether. Thus, the child who gives an unusually high number of form responses, who adheres rigidly to those limited and selected aspects of a situation that he feels he can handle (many D and d, few W) is definitely anxious and must constantly invoke these defenses against his anxiety.

Similarly, the child who denies his own formulations almost as soon as they are expressed, who doubts and qualifies everything he says or does, who refuses to respond or who blocks because he is so conflict-ridden that he cannot deal with the circumstances, is also suffering from exaggerated anxiety. Thus, many rejections of the blots in the child above six, constant qualifications and denial of responses are Rorschach evidence for anxiety.

Again, the child who retreats sharply into himself and makes no emotional response to his environment does so because his experiences with the world about him have led him to see emotional involvements as conflict-provoking and therefore sources of anxiety. His protocols will be conspicuous for their lack of color responses, something that is rare in children, especially children below eight or nine years of age. He may even be so disturbed that he will deny himself the comfort of emotional release in fantasy. On the other hand, the child may show exaggerated dependence on his environment and a complete repression or denial of his own inner life. In such cases there is a complete detachment from the emotions associated with his fantasies. Instead, the energy that would ordinarily be employed in the fantasy activity is used for establishing emotional contacts with the outside world, contacts which are usually characterized by the subject's infantile needs and demands. Consequently there will be no human movement interpretations, but many color responses.

Finally, loss of control, sporadic explosive emotional outbursts, intense strivings for prestige and status, all betray the presence of anxiety. When the tensions and anxiety he is experiencing get out of hand, the child will manifest a loss of objectivity and indulge in inadequate, unacceptable, disorganized, and inappropriate behavior.

It should be noted that the actual presence of anxiety is not in itself of significance in evaluating the degree of maturity and stability the individual has attained.[57] Some measure of anxiety is present in practically everyone. What must be determined is the intensity of the anxiety, what causes it, and what methods for handling it the individual has developed. This can be best discussed under the defense mechanisms.

The Defense Mechanisms

The way in which an individual tries to achieve satisfaction and security can take a variety of forms. These are almost always influenced by the need to allay the anxiety that the strivings for satisfaction and threats to self-concept may arouse. In our culture, activation of sexual and aggressive impulses is most likely to mobilize this anxiety. To avoid this, the individual develops ways to handle his impulses and drives, and so evolves ways of avoiding anxiety. In general these methods consist of repression; denial; flight from anxiety producing experiences; identification; reaction formation; doing and undoing; projection; detachment; regression; and deflection or sublimation.[12, 15] These mechanisms are employed by everyone but it is the appropriateness and effectiveness of their application and the amount of emotional freedom and constructive personality development they permit that determine whether or not the individual's adjustment is a healthy or unhealthy one. In the healthy individual, the defenses he musters when anxiety threatens operate well enough to reduce or allay that anxiety. There is no need, in his case, for the continued emphasis on certain mechanisms regardless of the nature of the circumstances. However, where the defenses do not operate successfully, there is a continual, compulsive need for them, and they are invoked even when the immediate situation does not demand their presence and activity.

The individual's adjustive mechanisms are reflected in the Rorschach and reveal the ways he seeks to deal with his anxiety. It is through these as well as direct evidence of anxiety that its intensity and nature can be determined.

Repression manifests itself in the inkblot test primarily through an extreme emphasis on the form responses with a concomitant neglect of emotional reactions. By avoiding emotional involvement, whether the emotional stimuli come from within or without, the subject strives to maintain conscious control over his reactions and this keeps them in line with the standards of behavior he has set for himself. It is the form responses that reflect the formal, controlled, intellectual approach and, when a large amount of energy is employed in maintaining such an approach, there is little or none of it available for emotional experiences.

An overemphasis on form responses cannot always be interpreted as the result of repressive efforts. In the very young child a high form percentage, 70 per cent or more, is the rule rather than the exception. His overabundance of form responses does not come from any attempt on his part to inhibit his affect (p. 25), but is caused by his lack of rich and varied emotional resources. Actually repression is not too frequently employed as an adjustive mechanism before the age of four or four and a half. At this time there is relatively little tolerance for anxiety and much of it is likely to be reacted to in direct, overt behavior. When repression is invoked it may show itself in complete refusal to respond to a card, in refusal to look at the cards, and in long time delays.

After four and a half, the absence of emotional responses must be considered a significant deviation. It may be a function of inhibitory efforts or may be the result of a developmental lag such as is sometimes seen in dull children, and also in children who, because of organic disorders or other disturbances, cannot develop a self-concept and then handle their feeling experiences in terms of such a concept. Which factors are operative can best be determined by the quality of the total record. If the child is still functioning like a two and a half or three year old, then his lack of emotional spontaneity may be the result of a developmental lag. On the other hand, if his reactions are more typical of the four and a half to six year olds, then his lack of spontaneity may well be the result of his efforts at dealing with anxiety by recourse to inhibition, overcontrol and repression.

In children of school age the problem is simpler. For these subjects the average number of form interpretations constitutes between 50 and 60 per cent of the total number of responses. When the form per cent rises much above 60, either strong inhibitory efforts or an absence of the capacity for emotional experience must be inferred. Where the high form percentage is the result of inhibitory efforts, the form response will be generally good, that is, the F+ per cent will be in line with and possibly even better than expectancy for the child's age, in contrast to those cases where the high form per cent is the result of developmental lag or serious personality difficulties, as might be encountered in mental deficiency, schizophrenia, or organic disorders of the central nervous system. In these latter cases the responses will frequently be vaguely perceived and weakly organized.

Some children, even relatively young ones, reinforce their inhibitory efforts by limiting the sphere of their activity. They do not try to meet total situations, but pick from each experience limited aspects of it which they feel they can handle (see p. 23). This not only gives them a sense of accomplishment and provides some feeling of security, but also helps them avoid anything that might mobilize anxiety. In these cases the Rorschach will show many D and d responses, far more than are ordinarily obtained from children of comparable age. There are strong efforts at *detachment* in such instances, along with other elements that mark the beginnings of the compulsive personality. In some cases, the emphasis on details is compensated for by quantity production.

In many instances where repression is employed, the effectiveness of the mechanisms can be evaluated in terms of the degree to which affect is avoided. In most cases the control is not strong enough to do this completely, and the child's helplessness in the face of his disorganizing emotions will become manifest in the abrupt appearance of a color answer, of the CF or C variety, or of an aggressive FM or M, quickly followed by a retreated-into, overcontrolled reaction, or by complete blocking. Recourse to white space responses may also occur at such times, being part of the total avoidance effort.

Reinforcement of repressive efforts by making definite character changes which, in a sense, obviate the need for the repressive efforts is known as *reaction formation*. For example, in the place of aggression, passive, conforming attitudes are developed and there is therefore no need to avoid situations which stimulate aggressive response or to deny the aggressive impulses. In the Rorschach, recourse to reaction formation is manifested by emphasis on conforming types of response, namely the controlled color (FC), good form (F+), and popular answers. Also, any marked emphasis on interpretations suggesting passivity and conformity may be a manifestation of reaction formation, providing the rest of the protocol is in keeping with such an evaluation of the personality structure.

In his efforts to deny the unacceptable impulse, the individual may resort to *doing and undoing*. This form of defense shows itself in the Rorschach in the giving and denying of responses, either in toto or in part, that is, the subject questions, alters, or actually rejects his response. Sometimes this takes very direct form in children, when an undesirable form of response is immediately followed by a denial of it (Record 4, page 92); or it may be carried out less directly, as when the same area is interpreted and reinterpreted a number of times, each new interpretation constituting a denial of the previous one.

Denial is one of the simplest mechanisms and is used largely by the youngest age group. "It isn't nothing," "I don't see nothing" and similar answers frequently stem more from anxiety about the circumstances confronting them than from any other reason. Other forms of denial are found in responses like, "It can't hurt you" or "It isn't anything bad." These and similar reactions are most frequent in the child under five. In older children denial sometimes occurs concomitantly with the expression of a forbidden impulse: for example, on Card III, "These two men aren't fighting, no they wouldn't be fighting, they're talking."

By *identifying* with the important figures in his environment, the child takes on the patterns of behavior he feels will enable him to conform with environmental demands and strengthen him in his struggle against his unacceptable drives. These identifications constitute a reinforcement of his own superego. The evidence of the capacity for internalization, the acceptance of demands of reality, efforts at control and conformity, when present in a Rorschach record, all give evidence that identification is an important factor in the individual's adjustment.

Flight from anxiety-producing situations involves escape from emotional demands that are too disturbing, or escape from fantasies that arouse anxiety. In the first instance, emotional involvement with the outside world is eschewed and emotions are turned back on the self. In such cases the M and FM responses will be very numerous, color answers completely or almost completely absent. On the other hand, when it is the fantasies that the individual cannot accept without anxiety, these will be avoided and escape from them sought through emotional involvement with the environment. In such cases there will be many color answers, and few or no animal and human movement interpretations. Where both the fantasies and emotional contacts are too distressing, the flight becomes repression. In those cases the form responses are very numerous, as indicated above, and may be accompanied by refusals of certain cards because of their particular significance for the individual subject.

Projection as a mechanism of defense must be distinguished from projection as a means of studying personality structure. As a defense, projection avoids the disturbances caused by unacceptable drives and impulses by ascribing these to others. Such activity, when carried to any lengths, interferes with the acceptance of reality and leads to the development of paranoid trends. In the Rorschach, it is usually accompanied by evidence that the individual finds his environment an evil, threatening place as a result of the activities and attitudes he has attributed to it. Accompanying this perception of the world he has created, there go strong feelings of being watched and threatened, these feelings being a counterpart of the guilt that the individual experiences in connection with his projected feelings and impulses. Thus his protocol will show humans in frightening, brutal, morbid forms of activity, and will also contain a number of interpretations of faces, eyes, pointing hands, etc.

Regression is the term used to define the retreat of the individual to stages of his development in which he felt more secure and satisfied. Such retreat is not uncommon in young children, and may often be indicative only of a very temporary disruption in their development. On the other hand, radical and prolonged retreats point to more serious disturbances.

In the Rorschach protocol, regression may be reflected in the presence of behavorial patterns characteristic of children much younger than the subject. In particular, the appearance of total or partial perserveration, so typical of the three year old (see p. 67), in the protocol of a school age child would be suggestive of such regression. However, it is also possible that the child never moved on from the level of development suggested by the reactions he is now giving. It is important that the distinction between regression and fixation be made. Where the behavior is of a regressive order, there will usually be some indications in the record of the capacity for more mature forms of response than would be expected on the basis of the overall picture. For example, the record may be strongly perseverative yet also contain one or two good movement responses, or indications of the capacity to deal with anxiety most maturely (Fc).

Other evidences of regression consist of the presence of pure color answers where there is indication that the individual can also give well controlled emotional responses (FC).

It is not clear just how *sublimation* and *deflection of impulse* manifest themselves in the Rorschach method. This is not surprising in view of the fact that it is not always easy to establish this through other procedures. Fenichel says, ". . . sometimes it is not possible to distinguish between 'a drive changed by the influence of the ego' and 'a drive that breaks through in a distorted way against the will of the ego and unrecognized by it.' "[12]

In a study of the defenses against anxiety employed by 190 children including normal, neurotic and schizophrenic children,[26] it developed that repression was the most frequently employed defense, outweighing by far all the other defenses. Flight and projection were next in order. However, all possible defenses were not included in the investigation, and it is possible that an inclusion of these might alter the picture somewhat.

Ego Strength

The ego is the name commonly given to those activities of the individual which aim toward the understanding and acceptance of the realities to which the individual must adjust. These activities involve not only the understanding or cognitive functions, but also are concerned with the power or energy necessary to enforce the behavior which follows this understanding of reality. With the aid of the sensory apparatus, the ego determines the nature of the physical, emotional, and social world in which the individual lives. It also must know the individual, that is, the strength of the instinctual drives and the pressures exerted by the superego. The ego then is the force that regulates the interplay between the various pressures placed on the individual from within and without. The better the ego's understanding of the demands of reality on the one hand and the strength and nature of the inner forces on the other, the better its directive power can be. Furthermore, it must have sufficient energy to enforce the responses which it has determined are the healthy ones. In general, then, the functions of the ego can be summed up under the following activities: selecting, understanding, directing, and enforcing. The ego is strong if it is able to integrate the needs of the conflict- and anxiety-provoking drives with the demands of reality in a way that does not interfere with reasonable fulfillment of the individual's potentialities and his desires. On the other hand, the ego is weak if either the handling of the drives is unsuccessful or the development of the personality resources is seriously curtailed. Some compromises must, of course, be made and some curtailment of personality potential is inevitable, as well as some break through of drives. It is when such curtailment and such break through exceed the so-called normal or expected limits that the ego is not functioning effectively.

On the basis of the above description of the ego and its functions, it becomes immediately apparent that the ego of the child cannot be a strong one when compared with standards set for adults. Moreover, the younger the child, the weaker the ego is likely to be. As the child's understanding of reality grows, as he learns to select from his experiences the important or essential aspects of them and correspondingly to subordinate trivia, as his control over his instinctual drives becomes stronger, the ego can operate more and more effectively. However, at each age level there is a certain amount of ego strength that is normal for that age.

Every reaction of the individual affords evidence of his ego strength since, in all behavioral responses, his appreciation of reality and his handling of his own impulses are reflected. From the point of view of ego strength, responses can be divided into four categories: 1) there is an understanding of the realities of the circumstances, the appropriate response is available and the ego has sufficient strength to implement such a response; 2) there is an appreciation of the realities involved but the appropriate response is not available; 3) there is an understanding of the realities, the appropriate response is available but cannot be enforced; 4) the nature of the reality factors are not understood and therefore the appropriate response is not made. The failure to appreciate the nature of the realities may be a failure to understand the nature of external reality, of internal reality, or both.

On the Rorschach test, good form (F+ %) has always been considered the primary indicator of the indivi   nderstanding of the nature of objective reality. The extent to whi   hild recognizes this reality should be in accord with expectancy for h   Similarly, his ability to face this reality should find reflection in the r   onship between his whole and his large detail responses. The child who   oes not grasp the obvious aspects of a circumstance at a level commensurate with his age, either because he is dull or because he is disturbed, is not meeting reality adequately. The good form answers and the relationship between the whole and large detail responses are among the primary indicators on the Rorschach of understanding of reality.

Appreciation of the realities but inability to give the appropriate form of response is caused by a variety of factors. An individual may not have at his disposal the resources necessary for giving the required form of reaction. Young children, for example, when they first get involved in a conflict with a strange child, indicate by their behavior that they understand what the circumstances hold, but they do not know how to respond. They may have been trained to avoid aggression, yet at the same time been expected to be self-reliant. In such cases the child recognizes the circumstances for what they are, but cannot select from among his responses the one he thinks will fit the case. Such disturbance may be reflected in the Rorschach in complete blocking;* in giving a poor response; in giving a response and then denying it; in much card turning and long time delays; in statements revealing feelings of helplessness and inadequacy.

Sometimes an individual recognizes the nature of the circumstance, knows what the expected response should be, but is so pushed by his own needs and anxieties that he cannot muster enough control to give the appropriate reaction. The ego's power to enforce this adequate reaction is missing. In such instances there are likely to be sudden breaks in form level, abrupt appearance of emotional outbursts $(CF-, C)$; breaks in sequence; impulsive formulations (DW).

Finally there is the inability to understand the nature of reality. This limitation can be caused by lack of experience; by organic disturbance which interferes with perception and organization; by distortions resulting from the intensity of the individual's own needs and impulses. In the young child, the many poor form responses he gives and his generally arbitrary treatment of the test stimuli give evidence of his weak grasp on reality. Similarly, in the "organic" individual distortions in perception make it impossible for him to understand the nature of the situation confronting him and his response to it will, therefore, reflect this weakness in understanding. In others the failure in perception is caused by their need to find in the cir-

---

* Such disturbance is not the only reason for blocking. In all cases, the total protocol must be taken into consideration.

cumstances what they seek there. They therefore distort their perceptions with frequency and naturally cannot then respond appropriately. In all these cases, poor form, whether it be present in the pure form responses (F), or in those where, among other factors, form is involved, as in the M, FM, FC, Fc, indicates deviant perception and response.

In general, weakness of the ego may stem from intellectual lack, with the result that understanding will be decidedly inferior to what is ordinarily found at a given age. It may be caused by disturbances in visual perceptions arising from an organic disturbance of the central nervous system, or may result from intense emotional impact which overwhelms control and objectivity, and produces distortions in perception. Such a state of affairs occurs where there are emotional disturbances of a neurotic and/or psychotic order. Again, where reality is correctly perceived but not accepted, it is very likely to be the push of impulse and feeling that produces the deviant and inadequate response to reality. The executive function of the ego, the carrying out of the activities which are necessary to effect an adequate adaptation of inner needs to external demands, is likely to be most hampered when impulses are unduly strong and emotions out of control.

It is important to note that ego strength cannot be measured solely in terms of the control that the individual is exercising. Rather, its strength depends upon its capacity to mobilize all the assets available to it and likewise to use these in appropriate fashion. Control by itself is certainly not an index of ego strength and good adjustment. In fact, exaggerated recourse to control is as much a sign of weakness as is absence of control. Indeed, in all personality measurements, extremes are never of value, even when the trait or attribute that is being emphasized seems to be a positive one. It is in this respect probably more than any other that personality testing differs from other kinds of evaluation. When measuring intelligence, artistic ability, manual skill, the more of the particular trait the individual has, the better. In judging personality traits, among them ego strength, this does not follow. It is not a matter of control being good and more control being better. Rather, there is a point beyond which the exercise of control (or of any function) hampers personality functioning and reflects weakness as surely as does too little. A strong ego is one which can use other mechanisms beside control, mechanisms which enrich and resolve conflicts, thereby reducing the necessity for extremes of any kind.

CHAPTER VII

General Interpretive Problems (continued)

Age Patterns

THE CHILD'S APPROACH to his experiences, the way he meets the problems typical for his age as well as the daily routines of living, is determined not only by his particular background, training and ability, but also by the general level of development, physical, intellectual, emotional and social, that he has attained. There are certain patterns of response typical for certain stages of development, evolving out of the child's needs and abilities at that particular time. These patterns are reflected in the Rorschach records and it is essential to recognize these as typical of a given age level in order to determine whether the child's development is keeping pace with his chronological growth.

Two and a Half to Four Year Olds

From all that has been said up to this point regarding the meaning of the Rorschach factors and of the child's specific problems at this age, it becomes obvious that the prevailing test pattern at this period will consist of relatively few answers (about 8 to 12), a large preponderance of whole responses, many of them poor, a number of them possibly combined with the inner or outer white space (WS). Interpretation will be made predominantly, in some cases almost exclusively, on the basis of form, and again much of this form will be scored minus. If any color answers occur they will be of the C or CF variety. Movement is as likely to be ascribed to inanimate objects as to animate ones. The content will deal largely with animals, nature, plants, and architecture.

Another important reaction typical for this age group is striking recourse to perseveration. It is not unusual in the record of a two and a half year old to find the same response carried through all ten cards. In some children this perseveration is found only in part of the record but, until about four, perseverative trends of a greater or lesser order almost inevitably occur.[1, 38] Klopfer refers to this as the "magic key." He suggests that the child uses the same response over and over because, having given it once and found it met the demands of the moment, he feels he can use it safely on other occasions. There is no doubt that such considerations must play a most important part in the magic repetition so typical for the young child. Other factors, however, are probably also operative here. The child's need to reassure himself about all his experiences demands an endless repetition of the same activity or response. One has only to watch a child open and close a door, or turn on and off an electric light to know how true this is. Similarly, his demand for endless repetitions of jingles and games, which must not deviate in the repeating by a single jot, bears witness to this need to go over and over things to ensure their substance and reality. This is one way that the child has of making sure of his environment and of making his ideas solidly his own.

Again, the child's unique way of perceiving and evaluating concepts may also play an important part here. What the child sees is a certain size card with a white shiny background and a superimposed blot. For him the minor differences in the shapes of the blots are probably of little moment. Therefore, if he has called the first card a mountain, he will probably feel that the second card is much the same and call it a mountain too. He may even indicate by a slight qualifying of his answer that he recognizes some minor difference in the circumstances, but his overall perception remains the same. Thus, Card II may be a prettier mountain or a bigger mountain, but it is still a mountain.

It is of considerable importance to note what the content of the response is. The child who stresses mountains is probably someone who feels overwhelmed by the size of his environment[8, 60, 62] and/or may be identifying with this size. Emphasis on tunnels is often indicative of a need for shelter and protection, and so on.

The place in the record where the perseveration breaks is definitely significant. In some cases the introduction of the all-colored cards is the point at which the repetition of the answer stops. In such cases it is obvious that the child is aware of the changing nature of the environment, and even if he does not include color in his interpretation of the last three cards, one can nevertheless be sure that he is not unaware of environmental pressures. The nature of the response he gives at this point, whether he shows a positive response to the emotionally charged stimuli, rejects them, or is disturbed by them, gives an indication of his perception of the environment. Sometimes it is the concentrated darkness of Card IV that makes itself felt and alters the pattern of the subject's reaction.

In this age group adult populars occur infrequently, and in some cases are altogether absent. On the other hand, if strict scoring is employed, there is likely to be a number of original minus answers.

As has already been indicated, initial shock is very common at this age period, reflecting the child's limited capacity for facing up to new and unexpected circumstances. Thus his reactions to Card I give some indication of his self-confidence and his ability to adjust to new situations (pp. 8, 35).

Dark shock also appears, though not as frequently as it does in the following age period, that is, between four and a half and six. When it does occur, it is generally indicative of conflicts with authority which have already left their mark on the developing personality (see p. 35).

Color shock (see p. 35) as seen in adults is not found at this age. The absence of color responses or the disorganized nature of those that do appear cannot be considered indicative of such shock. There are children who have had pleasant and reassuring emotional experiences, and children who have had negative ones. Their response to emotionally charged circumstances may reflect the nature of these experiences. However, their capacity for emotional control and modulation is so weak and limited, and proneness to disorganization so characteristic, that the concept of color shock, as it is generally used, can rarely apply.

In general the picture presented in the Rorschach findings of this youngest age group is in many ways like that obtained from seriously disturbed adults. In fact, children of this age have been characterized as "healthy schizophrenics," and their Rorschach protocols bear out this description.

Because of the generally unstructured nature of the personality, deviations at this age are not easily detected. Even complete refusal to respond may not be especially significant. More conclusive are evidences of precocity intermingled with the typical age patterns. Thus the appearance of a few human movement responses (M) or of well controlled shading answers (Fc), along with poor form and possible perseveration, points to such uneven and erratic development that it can only be indicative of the variability associated with personality disorders and serious maladjustment. However, if precocious reactions are present, but are part of a general mature integration (see Record No. 2), then no gross personality difficulties can be assumed.

Four and a Half to Six Year Olds

There are striking differences in the child's Rorschach responses at this period when compared with the period just preceding. Although still struggling with many new concepts and experiences, still uncertain about their meaning and place in the world and in relation to himself, the child nevertheless has a better grasp of reality, shows a somewhat greater capacity for discriminating between essentials and nonessentials, between animate and inanimate, and begins to have some recognition of his need to conform to society's demands. Above all, he has established himself as a "self" apart from the environment, and can therefore deal more objectively and realistically with the situations in which he finds himself.

As a result of the changes that have taken place during this period, the Rorschach records show a definite increase in F+ per cent, the good form responses now consitituting between 70 and 80 per cent of the total number of form answers given. Perseveration has practically disappeared by the beginning of this age period and by the end of it should not be present at all. As part of his increased grasp of reality the child now also deals with his experiences in more practical fashion. The number of large detail answers increases, and they constitute at this time about 50 per cent of the responses.

As part of the development of the awareness of the self, emotional reactions take on different meaning and color. There is a need to relate to others, to share feeling experiences with them. At the same time there is some recognition of the fact that emotional response must make certain concessions to the demands of reality, must be somewhat controlled. Thus, the pure color responses tend to disappear and CF responses take over, and an occasional FC response may be present. The CF responses, however, will be by far the most numerous, and continue to be so throughout childhood.

There is also some realization of the fact that some experiences must be dealt with within the self rather than in direct, overt forms, or through emotional contact with others. The beginning of internalization marks another important step in the personality development. On the average this occurs at about four and a half years. Obviously there are children who arrive at this stage much earlier and some who hit it later. The child who cannot handle any of his feeling experiences on a symbolic and fantasy level by the time he reaches five and a half or six years of age is manifesting a lag or deviation in development. He is either incapable of such internalization or is afraid of his fantasies and so cannot permit them any expression.

It is during this period that the use of black, as color, reaches its peak. The concept of "black" interpretations as indicators of traumatic experiences ties in well with the emotional problems of the child at this time. Having now established himself as a person in his world, the child is coming up against the demands and pressures of that world, is feeling frustration in a different manner than ever before. It is now the outside world, an agent apart from himself that is frustrating him. At the same time he is trying to identify with various objects in that world and is accepting and internalizing the concepts they stress. In consequence, the child is torn by his need to conform and his resentment of the frustration and deprivation that this need produces. The more intense the conflict, the more numerous the responses using "black" are likely to be. This hypothesis has received clinical validation since it is primarily in the disturbed children, those who are having difficulty accepting reality demands and resolving their oedipal problem, that the interpretations involving the black as a determinant are likely to be numerous.

The problems in relation to authority are also reflected in the change that takes place in the interpretation of Card IV (pp. 48, 49). It now almost universally becomes a figure symbolic of power, usually a large masculine figure, a gorilla, giant, monster. Dark shock is frequent on this card, and this sometimes carries over to Card V.

With the increased recognition of what is involved in emotional relationships, color shock may make its appearance, though it is still relatively infrequent. In its classical form of color avoidance, it is not typical for the child of this age who usually is still trying, despite whatever unpleasant experiences he may have had with his environment, to relate to it and get some emotional response from it. Initial shock also occurs at this time, although with somewhat less frequency than it did in the younger group.

The child between four and a half and six who is not developing in line with expectancy may show his deviations in a number of ways. He may present reaction patterns very similar to those of the age period preceding his, that is, he may give a record that is almost 100 per cent perseverative, consisting mainly of whole and poor form responses. Such a child has either not moved on from this phase of his development or has regressed to it.

Deviations in development at this age also manifest themselves in the appearance of pure color answers without any color-form or form-color responses. In such a case the child is apparently unable to develop the control necessary for making affective responses of a more acceptable order.

Records which contain only whole responses reflect a lag in the ability to discriminate and differentiate. Associated with this there is generally a lag in reality testing. On the other hand, records which emphasize details to a degree all out of line with the norms for this age period are generally obtained from children who are markedly insecure and are trying in this compulsive fashion to find some stability (see p. 23). Associated with this focusing on details, there is generally an exceptionally large number of responses when compared with what is ordinarily produced by children at this age level.

Again, as at the early period, any mixture of extremely precocious and extremely infantile forms of behavior must be considered indicative of serious deviations in development, a general lack of personality integration

Six to Ten Year Olds

The school age child is a very different individual from the child that he was just a short period ago. Both because of his physiological development and his intellectual, emotional and social experiences, his grasp of objective reality is much improved. His acceptance of reality, with all its frustrations, as an inevitable part of life, is strong, and he has learned what the expected forms of reaction are and is motivated toward complying with them.

He has developed resources which will help him in his adjustive efforts; among these resources is his capacity for dealing with many of his experiences on a fantasy level and for finding satisfaction through emotional contacts with the world about him. He has developed considerable intellectual and emotional control and is capable of exercising a certain amount of objectivity when confronted with reality problems.

The personality attributes characteristic for this period are indicated in the Rorschach record by: 1) a definite increase in good form per cent; 2) a shift in the relationship between the whole and detail responses, with increasing emphasis on the details so that by about eight years of age the W:D ratio is similar to that found in adults; 3) an increase in the total number of interpretations in the record, sufficient to allow for the evaluation of the sequence of responses; 4) a growing number of color and movement answers; 5) the appearance of two or more adult popular responses, the number increasing steadily from six to ten years. In general, the picture for this age roughly approximates that found in adults. The similarity to adult reactions is, however, only a relative one, the child's lack of experience and comparatively limited understanding of many matters still manifesting itself in his responses.

At the outset of this period the child has just completed his joust with authority and has come to accept the fact that he must go along with the demands of reality and play the game according to the rules. He is therefore unduly "rule" conscious. His experience with the rules is, as yet, so limited that he cannot be flexible about them but adheres to them rigidly. Emphasis is therefore strongly on "right" and "wrong," "good" and "bad." In consequence, the good form percentage at this age (six to seven) is likely to be unusually high, higher than it is later when the child is willing to take a chance (see p. 25). At the same time he is not always able to maintain the control which his own rigidity demands of him, and therefore sudden breaks, indicated by the appearance of a pure color answer or an unexpected poor form response, occur. There is likely to be a sharp fluctuation between rigid control and loss of control, between emotional outbursts and self-restraint. Not only the formal aspects of the responses, but their content likewise attest to this. His responses will stress the realistic, clear cut aspects of his experiences, the things about which he is sure, and he will have good explanations for his reactions, yet at the same time he will indulge in explosive, diffuse responses like "fire and smoke." The predominant trend, however, emphasizes reality factors and acceptable forms of response. The child will say, "This really looks like a bird," and will also ask for confirmation from the examiner who represents authority at the moment. He will also want reassurance that he is doing what is expected of him.

As the child becomes more accustomed to following the dictates of internalized authority, and grows more familiar with himself in the role of mentor, his rigidities pass. He takes chances with his impulses, tries out some of his ideas. At the same time, as the novelty of being his own guiding spirit wears off, he has less need to be aggressively positive. He also begins to compare his ideas and standards, as he has absorbed them from the parental figures, with those he is running up against in the larger environment. This is likely to produce some anxiety and confusion.

The Rorschach picture around seven is therefore likely to show a mixture of aggression, withdrawal and anxiety. Explosive and morbid responses are frequent. Reevaluation of the self in fantasy makes for an increase in movement answers. Occasionally shading responses appear for the first time, and color shock may be manifested.

Around eight the child achieves a reasonable integration of his personal problems and social demands. With this there goes a state of satisfaction and contentment not found at any other age. In a sense, eight may be said to be the peak of childhood, the time when the accumulated experiences are operating for the most satisfactory and satisfying adjustments. The child knows now that concessions must be made, that there are no absolutes, and he accepts this. He recognizes the need for modulation and qualification and he acts accordingly.

His Rorschach records in many ways come closer to those of the adult at this time than at any other period. The relationship between whole and detail answers is like that of the grown-up.[30] The same is true of his form and good form percentages. While his color-form responses may still outweigh his form-color responses, pure color reactions will probably be negligible. Human movement responses will often be as numerous as the animal movement answers. Likewise the number of adult popular responses will increase.

The reactions typical of the eight year old may continue for a year or so, or may be cut short by the appearance of prepuberty problems. Certainly by ten the picture for the majority of the children has altered considerably. The uncertainties produced by new feelings, thoughts and experiences make for withdrawal, caution and exaggerated control. Sometime during this period, it may be at nine, at ten or at eleven, the child no longer reacts in spontaneous outgoing fashion. Instead, he retreats into himself and tries to evaluate what is taking place in himself and in the world about him which he begins to perceive differently than ever before. Because he is unsure of what all this means, he has to refind himself, and he does this largely through his fantasy activity, with Rorschach emphasis on movement responses to the neglect of color answers. He also strives to act with great discretion, and attains this by imposing conscious control on his reactions (high F and F+ per cents). This control in part offsets the disturbances that are clearly indicated by the numerous and severe shock reactions the child experiences at this time. He now has a deeper understanding and awareness of the nature of emotional demands and experiences than he ever had before and, in view of his new feelings and undecided orientation, he is not able to meet these adequately. Instead, he is likely to withdraw sharply from all emotional pressures and, as has been indicated, turn his feelings back on himself in his efforts to refind and reevaluate himself.

Uncertainty further manifests itself in the child's qualifying of his responses and his concern about their correctness. Body tensions are reflected in the sudden appearance of a relatively large number of anatomical responses, especially in girls.

This period, like the very earliest period, has a distinct pattern. The trends found at this time are much more common and the differences between the individual children less marked than at almost any age since three to four. This similarity suggests that the group as a whole is facing a common problem, the coming of adolescence, and that the mechanisms that develop for meeting this problem have considerable similarity despite obvious individual differences.

The healthy child makes his adjustment at this time primarily through his withdrawal, his exaggerated control, his blocking. In other words, he uses mainly avoidance techniques as far as the environment is concerned while trying to work out his problems within himself. The disturbed child is unable to exercise the rigid control that the better adjusted child can command. For the disturbed child there may be shock reactions and withdrawal, along with a loss of objectivity and good reality concepts. It is primarily the difference in control that distinguishes the well adjusted from the poorly adjusted subject during this period. The other phenomena typical for this period, the withdrawal and shock, would under other circumstances spell disturbance of considerable magnitude. At this age, too, they reflect disturbance but since it is a typical and universal experience, it is not out of line with the normal reactions in our culture. Instead, the child who, at this age, does not show deep concern about himself, his role in life, and his relationships to others, is the deviate, rather than the child whose reactions reflect turmoil and conflict—always provided there is sufficient control to keep the disturbances within the limits of reality.

CHAPTER VIII

The Well Adjusted Child

ADJUSTMENT CONSISTS of a series of checks and balances or compromise formations, by means of which the individual attempts to get along in his particular environment in the way that is most comfortable and rewarding for him. "Good adjustment" cannot be measured in absolute terms, but rather on the bases of the criteria postulated above (see p. 5), namely the consistency of the individual's behavior in relation to inner and outer forces and circumstances. Thus it is not enough for the individual to feel secure and comfortable. The way he has achieved his security and comfort must also be acceptable to his environment. Similarly, environmental approval of his behavior does not spell good adjustment if this behavior has been achieved at the expense of the subject's sense of well being and happiness, if adequate self-realization is not achieved. Obviously the perfect dovetailing of inner and outer needs and conditions is never attained. Where the cut-off point between good and poor adjustment falls is, therefore, a somewhat subjective decision, varying from individual to individual and culture to culture.

In his adjustive efforts, there are, broadly speaking, two courses open to the individual. He can alter the strength, direction and goals of his inner needs, or he can alter the nature and the demands of the environment. In our culture, training emphasizes the modification of the individual's drives and the development of traits of character which in a sense constitute a synthesis of "instinctual drives and superego control."[51]

In general, adjustment must be measured in terms of the total personality picture, the richness of the resources that have been developed and the way these resources are employed. The mature, well adjusted individual is one whose emotions are so stable and so well integrated with social demands and standards that he can express them easily and appropriately, without producing anxiety, and without anticipating that such emotional release will prove disruptive to his equilibrium; who can accept his fantasies and use them to help him resolve his conflicts, but who does not permit them to interfere with his appreciation of reality or with the establishment of social and interpersonal relationships; who has sufficient sensitivity to be able to modulate his reactions so that they are in line with social norms, but whose sensitive awareness does not develop into overcaution and crippling anxiety; who can participate in group attitudes and reactions but who does not carry such participation to the point where his individuality is submerged

in that of the group; who can exercise good control and judgment, but is
not so rigid and exacting that he never dares take a chance or err; who has
appropriate and varied interests, not haphazard, scattered ones; who accepts and respects himself and extends this respect to those with whom he
has contact; who does not permit conflict to drain his energy, but uses
his energy in constructive, goal-directed fashion. Such a level of adjustment
is obviously not possible for the child. In his case, adjustment must be
measured in terms of the specific problems he has to face at specific age
periods, always bearing in mind what strengths can be expected from children at each age. Measurement of adjustment in children, therefore, cannot
employ the same criteria that are used with adults, and efforts to do so
result in misleading information.

Since the individual's adjustment is made because of his need to handle
his conflicts and the anxiety associated with these conflicts, the way he
deals with his anxiety, an evaluation of the nature and intensity of that
anxiety and the defenses developed against it, constitutes one of the more
objective methods for assessing personality adjustment. The nature of
children's anxiety, as well as the way they react to it, will be different at
different age levels. In using anxiety as a criteria of adjustment, the differences that pertain at different ages must be recognized and evaluation
made in terms of this understanding.

Two and a Half to Four Year Olds

At this age the child's energies should be primarily directed toward establishing both a concept of self and an understanding of objective reality.
Since, generally, only the feeble beginnings of a superego are operative,
relatively little anxiety is aroused by the conflicts that occur between the
child and his environment. As has already been indicated (see p. 69),
the personality structure of the child in this age group is still largely of a
diffuse, undifferentiated order. What the child experiences at this time is
essentially fear and frustration, rather than anxiety, and his reactions to
these are generally abrupt, direct, intense and short-lived.

Measures of adjustment for this age group therefore can only be based
on the nature of the child's efforts to meet his specific age problems, and
the success he achieves in these efforts. Obviously the child who is constantly gaining a better understanding of reality, and who is learning to
use this understanding constructively, is healthier than the child who shows
no growth in this connection. However, as predictive measures, such evalua-
tions must be treated with caution, since they give relatively little indication
of the way the child will handle the anxiety he will experience a little later
in life, during the four and a half to six year period and beyond that.

The diffuse, unstructured nature of the child's personality at this time finds reflection in the Rorschach protocol, and thus limits its value as a prognostic aid. The records obtained from children of this age are short and highly perseverative, revealing their inadequate grasp of reality and lack of personality resources. The findings can give some indication of the adequancy of the child's efforts to meet his specific problems, can indicate the extent of his understanding of reality, and the quality and nature of the resources he has developed to this point. However, prediction as to future adjustment can generally be only of a most tentative order.

Measurement of the effectiveness of the child's present functioning can be determined in terms of the amount of discrimination and objectivity he manifests in his test reactions. One such indicator can be found in the very first response to the test. If this initial interpretation shows an appreciation of the objective nature of the stimulus, that is, if the form of the response is reasonably good, there is evidence that the child is beginning to deal with his experiences in discriminating and realistic fashion. The fact that this response may then be inappropriately carried along through subsequent blots simply reflects typical limitations in the child's control and discriminatory capacities, but does not negate the relatively good judgment he displayed at the outset. The child who gives a good first response is definitely grappling with problems of his age.

Some children are less effective in their initial contact with a situation than they are subsequently. They need time to study the circumstances and become familiar with them. In such cases, efforts at coming to terms with reality may be delayed, but will eventually make their appearance as the child comes to understand what is expected of him, or when he encounters something he recognizes as part of a former experience (see Record No. 1). It follows then that any effort at exercising discrimination and objective control, in the form of an F+ response or a few large detail answers, points to constructive strivings. How successful the subject's efforts are can be determined by the number of adequate responses he gives, the extent of his perseveration, where it breaks, what responses come in at the time perseveration stops, and what emotional resources he has at his disposal. Among the youngest children in this group, the number of good form responses is often quite limited and additional resources consist largely of impulsive, demanding emotional reactions. Where there is absolutely no indication of a capacity for discriminatory reactions and objectivity, personality growth is certainly not proceeding in expected fashion. This is particularly true in the case of the child who is nearer four than two years of age.

In the evaluation of personality development, marked spurts in growth are as significant as lags. Thus, the occurrence of any unusual or unexpected forms of response, recourse to forms of adjustment that are out of line with the child's general level of development, are usually indicative of disturbance. For example, the child of four who is still perseverating and giving a number of poor form responses, yet also produces one or two FC answers, is manifesting emotional control that cannot have its foundations in real understanding or successful integration of affect and control. Rather it points to a precocity in one area and lags in others which are bound to produce disrupting effects. On the other hand, when the precocity is universal, that is, is present in all areas and therefore reflects a generally accelerated development, it may represent a comparatively mature, well integrated form of adjustment not typical for that age, but appropriate in terms of the particular child's endowment (see Record No. 2).

Four and a Half to Six Years Olds

By the time the child is four and a half or five, his personality has acquired structure. The self is differentiated from the rest of the world, and efforts at adjusting to that world must therefore be undertaken. Reality must be objectively perceived and must be accepted with some degree of consistency. The beginnings of the capacity for internalization and symbolization should be present, as well as the capacity for establishing emotional contact with others.

The major problems confronting the child at this period stem from the fact that, for the first time, he is aware of his responsibility in connection with his impulses and drives, is aware that he must do something about integrating these with the demands of his environment. Prior to this, he has experienced frustration, but little if any conflict and anxiety. Now he has many difficult, frustrating and anxiety-producing experiences to work through. If he can do this in reasonably adequate fashion, without crippling his own potentialities, his adjustment can be counted a good one.

In Rorschach terms his assets now consist of a relatively high good form per cent, the capacity to give FM and possibly even M responses, and also CF rather than C reactions. Large detail answers will now comprise about 50 per cent of all the responses given. How consistently and effectively the child applies his assets and how frequently he fails in their application constitute the measure of his adjustment. Certainly at this age the child cannot be expected to be objective at all times. Rather, he may lose control in unfamiliar and difficult circumstances, may give poor form responses particularly on such cards as VI; may show momentary regression, inappropriately carrying one response over to a succeeding card because of the stress he is experiencing at the time; may show helplessness in the face of conflict by blocking and failing to interpret; may show emotional regression by indulgence in a C answer. However, if such indications of disturbance and inadequacy are relatively infrequent and acceptable forms of response prevail, adjustment can be described as good.

Adjustive efforts that are all out of line with expectancy for the child's age must be evaluated in terms of the total picture. In particular, over-control (in the form of an exceptionally high F and F+ per cent), exaggerated efforts at discrimination and selectivity (many D and very few W responses), and flight from emotional involvement (no color answers, although from the quality of the responses it is evident that the child is mature enough to give them) often point to the beginnings of neurotic character structures. These efforts at adjustment may give a superficial impression of stability, but, insofar as they interfere with the development of resources and self-realization, they cannot be considered to have positive value. At this age it can be expected that the child's response to feeling experiences will be impulsive (CF greater than FC), his fantasies largely of an immature, primitive order (FM greater than M), and his control variable.

Six to Ten Year Olds

When the child reaches school age, his self-concept should be reasonably well crystallized and his personality well structured. He should be working through his basic conflicts with reality and authority. His resolution of these problems will be a function of many factors, internal and external. The form of adjustment stressed by any one particular child will not necessarily be the form used by another child of the same age. In one instance conformity may be emphasized, in another withdrawal and, in still a third, stress may be placed on fantasy activity. It is not the particular adjustive mechanisms that are employed, but the appropriateness and effectiveness of their application that determine the quality of the adjustment.

The manifestations of anxiety will be much the same for this age group as they were for the preceding group; they consist either of breaks in control with resulting disorganization and possible regression, or of exaggerated, inappropriate recourse to defenses. The latter are likely to be the more conspicuous at this period, in contrast to the earlier one where loss of control is frequent.

The good reality testing and control that the six to ten year olds have achieved is reflected in their Rorschach records in the form of a high F+ per cent (80 or better). Their ability to mobilize a variety of resources keeps the form per cent below 60, and produces CF, FC, FM and M responses. Emotional disorganization (C) is rare, and emotional control and maturity make an appearance in the form of FC answers (at least one at six, gradually increasing in number until around ten the FC answers exceed the CF responses). Inner life should be active, the more immature forms as represented by FM prevailing in the early years of this period, with the M increasing until they equal or exceed the FM answers.

With the onset of prepuberty which in many children occurs at nine or ten, a strongly introversive tendency makes itself manifest.* Aside from this exaggerated emphasis on fantasy at this time, there should be no marked stress on any one form of adjustment, no exaggerated control, no extreme dependency, no serious withdrawal. Defenses should be appropriate, and not called into use unnecessarily. A well rounded, smoothly functioning individual who is using his potentialities effectively and acceptably should be the standard for good adjustment.

The Rorschach records which follow were part of a complete psychological battery. The findings therefore do not constitute a full report, nor are they presented in report form. They simply state what the Rorchsach can contribute to the total picture.

* Where prepuberty occurs later than nine or ten, the characteristic emphasis on fantasy will not be manifested in the Rorschach until the appropriate time.

RECORD No. 1

Well Adjusted Boy, Age 2 Years 9 Months, I.Q. 108

I.	WS	F—	Arch	1. House.	(points to the four spaces) Windows.
II.	WS	F—	Arch	1. Another house.	(points to center space)
III.	WS	F—	Arch	(long delay) 1. House.	(no explanation)
IV.	W	F+	Pl	1. Tree.	Big, with a thing in the middle. (points to lower center D as "thing in middle")
V.	W	F—	Pl	1. Tree.	It's big too.
VI.	W	F—	Pl	1. Tree.	I don't know—no more.
VII.	W	F—	Pl	1. Tree.	It's big.
VIII.	W	CF—	Pl	1. Flowers.	So pretty.
IX.	W	CF—	Pl	1. Flowers.	It's pretty too, and here's leaves. (points to green)
X.	W	CF—	Pl	1. Flowers.	All flowers—no more.

R   10

W	7)10		F+	1)7		Arch	3		P	0
WS	3)		F−	6)		Pl	7			
			CF	3−						
W	70%		F	70%		A	0%			
D	30%		F+	14%						

$$M : C$$
$$0 : 3$$

$$Fm + FM : C' + c$$
$$0 : 0$$

$$VIII + IX + X = 30\%$$

This record is quite typical of reactions of two and a half to three year olds. All the responses are whole answers, the only determinants are form and color form, and the content is limited to two categories, architecture and trees. It is evident that this child's reality concepts are not in line with the more usual adult ones; rather, he tends to react to his experiences in a highly subjective fashion, projecting into them what is of concern or interest to him at the moment, with little awareness of what is actually intended. However, there is some capacity for discrimination and differentiation, as much as is ordinarily found at this age. This discrimination, which marks the beginnings of an objective attitude, manifests itself in the following ways: on Card I the subject points out the four spaces; on Card III there is a long time delay suggesting that he has some awareness of the difference between that blot and the preceding ones and therefore hesitates to use the same response. On Card IV he is able to act on his awareness of a difference between this blot and the preceding one and give a good form response; on Card IX on the basis of color discrimination, he separates the leaves from the flowers. Thus he gives indication that not only can he vary his concepts and, on occasion, bring them in line with more generally accepted reality, but he even shows some discrimination in his use of emotional stimuli (uses green correctly on IX).

The content of his responses suggests that this child's major concerns are his security and his relationship to his family. His emphasis on these matters is such as to raise the possibility of deeper feelings of insecurity than are ordinarily encountered at this age. However, the way he goes about responding to his disturbance is quite in line with expectancy. The present findings can be used to point up this boy's problems. These are typical for his age and his handling of them at this time is in line with expectancy.

The subject is an only child who is somewhat oversheltered. He tends to be rather passive and quiet, but is essentially happy. He is easily contacted. The parents report no special problems.

RECORD No. 2

Well Adjusted Girl, Age 4 Years 9 Months, I.Q. 142

		Response	Inquiry				
I.	11″	Piece of thing spilled all over paper and can't get it off. (urged to tell what it might look like)					
		1. Some people want not to stick together, but they are sticking together. I can't tell what they are doing. Where one goes the other goes. This man is so big, somebody stuck to him. These silly men have their hands on him.	(two side figures are men to which other [center] figure is stuck) Man is stupid, he's stuck to other guy. So stupid, have nothing on their heads, only hats.	W	M	H	
		2. Hole and you can stick your finger through. Can't find anything else.	(one of four center spaces)	S	F→FK	Hole	
II.	6″	1. Firemen hats on top. Firemen splashing each other. Look like they're putting their foot on a stool. The stool is breaking up and their foot is on it.	Because of the hats and they splashed each other. One wanted to help the other with hoses and the other wouldn't let him so they started a fight.	W	MC	H	P
III.	5″	1. This guy has a tie and he pulled it off and he sees a clock striking, and the other guy wanted the tie. He had no tie and pulled it off. He's trying to run backward. This guy pulled off the tie and the tie stayed there. They're not stuck together. (notes space between leg and body)	(upper side red is clocks, one is 8 o'clock, other 9 o'clock) Because of the points on them. One point is a little far back and one far front. (tie is center red and explained on basis of fact that her father wears bowties)	W	M	H	P
				D	F+	Clo	P
				D	Fm−	Obj	O−

look like bigger than an elephant is. these are hard needles, ears, paws. ([Can you think of anything else?] Yes, he's trying to put a foot on somebody with the needles and kill him. [Kill who?] Somebody trying to feed him and bother him. Said "no" twice, and wanted to kill him. Not hungry.)

	Loc.	Det.	Cont.	Pop.	Time	Response	Inquiry
V.	W	F+	A	P	5"	1. Looks like butterfly with wings and things on top.	(points to parts) (Doing anything?) No, just standing on the ground, he doesn't know how to kill people so he flies away.
VI.	......					Not look like anything to me. Ink spills it looks like something, but this one doesn't.	(rejected)
VII.	W	F−	Obj		3"	1. Some kind of a ring, it opens so you can put it on your finger or closes so you can put it on tight.	Because it's round.
VIII.	W	CF	Pl		3"	1. Some kind of a Christmas tree to me. I know, color red, orange, pink. All different colors. Look the same because they are colored. They must come from different ink boxes. (Add. Frogs climbing up. Because of feet and heads.)	Because of the different colors and the point on top.
	(D FM− A)						Everytime ink spills it spills same way on the other side.
IX.	......					Doesn't look like anything to me.	(rejected)
X.	D	CF−	N		4"	1. Rainbow in the sky that was painted all different colors. This part isn't stuck together so well.	(omits bottom center detail and outer details) Colors spread out.

R   11 + 1 (2 Rejections)

W	6⎞₇	F+	2⎞	A	2 + 1	P	4
W	1⎠	F→FK	1⎫4	H	3	O	1−
		F−	1⎭	Pl	1		
D	3 + 1			N	1		
		M	2	Obj	2		
S	1	MC	1	Hole	1		
		FM	1− (+ 1−)	Clo	1		
		Fm	1−				
		CF	2 (1−)				

W	64%	F	36%	A	18%
D	27%	F+	75%		
S	9%				

$$\begin{array}{ccc} M & : & C \\ 3 & : & 3 \end{array}$$

$$\begin{array}{ccc} Fm + FM & : & C' + c \\ 2 & : & 0 \end{array}$$

$$VIII + IX + X = 18\%$$

This record well illustrates the degree of maturity a young child may achieve. In this case the maturity is part of a well integrated personality structure, with development proceeding more or less consistently in all areas. In consequence, the rather startling findings—the three good human movement responses, the relatively high F+ per cent, the well integrated whole responses—cannot be considered out of line or reflecting personality deviations.

This is obviously a very well endowed child who is indulging in elaborate fantasy as a means of handling her strong aggressive impulses. Her responses on Cards I, II, III, and IV definitely give evidence of this aggression. To a large extent the aggression she experiences is typical for her age. This is the period when the child must learn to accept the fact that there are certain demands to be met, certain standards by which to abide, certain limits that must be recognized. The fact that all this child's movement responses, human and animal, are of an aggressive order while her color responses are mainly of a pleasurable nature points up the nature of her adjustment. In her inner life she indulges her aggressive drives, while in her contacts with the world about her, in the emotional relationships she establishes, she achieves satisfaction. There seems little doubt that this girl is somewhat in conflict with regard to her feelings for others, has aggressive and possibly even hostile impulses toward them, but she also has a sufficient number of satisfying experiences and reassuring emotional relationships to motivate her toward conforming behavior without causing her to feel unduly tense or anxious.

In addition to her recourse to fantasy, this girl has met her problems by identifying very strongly with the figures who are imposing their will on her. Like all children when they first become aware of "right" and "wrong," there is an exaggerated emphasis on these concepts and on the importance of exact compliance. The indications for this identification are to be found not only in the intensity and detailedness with which she enters into adult roles and adult activities, but in such remarks as "one wanted to help the other," in other words, actually being a part of the adult world; and again on Card IV when she says, "Somebody trying to feed him and bother him. Said 'no' twice," she is certainly repeating adult statements— "I said 'no' twice." There is a kind of smugness in her attitude, stemming from her sure knowledge of what is expected and her conviction that she will do the right thing.

That her conflicts at this time seem to focus about her resentment of authority is evident from the reference to constant supervision (Card I, "Where one goes the other goes"), the awareness of the heavy hand or foot of authority (Card IV, "He tries to put a foot on somebody and kill him"). This resentment of authority apparently also involves competitive activity (Card II, "Firemen splashing each other—they wanted to help the other with the hoses and the other wouldn't let him," etc.); also the conflict over the tie on Card III.

In spite of her abilities and resourcefulness, it is also apparent that this girl is not always secure and confident. The fear of not being "whole" is reflected in her observation that the figures are not stuck together on Card III. Similarly the response to Card VII suggests that while she would like to be released from the sheltering circle provided by the mother, feels that that circle is restraining and "tight," nevertheless she probably also finds some security in this tightness.

The breaks in control and judgment that the subject shows seem related primarily to the competition with the parents and the resulting distortion of the immediate circumstances. On the whole, however, she handles her difficulties well, does not seem anxiety ridden, and has a strong ego structure. Similarly she seems to be incorporating a strict superego, the "heavy footed elephant," but this is not curtailing her spontaneity or her energy. Rather, she finds many pleasures and satisfactions in her experiences.

Her response on Card V strongly suggests that her trend is away from overt aggression, and that conflict and aggression are not what she seeks in her contacts with others. At best, this aggression is likely to manifest itself in verbal derogation, "silly," "stupid," etc. It also points up the fact that her own excellent verbal and intellectual capacities are likely to be used to a marked degree as a means of building up her self-esteem and also as a way of channelizing aggression.

The complete blocking which she shows on Cards VI and IX has positive as well as negative implications. It is evident that certain situations are too much for this girl. However, it is equally evident that her control is sufficient to keep her from dealing with such situations in inadequate fashion. What she does not understand, what she cannot handle adequately, she leaves alone.

This child is the older of two girls. The parents are professional people who take their parenthood very seriously. They have dealt with this child almost exclusively on a "rational" basis and have rarely had to resort to punishment. However, the rationality has been counteracted by much emotional warmth which has evidently led this child to feel basically secure and accepted. Her present righteousness and overemphasis on correct, acceptable behavior is in part a function of her particular age period and in part the result of the position in which she finds herself in relation to her younger sister. The younger sister (aged two and a half years) is a much less conforming child, and the older one has identified strongly with the parents in criticizing the behavior of the little one.

Well Adjusted Boy, Age 6 Years 7 Months, I.Q. 112

Card	Location	Determinant	Content	Response	Inquiry
I. 38"	W	FM	A	1. Sorta like an eagle.	It's big, got big wings, it's going up.
	W	F+	Pl	2. Like a tree.	Tree comes round like that on both sides.
II. 61"	WS	mCF	Fire-crackers	V16" 1. It's a design when the firecrackers blow out.	Shoots out and its all red.
III. 46"	D	F+	A P	3" 1. Sorta like a butterfly.	(center red) Got two wings sorta.
	W	M	H P	2. Two boys.	Like they're gonna catch the butterfly.
IV. 63"	W	F+	A	16" 1. Looks sorta like a bird.	Pigeon maybe, no an eagle.
	W	Fm	Pl	2. Weeping willow tree.	This stuff goes down like on a weeping willow tree.
V. 24"	W	F+	A P	4" 1. Butterfly or moth maybe.	Got big wings and things in front sorta.
VI. 74"	W	F-	A Obj	8" 1. If I left this out it could be a spider's web.	(large lower section) The shape of it is like it.
	D	FM	A	2. This is a snake coming out of his hole.	(top detail) Long and skinny.
VII. 47"	W	F+	(H)	14" I can't make out anything. 1. Statue.	Two things like on two stones. (Statue of what?) Two ladies maybe.
VIII 51"	D	FM	A P	8" 1. Two lions sorta climbing along.	(usual) Just like I saw them in the zoo.
	D	F+	At	2. Some bones.	(center riblike area) All straight sorta.
IX. 61"	D	FC	Pl	V11" 1. Like a tree this was.	(midline and green area) Got the middle part and green leaves sorta.
	D	mCF	Explosion	2. Splosion.	(midline and pink) Red stuff shooting up.
X. 70"	D	F+	A P	8" 1. Spider.	(side blue) All legs.
	D	F+	Ad P	2. Rabbit.	(usual) See his ears, just his face.
	D	FM	A	3. Like a reindeer.	(side brown) Horns and it's running.

R   18

W	6		F+	8		A	8		P	6
W	2	}9	F−	1	}9	Ad	1	}9		
WS	1					H	2(1)			
			M	1		At	1			
D	9		FM	4		Pl	3			
			Fm	1		Obj	1			
						Expl	1			
			FC	1		Fire cr.	1			
			mCF	2						

W	50%	F	50%	A	50%
D	50%	F+	89%		

$$M \ : \ C$$
$$1 \ : \ 2\tfrac{1}{2}$$

$$Fm + FM \ : \ C' + c$$
$$7 \ : \ 0$$
$$VIII + IX + X = 39\%$$

This six year old gives evidence of possessing a number of resources which he can use quite effectively. Thus, although there is no doubt that, on occasion, he experiences considerable tension (mCF on Cards II and IX), he manages to handle this acceptably much of the time. He is a boy with strong aggressive impulses (flying eagle, snake coming out of hole, lions climbing; even his butterfly has big wings and his pigeon changes into an eagle), but he appears to have accepted the demands of reality and with this has achieved considerable control and objectivity (high F+ per cent). The fact that he has attained this without producing any serious curtailment of his affect or any reduction in fantasy indicates that he is not overwhelmed by his anxiety, but rather is developing in healthy fashion.

The content of the subject's interpretations suggests considerable concern about his relationship to the family. Three tree responses is unusual for a boy of this age. The response on Card IV, the weeping willow tree, would seem to have some special significance in this case. Responses of this type, weeping willow tree, dead tree, tree cut down (see p. 49), are given almost exclusively by subjects who have lost a parent figure, or where the figure is so ill or inadequate as to be completely ineffectual. In this case there was an uncle, a young man in his twenties, to whom this boy was very much attached. The uncle lived right above this boy, saw him every day, played a great deal with him, and was really a father figure for the child. He was killed in a car accident a few months before the Rorschach record was taken. The child's disturbance in connection with the loss of a father figure is symbolized in the response to Card IV.

Several factors in the test productions point to a disturbed maternal relationship. The subject's associations to the mother, as suggested by his responses to Card VII, are such as to indicate that he sees her as hard, unyielding and unresponsive. The interpretation also reflects his need to "immobilize" her in order to maintain control and stability. Certainly the relationship to her does not appear to be too positive a one. This impression is even further borne out by his "spider"* and "spider web" interpretations. It is the spider web which the snake must break through to come out of his hole, and it is after the response "spider" in Card X that he retreats to the furthest end of the card and comes up with a timid answer, "rabbit." The interpretations here suggest that in order to express himself, release his fantasies and adopt masculine roles, this boy will have to engage in conflict with the mother. It is his anxiety in relation to this conflict, his fear lest it get out of hand, that causes him to strive for control (only one $F-$). So far his efforts have been successful in that they have not curtailed his potentialities nor left him with too great a sense of instability. His concept of himself appears to be that of a vigorous person, though one who must struggle not only to maintain control, but also to establish himself, in order to avoid being enveloped by overpowering and "smothering" maternal forces.

This child is the older of two boys. Consensus of opinion among those who know him well is that he's just a "regular boy." He has moments when he is difficult to handle, has occasional temper outbursts, but these are not more frequent or intense than found in many children. The difficulties he has are primarily with the mother, the father being absent much of the time on business.

* For most children, the spider appears to be symbolic of the all-absorbing, devouring, frightening mother figure.

RECORD No. 4

Well Adjusted Girl, Age 6 years 8 months, I.Q. 118

Card / Time	Response	Inquiry	Loc.	Det.	Content	P
I. 20″	1. Butterfly.	He has big wings and he's flying.	W	FM	A	P
II.	Oh gee, phew.	(Add. Now it's somebody's hands with red gloves on—mittens.)		......		
			(D	F/C	Hd)	
III. 10″	1. Two lambs.	(all the black area) Cause it shapes like this, has a head and feet.	W	F+	A	
	2. Bow, red bow like mine.	(center red) Comes out like a bow.	D	F/C	Obj	P
IV. 11″	1. Fly.	Now it don't look like a fly, but before I thought so.	W	F−	A	
	2. Bear.	I see two feet and arms, he's big.	W	F+	A	
V. 20″	1. Girl.	(center) She's wearing pants, like cowboy pants, and her hands are up like this, waving. (illustrates)	D	M	H	
VI. 33″	Looks like nothing.					
	1. Butterfly.	(top) Got wings like.	D	F+	A	
	2. Leaf.	(lower large detail) Goes in and out, maybe it's poison ivy. (laughs) Don't look like it, I made it up.	D	M−	Pl	
VII. 10″	1. Deer's horns.	Two big pointy things that could stick you.	W	F+	Ad	

VIII. 19"	W	FM	A	P	10" 1. Two mice crawling up a little tree.	Has a head and feet and a tail—the stem for the tree goes way down into the ground.
	D	CF	Food		2. Plate of ice cream.	Orange and strawberry. (lower center)
IX. 15"	D	FM—	A		4" 1. Two rhinoceroses trying to fight. I know that's not right.	(orange) Cause I think they have a big nose like that.
	[D F (H)]				(Add. Looks like a witch, cause here's the head and the big nose.)	
X. 32"	D	C/F	Spot		5" 1. Two spots.	(side blue) Like something spilled.
	DS	F+	A		2. Two flies.	(top gray) Head and eyes and thing sticking out of head.
	D	FM,FC	A	P	3. Little rabbit peeking.	(usual) Big ears and green eyes.

R   15 + 2

W	5	} 6	F+	5	} 6	A	9
W	1		F−	1		Ad	1	} 10

H   1 + 1

D	8	} 9 + 2	M	2 (1 −)	Hd	0 + 1
DS	1		FM	4 (1 −)	Obj	1

Spot 1

FC	1 + 1	Pl	1
C/F	1	Food	1
CF	1		
F/C	0 + 1		

W	40%	F	40%	A	67%
D	60%	F+	67%		

M : C
2 : 2½

Fm + FM : C' + c
4 : 0

VIII + IX + X = 40%

This little girl's test responses give evidence of the presence of considerable underlying aggression. In this connection there are the "two rhinoceroses" answers, the "leaf" that "may be poison ivy" and the "deer's horns" that "stick." It is toward the handling of this aggression that much of her energy is being directed. To this end she employs a number of mechanisms, the major ones being a kind of "doing and undoing," as she gives and denies answers on Cards IV and IX, and makes a laughing denial on VI. Moreover, the way she expresses her aggression, even in fantasy, indicates that emphasis is on its inhibition and curtailment. Thus the mice on Card VIII are "crawling," the "rhinoceroses" on IX are "trying to fight." When there is danger of losing control, she blocks completely (Card II).

Her efforts at controlling her aggression lead to some constriction, particularly in the intellectual area. This can be seen in her relatively low W per cent and high A per cent. She tends to pick from her experiences isolated aspects of them (many D) and goes along in somewhat stereotyped fashion, with limited interests.

Her story is easily read in the sequence of her responses. There is some caution, as well as a capacity for control, indicated by the relatively long time that elapses between the presentation of the first card and the giving of the first response. However, once having sized up the situation, she gives a good answer and one which reveals spontaneity and freedom in her fantasy activity. This spontaneity and self-confidence do not survive the shock of

Card II. The emotional demands made by the card, and very probably the associations aroused by the two black figures, prove seriously disturbing and she handles this disturbance by permitting no associations to come through. However, by the time this card is reached in the inquiry she has sufficient control to give a color response, but it is an emotionally shallow (F/C) one. It is almost as though this child were saying, "The world frightens me, I don't know how to respond to it, but I would like to relate to it and I'm willing and trying to do so, as I think the people around me want me to."

Her shock on Card II is followed by the interpretation of a very mild gentle order on Card III, the lamb, which is permitted no activity. Similarly, she is attracted to the red center area, but does not respond to its emotional implications. In a sense then, the shock she experienced on Card II carries over into Card III, in that it robs her of all affective freedom, although the potentialities for this were clearly evident in Card I.

Contact with authority again proves disturbing, showing itself on Card IV in the form of loss of judgment and control. Again recovery takes place, but in a way that indicates how she feels in relation to the authority figure—"he's big."

Her reactions to Card V point up her concern about herself. She goes directly to the midline area and interprets a "girl." Her elaboration of this response emphasizes her feeling that she may have certain attributes which are more like those associated with boys than with girls. However, the identification is a secure one, and the girl is "waving." It would have been important to know if the waving were a greeting or a farewell. Unfortunately this information was not obtained.

Her long delay on Card VI is, in good part, a function of the difficulty that children generally have with this card. It is interesting to note that she helps herself by picking out a detail that is obvious and giving an acceptable answer. However, she cannot leave well enough alone, but instead follows this with an immature and inadequate response. The giving of a leaf response in a child this age is suggestive of a trend toward regression under stress. Furthermore, she is sufficiently pushed by her aggressive impulses to distort her response. As before, there is recognition of her own inadequacy and quick recovery in the denial of the response. Nevertheless, if the leaf is considered as symbolic of the child (see p. 37), her unpleasant association to it suggests that she has come to see herself as harmful and unliked. The efforts at control that she has manifested thus far, and that continue throughout, are undoubtedly most strongly motivated by this feeling and the consequent exaggerated need to please the significant objects in her environment and act in accordance with their wishes.

The aggression reflected in her interpretation of Card VII strongly suggests that this child sees the mother as an aggressive, commanding figure. Since she has already given indication that she sees herself as a feminine figure, possibly with some masculine attributes (Card V), it seems evident that she has identified with this aggressive "antlered" mother, and along with this identification has incorporated standards of behavior which demand much control and submission to authority.

There is a rather long delay on Card VIII as compared with the time the subject needs to respond to most of the other cards. Here again emotionally charged circumstances prove disturbing. The drives and feelings aroused by the test stimuli are shaded down, the mice crawl, the tree is little. In this way control holds.

The two rhinoceroses fighting on Card IX once more reflect the aggressive activity she perceives in the parents and with which she apparently identifies. Again it is immediately denied, but the concept remains an unpleasant one—a witch. Her comment, "I know that's not right" was taken to mean that she was criticizing her own response. However, it may well be that what she was saying is "I know it's not right to fight."

The multiplicity of stimuli on Card X are too much for this girl's control and she comes up with a poorly organized response, "two spots." She then retreats to the gray area on the top of the card, thus avoiding color and also escaping the need to penetrate into the blot. Her final response, "the rabbit peeking," is significant because it is the last thing she says as though, having offered this, she can add nothing further about herself. This is a word picture of a small, timid, gentle creature, only looking on, or peeking at life, not too actively taking part.

The overall picture is that of a girl with a strong ego and superego. She tries to meet the high standards she has set for herself by denying spontaneity and aggression. To a large extent she achieves this; in fact she strains to give the form of response she feels is expected of her (FC and P). However, her spontaneity is not by any means completely inhibited. She finds pleasure in fantasy and is relating to the environment, albeit in somewhat overcontrolled and shallow fashion. Some compulsive trends are indicated (doing and undoing). However, the curtailment she manifests is not so extreme as to be of a crippling order. While she certainly is not realizing all her potentialities, she is not without satisfactions. It is evident from her responses that she has had many happy reassuring experiences.

The subject is the older of two girls, the sister being almost four years old. The parents are intelligent young college people. Emotional control and rational attitudes are stressed in the home. The subject is considered a happy, well liked child, both in school and in the neighborhood. According to the mother she presents no special problems, other than a tendency to be bossy with her sister and her friends. This has been observed by the teacher too, but is not considered to be too serious a manifestation.

The patterns of behavior this child has adopted are apparently very similar to those of the parents. If she continues with her present methods for handling her conflicts and anxieties, this child will undoubtedly develop into a very controlled person who can adapt herself to circumstances on a superficial level without much difficulty. She will find her real satisfactions within herself, in her fantasy, while her contacts with the environment will always remain somewhat shallow and relatively unrewarding. The adjustment she has made is one which enables her to keep her anxiety in check and, although it extracts a price in terms of emotional spontaneity, the price is still within relatively normal limits.

RECORD No. 5

Well Adjusted Girl, Age 7 Years 5 Months, I.Q. 98

Card	Response						Inquiry
I.	5"	1. A butterfly.	W	F+	A	P	These things here and it looks like it. We draw them in school.
II.	18"	1. Another butterfly.	D	F+	A		These things here that stick out. (lower red)
III.	4"	1. This looks like a bow.	D	F/C	Clo	P	(center red) I think it's just a bow with red.
		2. With a girl.	D	F−	Hd		(lower center) The eyes look like a girl. It's a girl because a girl has a bow.
IV.	2"	Oh, this is going to be hard.					
	14"	1. A gorilla.	W	FM	A		Head, arms, feet. I don't know what this part could be. He's mad the way he's holding his face and hands.
V.	6"	I can't make it out.					
	11"	1. It looks like another butterfly.	W	FM	A	P	The wings are spread out like its flying.
VI.	9"	1. This is a spider.	D	F−	A		It looks like it because of a lot of feet. (top detail)
VII.	5"	1. Two dogs looking at each other with their ears up. Some are easy and some are hard.	W	FM	A		They have tails and ears and a face—sitting on something.
VIII.	3"	Oh, this is going...					
	12"	1. Two lions climbing up a tree.	D	FM, F/C	A	P	No, they are tigers. These are red tigers even though I never saw one like it.
		2. With red and orange behind the tree.	D	CF−	Obj(?)		Just something red and orange.

IX.				4″	This, let's see. This is very hard this one.
	D	M	(H)	14″	1. This looks like two hands, two witches with hands out.

The witches are bringing their hands to-gether. These are bad witches, the nice ones have a nice face and long hair.

X.	D	F/C	A	P	6″	1. Oh, this is two crabs.
	D	FC	A			2. Two lions.
	D	F+	Ad	P		3. An animal with two things hanging down.

Two blue crabs. (side blue)

The shape is like lions and they're yellow like lions.

It looks like a bunny's head (usual), but the rest I don't know.

R 14

W	4	F+	3 }5	A	9 }10	P	6
		F−	2	Ad	1		
				H	(1)		
D	10	M	1	Hd	1		
		FM	4	Clo	1		
				Obj	1		
		FC	1				
		F/C	2 + 1				
		CF	1−				
W	29%	F	36%	A	71%		
D	71%	F+	60%				

$$M : C$$
$$1 : 2\tfrac{1}{2}$$

$$Fm + FM : C' + c$$
$$4 : 0$$

$$VII + IX + X = 43\%$$

The feelings of inadequacy and insecurity which this girl repeatedly manifests (Cards IV, V, VII, VIII, IX) are fairly typical for this age. The competitive relationships that are established in school and in play, as well as those which may exist in the family, come to their peak about this time in rather simple and direct form. The child either can or cannot do something as well as somebody else does, or as well as he is expected to. In this case it is evident that the subject is afraid she is not likely to do as well as she should. She questions her capacity to meet varying situations at an adequate level. Nevertheless, she strives to do what she feels is expected, thereby revealing strongly compliant trends. Further evidence of these trends is found in the relatively large number of adult popular responses given, and in forcing of controlled affective responses (F/C).

Her perception of authority as prone to anger (Card IV, "he's mad") certainly intensifies her efforts to comply, and by the same token makes her feel serious doubts about her success along these particular lines. Her reactions in this connection strongly suggest that she is a child who has been held to high standards and has not been treated in a way that is especially reassuring to her. Her self-esteem has not been built up successfully.

Her attempts at doing just what she thinks is wanted have produced some curtailment of spontaneity, or rather a kind of forced emotional conformity (F/C), and have also made for some stereotypy in thinking (high

A% as well as initial tendency toward perseveration on Card II). Constriction of a sort is also reflected in the high D%. However, it is largely this high D% which permits this little girl to achieve as much stability as she has. By picking out certain aspects from her experiences, rather than trying to face total situations, she manages to achieve some feeling of accomplishment, with concomitant reassurance. This aid to her self-esteem would not be possible if she were more expansive. Her adjustive mechanisms have somewhat the coloring of the compulsive's defenses. However, in her case, they have not been carried to exaggerated lengths and, although they point a direction, they are not yet of a neurotic order.

In summary, this is a very "average" sort of child, anxious to get along with the world about her, but not always sure she will be able to meet the demands this world places on her. She feels it important to live up to the standards set for her, but questions her own effectiveness. Along with her self-doubts, and the anxiety associated with them, go feelings of aggression. This aggression she handles primarily by attributing it to the authority figures in her life ("mad gorilla," Card IV). The attitude she has ascribed to them increases her need to do what she feels is expected of her, and she strains for conformity, achieving this primarily through the exercise of intellectual control. This control is, in turn, made possible by the fact that she tends to delimit her reactions and confine them to aspects of her experiences which she feels capable of handling successfully. If this child were helped to feel more adequate, her total adjustment would probably be a more vigorous and effective one. However, despite her self-doubts, there are no gross deviations.

This child is the youngest of three siblings. She has been made to feel that she cannot compete with the other two, both because she is younger and because she is not as bright as they are. The parents are fond of the child and try to do what is "right" in relation to her, but they do not have good understanding of her special problems, as the youngest and least gifted of their offspring. The child is reasonably happy, gets along at home and in school, has many friends and presents no problems in that she is "no trouble."

RECORD No. 6

Well Adjusted Boy, Age 10 Years 1 Month, I.Q. 118

Card	Response	Loc.	Det.	Cont.	P	Inquiry
I. 39″	1. Dog's face.	WS	F+	Ad		Got ears like a dog and eyes, nose, mouth.
	2. Another dog's face. (somewhat questioningly)	D	F+	Ad		(upper side detail) Big snout coming out, ear.
II. 42″	1. Two bears.	W	F+	A	P	I see the snout and the fat body, little legs.
	2. Two men fighting.	W	M	H	P	Head, body, hands up. (Why men?) Women don't fight like that.
III. 55″	1. Two men bowling.	W	M	H	P	Bent over like, ready to throw ball.
	2. Eyeglasses.	D	F+	Obj		(center red) Piece that goes over nose and two eye parts.
	3. Fish swimming.	D	FM	A		(usual man's leg) Has long body, fin.
IV.	1. Fur from an animal.	W	Fc	A Obj		It's like an animal skin, you can see the legs and the head. It's flattened out. (Why fur?) Looks rough, the different blacks makes it look rough.
	2. Animal's head.	D	F+	Ad		(lower center detail) See eyes and horns. (what animal?) Cow or bull.
V. 18″	1. Bat.	W	F+	A	P	Big wings, head and hind feet.
VI. 61″	1. Wings spread, flying like a bird.	D	FM	A		(top detail) It just makes me think of a bird flying fast.
	2. Another fur from an animal.	W	Fc	A Obj	P	(large lower section) It's shaped like those rugs you see.

VII. 68"	D	Fm	N		1. Like a water fall on a mountain.	(lower center detail) Comes down like a waterfall.
	D	F−	A		2. Dog.	(top two thirds, but poorly seen) Head, and paw sticking up in front. (usual feather)
	D	F+	Hd		3. Two men.	(top third) Heads of two men, maybe Indians.
VIII.	D	FM	A	P	1. Lion or tiger.	(usual) Look like they're stalking something.
	D	F+	Rocks		2. Rocks.	(lower center) Shaped like rocks.
	D	FC	Pl		3. Tree.	(top center) shaped like a tree—comes to a point and its sort of green.
IX. 53"	D	KCF	Cl		1. Clouds.	(pink) Round and fluffy like clouds, pink clouds.
	D	M	H		2. Like two men playing dice or something.	(orange) Heads bent down, hands out, holding dice.
X. 61"	D	F+	A		1. Octopus.	(side blue) Lots of arms.
	D	FM	A		2. Deer running.	(side brown) See the antlers and the feet out in back.
	D	M	H&N		3. Two men climbing up the side of a mountain, shaking hands because they made it.	(center blue is men, pink is mountain) See them reaching across, one hand holding onto the mountain.

R   23

W	3⎫		F+	9⎫10		A	8⎫11	P	6
W	3⎬7		F−	1⎭		Ad	3⎭		
WS	1⎭					H	4		
			M	4		Hd	1		
D	16		FM	4		A Obj	2		
			Fm	1		Rocks	1		
						N	1 + 1		
			FC	1		Pl	1		
			KCF	1		Cl	1		
			Fc	2		Obj	1		
W	30%		F	43%		A	48%		
D	70%		F+	90%					

$$M : C$$
$$4 : 1\tfrac{1}{2}$$

$$Fm + FM : C' + c$$
$$5 : 1$$

$$VIII + IX + X = 35\%$$

The Rorschach productions in this case point to a definitely masculine identification and a concept of the self as a vigorous, achieving and participating individual. All the human movement responses this boy gives are concerned with men who are engaged in competitive and aggressive activities (fighting, bowling, playing dice, climbing mountains). At the end, however, these activities also reflect positive, cooperative relationship, "shaking hands." The animal movement answers are also of a vigorous order—the fish are swimming, the bird flying, the lion stalking, and the deer running.

The emphasis on fantasy activity is one of the main ways that this boy has developed for dealing with unacceptable impulses or feelings. However, he also shares his feelings with the people who are emotionally important to him and makes emotional contact with the world about him. It is very probable that the extent to which he withdraws into fantasy, the extent to which his energy is absorbed by the activities of his inner world, is caused by the special problems he is called upon to handle at this time. His stress on movement responses is characteristic for this period.

The problems this boy has, over and above those typical for his age, are in relation to his mother. The greatest shock he experiences in the whole test comes on Card VII. This shock shows itself not only in the long time delay that precedes the giving of his first response, but also in the presence of his only poor form answer, and in the absence of a whole answer. In fact Card VII is the only black card which the subject cannot integrate successfully. The disturbances in this relationship will naturally be aggravated at a time when sexual stirrings and interest in girls are about to become of prime importance. There can be little doubt that this boy feels more secure in his relations with men. His recovery on Card VII comes with the response "two men."

That sexual matters are also a focus of distress is evident from the relatively long time the subject needs to give a response on Card VI, and it is the first time that he begins his interpretation of a card with a detail rather than a whole answer. Here, however, he recovers in highly mature and conforming fashion (an Fc response and a popular one).

The relatively well integrated picture this boy presents, aside from the anxiety he experiences in relation to the mother, suggests that his problems in this area have not infiltrated too deeply, have not disrupted his general adjustment. On the whole, the ego is strong, energy and spontaneity free and vigorous, self-concept and self-esteem good. Only at the very outset, Card I, in the face of the new situation, does this boy show any serious doubt, or react in unduly childish fashion (Card I).

The overall picture is that of an able, well adjusted boy who is dealing with stress situations in relatively well integrated, controlled fashion. Recourse to fantasy is his primary adjustive mechanism, but this fantasy never gets too far away from the demands of reality. It thus serves an important adjustive function.

This boy is an only child in a middle class professional family. He is expected to be a controlled, conforming "little man," and to a large extent he complies with these expectations. However, he is not overcontrolled and he is a "real boy." He is very much interested in games and athletics and competes successfully in school and club events. He presents no special problems at school or at home.

RECORD No. 7

Well Adjusted Girl, Age 10 Years 5 Months, I.Q. 116

Card / Time	Loc.	Det.	Content	Response	Inquiry
I. 32"	W	M	(H)	1. Looks like a fairy with her wings out and her hands up.	Big wings and the fairy in the middle. (asked what the upraised hands signified) Just saying "hello" to someone.
	W	F+	A P	2. And it could be a butterfly too.	Big wings. When you make up in a fairy costume you put on "butterfly" wings.
II. 61"				6" I don't know.	
	W	M	H P	38" 1. Two people sitting together arguing or talking.	(Asked about the sex of the people) It's hard to tell. Funny clothes on.
	D	F+	A	2. Another butterfly.	(lower red) Shape of wings.
III. 57"	W	M	H P	8" 1. It's two people again, maybe two women hanging out the wash.	They have skirts on.
	D	F+	A	2. Dog.	See head and long tail. (side red)
	D	F+	Clo P	3. And bow in the middle.	(center red) Shaped like a bow.
IV. 72"				8" Gee, I don't know.	
	D	F+	Ad	17" 1. Heads of two snakes.	(usual armlike projections on side) Long and thin.
	W	Fc	A	2. Looks hairy, maybe a big animal, like a bear.	I don't know what this is. (lower center detail) Head, feet, like the skin of bear, fuzzy. (rubs finger over blot)
	W	Fc	A Obj	3. Really more like those rugs they have in hunting cabins.	Shaped like it, and fuzzy.
V. 34"	W	FM	A & Obj	9" 1. A little animal looking over a fence.	(center is animal, all rest is fence) Looks like he wants to see what's on other side.
	W	F+	A P	2. Could be another butterfly.	Wings, head with the things sticking up on it.

VI. 44"	W	F–	A	22" This I don't understand. 29" 1. A bug maybe. Nothing else.	Bug could be any shape.
VII.	D	FM	A	7" 1. Two dogs looking at each other.	(top two thirds) Heads like dogs and ears.
	D	M	H	2. Could be two children discussing something.	(top two thirds) Like children's heads too—arms pointing out, not sure which way to go.
VIII. 73"	D	FM	A P	9" This is pretty. 19" 1. Bear standing on a rock looking around.	(usual animal) Seeing if he's going the right way.
	D	F+	Rocks	2. Those are rocks or stones.	(lower center) Round like some rocks.
	D	CF	Pl	3. Or beautiful flowers.	(lower center) Color and also look like certain petals.
IX. 50"	D	F+	(H)	12" 1. Two fairies that have been turned into witches.	(orange) They're ugly with big noses. (why fairies?) In some way not so ugly, kind of graceful.
	D	F+	Obj	2. Candle.	(midline) Long and comes to a kind of point.
	D	F+	Ad	3. Claws of a lobster.	(orange projections) Stick out like claws do.
X. 52"	W	C/F	Fairyland	10" 1. This is like a fairyland.	All the different colors and things.
	D	FM	Ad P	2. Head of a rabbit.	(usual) Like watching the fairyland.

R 23

W	8 } 10	F+	10 } 11	A	9 } 12	P	7	
W	2	F−	1	Ad	3			
				H	5(2)			
D	13	M	4	Clo	1			
		FM	4	A Obj	1			
				Obj	1 + 1			
		CF	1	Rocks	1			
		C/F	1	Pl	1			
		Fc	2	Fairyland	1			
W	43%	F	48%	A	52%			
D	57%	F+	91%					

$$M : C$$
$$4 : 2$$

$$Fm + FM : C' + c$$
$$4 : 1$$

$$VIII + IX + X = 35\%$$

The high degree of fantasy activity in which this girl engages is most important to her at this time. It is through this recourse to fantasy that she is attempting to resolve the problems facing her at the moment. Both the problems and the method chosen for dealing with them are typical of the prepuberty child. If earlier records of this girl were available, it is most probable that the present emphasis on movement responses would be less marked and that the sensitivity reflected in the Fc responses would not be present. It is this sensitivity that is to a large extent responsible for the child's new awarenesses and the resulting need to reformulate the self-concept and alter the nature of the relationships that obtain between the self and the rest of the world.

In this case there is a kind of "standing with reluctant feet where the brook and river meet." The subject is not sure she wants to grow up, not sure what she will see on the other side (Card V), not sure which way to go (Card VII). A comparison of her human movement and animal movement responses is most revealing. All her animal movement responses are concerned with "looking," sizing up the situation; whereas her human movement answers are of a more participating order (fairy saying hello; people sitting and arguing, talking; women hanging out the wash; children discussing something). It would seem as though this girl has suddenly discovered that she could assert herself more positively than she did as a young child when she was really only an observer, but she has apparently not decided just what the nature of her participation should be. There is even some doubt as to whether she really wants to be a participant or whether she would not be happier escaping to the world of "make believe," the fairyland of childhood. Certainly being adult implies argument (Card II), drudgery (Card III) and the possibility that the lovely dreams of fairyland turn to ugliness (Card IX). In other words, at this time, she is not sure that remaining in fairyland, in the state of watching and dreaming rather than active involvement, might not be happier (rabbit watching fairyland, Card X).

In addition to concern about the aggression, drudgery and ugliness that she feels in connection with growing up, there is very evident disturbance in connection with sexual matters. The shock she experiences on Card IV and the sequence of her responses to this blot tell the story very succinctly. The associations to this large authoritarian figure are most disturbing because now they have sexual implications—two snakes' heads. She retreats from these to the more familiar animal, bear, that is a typical reaction to this card from five or six years on. However, her association with the strong authority figure now has changed from what it was in the earlier days. Shades of meaning which were not present in the early years now make themselves felt, and change the nature of the relationship with this figure. The anxiety that this figure arouses has new significance and must be met at a different level. It is no longer simply a matter of compliance or resistance to authority, but a matter of relating to this figure, with all that this implies, in more subtle and mature fashion. That it is the sexual implications in this relationship that prove disturbing to this girl seems further substantiated by her denial of the penislike detail. The resolution of conflict that she achieves is one that is typical for this age. The animal aspects of her response are denied, "killed," and the conventional, civilized answer—the animal rug—takes its place. The relationship between the child and the male parent now becomes a formal, acceptable one, in which all the animal drives are stilled.

Further evidence of sexual disturbance is demonstrated by her shock on Card VI. She states quite directly that she does not understand what is involved in sexual matters. Such uncertainty, blocking and avoidance are quite typical in prepuberty and early puberty records, especially among girls. That she is nevertheless engaged in fantasy which should eventually help her resolve her problems in this area is indicated by such responses as those given on Card VIII. In the area which frequently is considered representative of female genitalia,[8] she first gives the interpretation of rocks, but follows it immediately with beautiful flowers.

The overall picture is a typical prepuberty one, emphasizing fantasy activity and concern about sexual drives and sexual activity. Although this girl shows a number of "shock" reactions (II, IV, VI, VIII) she recovers from each of them, and only where sexual implications are strong, as on Card VI, is there any interference with her judgment or distortion of her perception. On the whole she exercises excellent control without hampering her total development in any way.

The subject is the second of three children, the oldest one being a girl of thirteen, the youngest a boy of nine. She is considered a quiet, happy child who gets along well with practically everyone and presents no special problems. There is some feeling on the part of the mother that she is the father's favorite and she is exceptionally fond of him. She is also closer to her little brother than she is to her older sister.

CHAPTER IX

The Emotionally Disturbed Child

THE EMOTIONALLY DISTURBED child is the one who has not been able to reconcile his primitive, instinctual, unacceptable impulses with the demands of the world about him in a way that leaves him feeling secure, satisfied and happy and at the same time makes for attitudes and reactions that are acceptable to the environment. To achieve such a resolution the child must have opportunity for emotional experience and emotional experimentation, so that he may develop his emotional resources and learn how best to express and direct them. It is in cases where no opportunity for such emotional expression and experience has been made available that emotional demands and interpersonal relationships prove disturbing and threatening. The child who has been permitted little or no affective freedom; the child who has had no consistent love objects to whom he can relate and who is therefore not motivated toward winning approval and love; the child who has been given so much freedom that he has not learned what is and is not acceptable, who does not know where to set limits; the child who has been handled so inconsistently that he does not learn what is and what is not expected by his environment; all such children will grow in ways that depart radically from healthy, constructive forms of behavior.

The manifestations of emotional disturbance may take a variety of forms. Overt behavior which is definitely out of line with expectancy, and characterized by unruliness, temper tantrums, nonconformity, minor delinquencies, is one such expression. Children who present such behavior are generally classified as primary behavior disorders. These children, in their efforts to find equilibrium, have developed traits of character, designed to protect them against the anxiety to which their own inadequacies and destructive impulses would otherwise expose them. Thus they act the "big shot," the bully, the aggressor, and do not face the realities.

There are other children who do not act out their conflict but instead develop symptoms which reflect their disturbed state. They manifest tics, are enuretic, have anxiety attacks and phobias, do not learn. There are also children in whom the tensions caused by their emotional conflicts produce somatic disturbances or aggravate somatic weaknesses that are already present.

Actually it is rare to find a child who can be said to present only neurotic symptoms or only deviant behavior. Rather, in most instances, there is likely to be a mixture of neurotic symptoms and deviant character traits.

111

The child who has phobias may also have temper tantrums and the child whose asthma is on a psychosomatic basis may also be a bed wetter and have learning difficulties. In itself the symptomatology gives relatively little indication of the underlying character structure. A child may be a poor eater primarily because he is too anxious to eat, cannot enjoy his food; because meal time has always been a period of conflict, a power contest between himself and authority; or he may use his noneating as a means of gaining attention from a mother who he feels is neglecting him. Undoubtedly, in the latter case, anxiety is also interfering with the pleasure he might otherwise have in eating, but in each instance one factor is likely to be primary in producing a specific form of reaction. Noneating or poor eating is therefore an indication of disturbance, but in itself gives no clue to the cause of the disturbance or to the personality structure of the subject manifesting this disturbance. It follows then that classifications made on the basis of symptomatology do not necessarily take into account differences in basic personality structure.

The fact that most emotionally disturbed children show both character deviations and neurotic symptoms also makes differentiation among the various groups of maladjusted children by means of the Rorschach a difficult, if not impossible, task. They all show emotional disturbances, but these disturbances take a variety of forms in the test, as they do in life, and only in certain instances is it possible to postulate from the test findings the exact way in which the child's disturbance will be reflected in his overt behavior. There will be no doubt from the test productions that his development is not proceeding smoothly and that he is a maladjusted child, but the test will not necessarily indicate whether this maladjustment will show itself in the form of unruliness, poor eating, bed wetting, negativism, phobias, etc. In practically all cases there will be a number of such behavioral deviations, not just one.

Actually the determination of symptomatology on the basis of the Rorschach is not essential, since such symptomatology is already known or easily established. One may speculate about a given child, and suspect, on the basis of the particular personality structure he reveals in his test performance and the indications his productions give concerning special areas of tension, that this child is a bed wetter. However, it is much simpler and certainly more reliable to get such information from the mother or some other member of the household who is in a position to know about this.

On the other hand, studies of groups of children showing specific, well defined symptoms have shown that there are certain significant personality trends common to the majority of such children. Piotrowski[53] studied a small number of children who manifested tics. He found that his subjects gave a large number of human movement responses and a low number of color responses, that they manifested deep color shock and what he calls "earthy" forms of color response. He interprets these results as indicative of the child's concern about his role in life and his need to establish a few intense relationships to the exclusion of many associations. He finds that these children respond more to inner than outer pressure, yet do not assert themselves in satisfying fashion, but rather remain emotionally immature.

Krugman[41] and his coworkers undertook a Rorschach study of a group of stuttering children. They describe the stutterer as seriously maladjusted with many neurotic trends. Outstanding is the obsessive-compulsive make-up of the personality structure of these subjects. Gann[20] and Vorhaus[70, 71] used the Rorschach test in their studies of nonreading and slow reading children.

Among the more significant researches employing the Rorschach with children have been those of Goldfarb[21-25] seeking to establish the effects of early institutionalization on personality development. The Rorschach records of the institutional child, when compared with those obtained from children who had lived all their lives in foster homes, were characterized by poor form perceptions, inaccurate, arbitrary whole responses (DW) and a preponderance of CF rather than FC answers. The results showed that these children suffered from severe limitations in intellectual and emotional control, lacked drive toward or interest in intellectual and social achievement and adjustment, and were emotionally most immature. His studies go a long way toward establishing the necessity for and the importance of consistent love objects in the environment as one of the primary factors in the development of an adequate personality structure.

All these studies of specific groups have considerable value in determining the personality factors and trends typical for the individuals comprising the group. However, it must be borne in mind that these personality descriptions also apply to individuals who do not show the symptomatology typical for the group. For example, the description of the personality of the stuttering child can apply to many disturbed children who do not stutter, and what has been said of the child with tics can also be said of others. It is a highly complex constellation of factors, inner and outer, which causes one rejected child to react to his emotional deprivation with negativism and aggression, and another to develop asthma, and determination of these factors is not yet well established. That the Rorschach can be helpful in determining some of the factors that go into such a constellation seems self-evident, but the Rorschach alone certainly does not hold all the answers. What it can provide is a good personality description, a measure of adjustment, and indications of areas of disturbance.

As has already been indicated, determination of emotional adjustment and maladjustment in the very young child (two and a half to four years old) by means of the Rorschach must be of a very limited and tentative order. Certainly, until there has been some structuring of the personality and therefore some way of gauging the amount of conflict and anxiety a child is experiencing, as well as the methods he is developing for dealing with that anxiety, such evaluation has little meaning or validity. At about three and a half or four there should be evidence of the beginnings of structure and the direction that adjustment is taking. However, in the very young child this can only be suggestive, never conclusive.

From about four and a half years on the picture becomes more definite. Lags can be more clearly discerned and uneven development detected. In the years from four and a half to six or seven, most children, no matter how disturbed they are, still try to establish some emotional relationship with the world about them. Their dependency needs are probably largely responsible for their continuing outgoing reactions, for the fact that they are still responsive to external pressure. It is the rare child at this age who has already withdrawn sharply from all emotional sharing. In other words, unhappy as they are and unfriendly as they find their surroundings, they still appear to battle it out with the world; they have not given up the struggle for reassurance and emotional response from others.

At about seven or eight some children give up this struggle and turn their backs on the environment. Their emotional energy becomes absorbed by fantasy life and by narcissistic involvements while external stimuli and pressures are ignored. This emotional withdrawal may manifest itself in withdrawn behavior, a failure to make friends, an unwillingness to participate in group activities. However, there are also instances in which this emotional withdrawal is not paralleled by social withdrawal. The child may still be very active in his group, but since his activity will all be determined by his inner promptings and not come in response to any wish to share his experiences with others, it will be of a highly individualistic order, and may therefore often have deviant and unacceptable form. In both cases this withdrawal will be reflected in the Rorschach by emphasis on the movement responses and a neglect or complete ignoring of color.

Where there is emotional response to the environment, it is likely to be exclusively of a demanding and possibly even disorganized order. While impulsiveness and egocentricity are an integral part of the child's emotional reactions, by the time he reaches seven or eight years of age an occasional evidence of the capacity for emotional control, FC, is expected and desirable. In the emotionally disturbed child, there is a flooding over of feeling usually in conjunction with a definite drop in effectiveness (as manifested in time delays, poor form responses, expressions of uncertainty) when the child is placed in emotionally charged circumstances. Very frequently in these cases there is also strong evidence that the child's experiences with his environment have been such as to leave him anxious, unhappy and anticipating trouble (responses using black). Regressive tendencies in the form of perseveration or recourse to infantile symbolism are frequent (Record No. 15).

Some children find their stability in extreme inhibitions of their emotional life, denying themselves any spontaneity. These are the children who do not develop their affective potentials or who repress what has been developed. They give Rorschach records which are not unlike those obtained from adult compulsives, with high F percentage and little lability. Their control will be sporadically shattered by some uncontrollable outburst.

In some cases, poverty of resource seems largely responsible for the child's unacceptable behavior. Failure to develop fantasy and an inability to find satisfaction in emotional sharing with others leave certain children without any way of dealing with their disturbances except through direct, overt expression of them. Failure to develop more constructive channels through which conflicts might be handled may stem from a number of causes. In some cases the opportunity for satisfying and sustained emotional contacts has not been available or has been discouraged, with consequent crippling of affective life. In other cases innate limitations, where there are gross defects, constitute the hampering factor.

Some children reveal their marked dissatisfaction with their environment and their unwillingness to accept that environment in very direct fashion. Given the test card they immediately turn it, as much as to say, "I take nothing from others on their terms." They also give interpretations which reflect their desire to change their world. They will say, "If you take this away, put this up here, and straighten this out, it might be a ———."

Differentiation, by means of the Rorschach, between a reasonably well adjusted child and a child who is presenting behavior problems or showing neurotic trends is not always possible. While the disturbed child may tend to show more anxiety than the well adjusted child, the difference in this respect is not statistically reliable,[28] showing only a tendency in the poorly adjusted child toward more anxiety. Likewise, both groups employ the same adjustive mechanism, though there is likely to be some difference in the intensity and appropriateness with which they are employed. Certainly there are times when the well adjusted child imposes constrictive control on his emotions, when he withdraws from emotional involvement and environmental pressure, when he attempts to alter the nature of his surroundings, when he regresses. However, his use of such a mechanism or mechanisms will produce security and an alleviation of anxiety and tension, and he can then proceed to act spontaneously and creatively in subsequent circumstances. The disturbed child, however, resorts to all the mechanisms used by the child who is not disturbed yet finds no security. He continues to be anxious and compulsively applies his adjustive techniques, even in circumstances which really do not demand such reactions and where such responses are actually inadequate and inappropriate. In consequence, any mechanism he employs will be grossly emphasized. If he is inhibiting, his lack of affective response will result in an extreme emphasis on form interpretations; if he is turning his affect on himself, there will be gross imbalance in the relationship between his movement and color responses; if he is resorting to detachment, he will not only fail to give emotional responses but will be likely to stress large details to a degree that is out of line with usual performance at his age; if he is retreating from the pressures placed on him at the moment, if his anxiety is causing him to resort to forms of behavior which are no longer appropriate for his age, he is likely to give a record that is somewhat perseverative and that may also have a content that is typical of the very young child where the emphasis is on nature, rocks, sky, rains, trees, leaves.

The records presented in this chapter will be those of children who have been diagnosed as behavior disorders with neurotic traits although, as the histories indicate, the pictures are definitely of a mixed order.

Card	Location	Score	Response	Inquiry
31"	(W F− Obj)		1. An animal, some kind of fish. (Add. Looks like a statue better, because it has this. [points to projections] Fish don't have these holes.)	This is the big nose (usual wing) and the tail.
II. 12"	W	CC'	Sunset	4" 1. Sunset. (looks at back of card) There's nothing on the other side.	Because it has orange and black.
III. 12"	W CC' (W F− Pl)		Sunset	5" 1. Sunset too, orange and black. (Add. Looks like a leaf too, because it has holes in it. Leaves always have holes in the middle.)	
IV. 12"	W	F+	Pl	V 7" 1. Looks like a flower.	Comes around like a flower.
V. 7"	W	F+	A P	4" 1. A butterfly.	Because of the wings and this. (points to center detail)
VI. 10"	D→W FC'	Fire	6" 1. Fire on top.	(top projections are fire, tries to indicate that they are like flames and lower section is smoke, because it's black)
VII. 8"	W	C'	Smoke	3" 1. Smoke.	Because it's black.
VIII. 7"	W	C	Sunset	2" 1. Sunset.	All colors.
IX. 8"	W	C	Sunset	3" 1. Sunset.	All colors.
X. 15"	W	C	Sunset	4" 1. Sunset, I know, because a sunset is all colors, pink, blue, yellow, green.	

R   10 + 2

W	8 + 1		F+	2		A	2		P	1
WS	1	10 + 2	F−	1	3 + 2	Sunset	5			
D→W	1		C	3		Pl	1 + 1			
			CC′	2		Smoke	1			
			FC′	1		Fire	1			
			C′	1		Obj	0 + 1			

W	100%		F	30%		A	20%
			F+	67%			

$$M : C$$
$$0 : 7\tfrac{1}{2}$$

$$Fm + FM : C' + c$$
$$0 : 5$$

VIII + IX + X = 30%

The general mode of response reflected in this record is typical for a four year old (small number of responses, only whole responses, nature of content). There are also indications that this child is developing in line with expectancy, that is, he is striving to determine the nature of the realities with which he must deal (effort at improving response on Card I, picking out of flames on VI) and to establish some emotional contact with his environment. In other words, he has passed the stage of arbitrary projection, and realizes that there are certain realities which must be faced. At the same time it is evident that this is not a happy or secure child. His emotional disturbances manifest themselves primarily in the depressive order of his feelings. It would seem as though he already viewed the world through saddened, disappointed eyes.

Nevertheless, he is trying to respond to that world, to understand it and relate to it. His prompt turning of Card IV, the only card that he does turn, suggests that it is the authority figures in his life that he would like to change. When he does attempt to alter them he comes through with something soft and beautiful. It can be inferred that this is a wish on the part of this child rather than a reality. At the same time the nature of his reactions, his many C and C′ answers, indicates that he is not withdrawing or dealing with his experiences passively, but is still "battling it out."

Diagnosed as a primary behavior disorder, this boy shows conspicuously aggressive behavior. He fights back whenever he has a chance, and acts as though he feels compelled to dominate every situation he meets. Thus, when first introduced to the toy room to select toys for the therapeutic sessions, his first reaction was to announce that he had bigger ones at home.

He appears to be under considerable tension, is physically restless and a poor sleeper. Jealousy of a seven month old brother adds to his problems. The mother is a rigid woman, with little understanding of his problems and the father meets the child's disturbances by using, or threatening to use, the strap.

RECORD No. 9

Disturbances in Eating in a Girl, 7 Years 6 Months, I.Q. 107

		Response	Inquiry	Loc.	Det.	Content
I. 30"	4"	1. Like an owl sitting in a tree. Something like a child but *not* really.	(owl is in center, rest is tree) (replaces owl with child, but then denies)	W	FM, FC'	A & Pl
		2. Something like reindeer horns. (Add. It's really like the shadow of a tree, black shadow.)	Just the horns, shape.	D (W C'F– Pl)	F+	Ad
II. 47"	V∧15"	1. Two little puppies.	Because they're dancing together (illustrates) and they're black.	W	FMC'	A P
	6"	Could I turn it upside down?				
		2. Something like an aeroplane, an atomic bomb, no. (laughs)	(space and lower red) Going up, looks like it's dropping bombs because it's red.	DS	mCF	Obj
III. 33"	11"	1. 'Them two look like, I forgot what animal, it has a beak. Is that a rooster?	Just the beak looks like a rooster, standing up.	W	FM–	A
		2. It's a bow.	(center red) Two things coming out.	D	F+	Clo P
IV. 41"	10"	Ugh, what in the heck is that?				
	18"	1. Some part looks like a monster. Eek, mama mia, the eyes now.	(asked what the monster is doing she says nothing and seems anxious to get away from the card)	W	FM	(H)
		2. Tree with monster sitting on it —something like a lady, but I don't know what it really is.	(lower center detail) I don't like it.	D	F+	Pl
V. 7"	2"	1. Butterfly.	Wings and things, 'cause it flies.	W	FM	A P
		2. Or a spider.	Spider has legs and points and wings.	W	F–	A

				Response	Inquiry
VI. 18"	D	F+	A	1. Fly.	Head things, wings and whiskers.
	W	C'F–	(A)	2. Shadow of butterfly.	(lower section) I don't know why a shadow —black and has wings.
VII. 14"	D	F+	A	1. Two little bunnies.	(top two thirds) Because of the ear and the tail and the body.
	D	F–	A	2. A spider.	(lower third) The wings and the legs and the face.
VIII. 28"				Hey nice colors, I begin to like it.	
	D	FM	A P	1. Two little squirrels.	(usual) Climbing up the tree, not really a tree. Just climbing, head, feet, one foot missing.
	D	CF	A	2. A butterfly. And that's all.	(lower center) Two colors and wings.
IX. 17"	D	Fm	Obj O	1. Something like a parachute. That's all.	(pink) Just blowing up, you know, like when they come down.
X. 41"				Looks like nothing to me.	
12"	D	C'F–	A	1. Two little snails.	(side brown) Gray snails or black.
20"	D	FMC	A	2. Two snakes.	(lower green) Snakes are green and they crawl like that.

R   19 + 1

W	5⎫7 + 1		F+	5⎫7		A	13(1)⎫14		P	4
W	2⎭		F−	2⎭		Ad	1 ⎭		O	1
						H	(1)			
D	11⎫12		FM	5 (1−)		Clo	1			
DS	1⎭		FMC′	1		Obj	2			
			FMC	1		Pl	1 + 2			
			Fm	1						
			mCF	1						
			CF	1						
			C′F	2− (+ 1−)						
			FC′	0 + 1						

W	37%		F	37%		A	74%
D	63%		F+	71%			

$$M : C$$
$$0 : 2\frac{1}{2}$$

$$Fm + FM : C' + c$$
$$9 : 2\frac{1}{2}$$

$$VIII + IX + X = 26\%$$

The content of this record by itself gives a very clear story of this girl's problems. This "wise" little one is definitely depending upon and using her family (Card I, "owl sitting in a tree"). In connection with this association there are also aggressive impulses (the "reindeer horns"). In fact in almost every situation her initial relatively pleasant reaction is likely to be followed by a more aggressive one. Thus, on Card II, she sees two puppies dancing, but immediately follows this with an atom bomb. Here the aggression which is evoked by associations to the parental figures assumes much stronger proportions and must be immediately denied. Her disturbance continues on Card III, primarily manifesting itself in her inability to perceive people on this card. She is still at a level of development when the activities of animals seem more meaningful to her than the reactions of people. It follows then that her relations with people have not led to identifications which are strong, satisfying and reassuring. The control and conformity she manifests stem from anxiety and fear of authority rather than a more positive form of motivation. The anxiety she feels in relation to authority is graphically portrayed by her reaction on Card IV. She is shocked, overwhelmed and guilt-ridden (the comment about eyes). That it is primarily the mother who constitutes the disturbing authoritarian comes out in her statement indicating that the monster is "something like a lady." This is further reflected in her two "spider" interpretations on Cards V and VII. (Psychiatrist's note states "This child's difficulties revolve around a demanding, anxious, overprotective mother.")

The significance of Card VI is not clear, but her reactions here follow a fairly consistent pattern, namely, that of producing a disturbed second response after giving a pleasant or at least an innocuous first one. This is certainly the case on Card VII where she follows two bunnies with another spider.

The sense of smallness and inadequacy that she has manifested previously—"little puppies" on Card II—receives special emphasis on VII in connection with the mother and this continues on the color cards ("little squirrels," "little snails"). She is less sure than she was on Card I that these animals can climb up and dominate this tree. At the end there is some resurgence of her aggressive impulses, in the "snake" interpretation, but it is toned down by their "crawling" activity.

To summarize what the content has revealed—this is a child who is afraid of and overwhelmed by authority, as represented in the mother figure. She feels aggressive and hostile as a result, but is afraid of and denies this hostility. In consequence she is left most uncertain and insecure and cannot develop in constructive fashion.

In her efforts to handle her conflict between hostility and dependency, she resorts mainly to denial and retreat into fantasy. There is only limited response to the environment (color sum 2½, FM 8). In addition she tries to deal with her experiences in a kind of piecemeal fashion (high D per cent), yet at the same time feels compelled to account for every aspect of a situation (on practically all cards tries to cover completely) lest, by leaving some detail unexplained, she expose herself in some way to further uncertainty and danger.

The heavy use of "black" indicates that this girl does not anticipate pleasant response from her contacts with the world about her. Instead, she feels that these are as likely, if not more likely, to be unpleasant and traumatic. Her uncertainty, her need to express her aggression and deny it, her vacillation between pleasant and unpleasant associations, all point to marked instability. Under such circumstances she certainly must have serious doubts about herself and how acceptable she is. It is these doubts which are largely responsible for her withdrawal, her limited interests and her efforts at detachment. These efforts at detachment are somewhat precocious, whereas her immature fantasy (8 FM, no M) indicates something of a lag. Personality growth is not progressing smoothly in this case, but has an erratic, uneven quality. The primitive impulses are strong and the authority figures threatening, with the resultant crippling and distortion of the true self.

This is a somewhat obese, thumb-sucking child who was brought to therapy by her mother because the mother has difficulty getting the child to conform and cooperate with her. The difficulties seem to focus largely around eating problems, and the whole eating situation seems to be a power contest between mother and child. Interestingly enough, the mother cannot see that the child's obesity has anything to do with her attempts to "stuff" the child, but rather suggests that it may be due to glandular difficulties. She also feels that the child is "unhappy," that she would like her to be lively and "happier," but again does not feel she is in any way responsible for this unhappiness. There is a nine year old sister who pushes the younger girl around. The psychiatric diagnosis was that of behavior problem with neurotic symptoms.

RECORD No. 10

Reading Disability and Behavior Disorder in a Boy, 7 Years 11 Months, I.Q. 116

				Response	Inquiry
I. 11"	W	FM	A	1. An eagle.	The way its spread out, it looks like it's flying.
	D	FC'	A	2. One of those things it's black and it has claws.	(top center detail) Wish I knew what it was called, have sharp claws. (means crab)
	W	F+, FK	A P	3. A mouse bird.	(means bat) Mouse—there's a hole through it. (light spot in center of body)
II. 20"	W	FMC'	A	1. Two funny birds dancing together, mouth open, teeth. Is this really ink? Baby birds dancing together.	They look like baby sparrows. Baby sparrows are black and have a beak and have little teeth in their mouth.
III. 18"	D	F+	A P	1. Butterfly.	(center red) Wings look like a butterfly, shaped like that.
	W	FM	A	2. Look like pulling something against each other, both these things.	Want to break it in half, some kind of funny birds, not people, can't exactly describe it, they have a beak.
IV. 25"	W	F−	A	1. This looks like some kind of baby sparrow. (I picked one up, shot it with a BB gun in the country.)	I can see the head and the wings.
V. 24"	W	F+	A P	1. This looks like a mouse bird.	Claws, feet, head, wings. Call it a mouse bird because I don't know the name of it.
	W	FM	(A)	2. A rabbit that's flying with wings.	Big ears and the wings here, like in the comics.
VI. 27"	W	FC'−	A	1. Some kind of butterfly, has a long neck, I would say African butterfly.	The neck and the face and the body and the wings. They're colored (?) black and white.

RECORD No. 10—continued

VII. 15"	D	F−	Map	5" 1. Looks like a map.	(top two thirds) Can't describe why.
	D	FM	Ad	2. Two faces, opened up their mouths, they're going to fight each other.	(top two thirds) Two heads. (Of what?) Animals, the mouths are open.
VIII. 28"	D	FM	A P	5" 1. It really looks like two mouses climbing against...	(usual) Shaped like mice.
	D	F+	At	2. Skeleton bones.	(center riblike area) Line here and like bones.
IX. 23"	D→W	M	Hd & Map	12" 1. Two heads looking down at a map.	(pink) Shape, people's heads and the beginnings of the body. (midline) Like in the back.
	D	F+	At	2. Skeleton bones.	
X. 29"	D	FM	A	6" 1. Two crabs on top looking at some object.	(top gray) Shaped like crabs. They want to know what it is.
	D	F+	Ad P	2. Face like a rabbit.	(usual)

R   18

W	7 } 9	F+	6 } 8	A	12(1) } 14(1)	P	5
W	1	F−	2	Ad	2		
D→W	1			Hd	1		
		M	1	At	2		
D	9	FM	6	Map	1 + 1		
		FMC′	1				
		FC′	2 (1−)				
		FK	0 + 1				
W	50%	F	44%	A	78%		
D	50%	F+	75%				

$$M : C$$
$$1 : 0$$

$$Fm + FM : C' + c$$
$$7 : 1\tfrac{1}{2}$$

$$VIII + IX + X = 33\%$$

This is a child who apparently no longer has any hope of winning positive response from his environment. He therefore makes no attempt to relate to it, nor does he react to emotional pressures from the outside world or seek to establish emotional relationships with it. Instead, he pours his energy into his fantasy activity. This activity is of a most immature order, and is not tested with any great frequency against reality standards. Rather, his formulations tend to have a strange, unrealistic quality which further emphasizes his disregard of the immediate realities he is expected to face.

The pretentiousness that is reflected in this boy's productions (his statements to the effect that "baby sparrows are black" as though he were an authority on such matter; his description of the butterfly on Card VI, "I would say an African butterfly"; his "map" responses) is essentially a façade intended to convince himself and others that he is an able, effective person. The extremes to which he goes in maintaining this front as in conjunction with his admission of his limitations (Card I, "I wish I knew what it was called"; Card VII, "I can't describe why"), as well as his essentially passive identifications (butterflies, birds, mice and rabbits) highlight his basic sense of inadequacy and his passivity. That he is a child who sees himself as essentially passive, ineffectual, is confirmed by this choice of animals, but he feels compelled to hide his insufficiencies and passivity from others. To this end he "puts on an act," forces issues and assumes attitudes of wisdom and assurance that he definitely does not possess.

His drastic withdrawal from emotional contacts points to disappointment, unhappiness and depression. Along with this there goes a decided narrowing of interests. Carrying along in the daily routines seems all that this boy can possibly be concerned with at this time.

The large number of teeth and mouth responses suggests that this boy experiences much oral tension. In conjunction with his failure to find emotional satisfaction in the environment, this emphasis and tension point to severe affect hunger. It is most probably the tension associated with this affect hunger that drives him into compulsive efforts to deal with all aspects of the situations he encounters and forces him, despite the generally limited and curtailed nature of his resources, to adopt an expansive attitude (W% high in relation to A %, a number of the whole responses being definitely forced).

The subject's marked immaturity finds expression in the high number of animal movement responses he gives. He finds symbolization of his dreams and problems in the activities of animals rather than of people. He verbalized this during his therapeutic sessions, saying that he liked animals better than people, that he understood animals and felt they were his friends. His problems, as reflected in his FM answers, focus about conflict and aggression (especially, the interpretations made on Cards III and VII). When not concerned with these matters he seems preoccupied with ideas of flight. In the final analysis, he is the timid figure, the rabbit with wings who would like to escape (Card V).

The associations mobilized by Card VII suggest that this boy sees the mother as someone with whom he must vigorously contend, and this need for self-assertion is something which he apparently does not find pleasant or comforting. Thus the mother becomes a figure who disturbs him and who arouses all the undesirable impulses he is trying to check or inhibit. The father, on the other hand, is apparently considered a weak helpless figure, someone against whom he can vent his hostility (Card IV). The reversal of roles on the part of the mother and father make it most difficult for this boy to achieve good masculine identification. If he identifies with the father, he feels he will be weak and easily destroyed; if he identifies with the mother, he must adopt contentious attitudes, something which produces tension and is distressing for him. Flight is his final solution, but since circumstances do not permit this, he also attempts to put up a "tough" front, hoping thereby to ward off external attack or exposure of his inadequacies.

In general, it is largely "power problems" which concern this boy and interfere with his sense of security. In meeting these he vacillates between "eagle" (first response) and "rabbit" (last response), from dominating predatory identifications, to timid, passive ones. In consequence, he cannot find himself and he fears to establish relationships with a world that is so confusing and distressing to him. Under such circumstances it is most probable that his behavior will be erratic and at times most unacceptable.

The presenting symptom in this case was inability to read, but this was actually a minor matter in comparison with this boy's basic problems. The younger of two boys, he lives with his father, mother and brother, aged 14. The mother is a relatively young, attractive woman, who is extremely tense, ambitious and dissatisfied. She finds no happiness in her relationship with her husband, who is a passive individual, content to spend his life working and watching television. He never takes her out or does anything with his boys, except to yell at them when they become exceptionally noisy. The mother, on the other hand, is after the boys all the time, especially the younger one, since he cannot fight back with any effectiveness. All her thwarted ambition and her anger is released in her contacts with her sons. In addition to the pressures which this boy suffers at the hands of the mother, the tongue lashings she gives him, the punishments and denials he sustains, he is also victimized by his brother who bullies and teases him. He has few friends, does not know how to get along with people, does poorly in school, and is in difficulties constantly with the teacher and the other children in his class and in his neighborhood. Much of the time he stays by himself, and the sporadic efforts he makes to establish social contacts generally end in disaster. It is not long before he feels rejected, insulted, and he then either withdraws or, on rare occasions, gives vent to an explosive outburst of violent proportions, threatening to kill people, once actually pursuing his opponent with a knife. In his sessions with the therapist he would tell stories of his exploits with the boys in the neighborhood, how he had beat them up, even how he had beat up their older brothers and fathers a few times. Similarly, he told about a dog he owned and gave very graphic pictures of the dog's activities and its devotion to him. None of these stories were true, there were no friends, no successful fights and no pets. However, his recounting of these fairy tales was so vivid and detailed that at first the therapist actually accepted them. Their realistic quality stemmed from their importance to this boy and indicated how intensely he lived in his fantasies to the neglect of participation in the world about him.

RECORD No. 11

Repeat Rorschach (See Record No. 10), Age 9 Years 6 Months, I.Q. 118

Card		Response	Inquiry	Loc.	Content	P	Det.
I. 65"	10"	1. That looks like a ...... doesn't exactly look like a bat.	(same as response 3)				
		2. Looks like a map, features look like a map.	(center detail) The bumps and shapes.	D	Map		F±
		3. Part of it looks like a bat, not the whole thing.	(side detail) Looks like a bat's head, two bumps and the darkness.	D	Ad		FC'
II. 40"	17"	1. Looks like the inside of an animal which is very ugly.	(top red) Meat and bones sticking out.	D	At		CF
		2. Head looks like a mouse's head.	(top center detail) Rat's head rather, pointy, black.	D	Ad		FC'
III. 57"	24"	1. Looks something like an ancient thing, a statue.	Eyes, hands sticking out, head. Maybe not ancient, but religious or Indian, like in India.	W	(H)		Fm
		2. Thing in middle looks like meat.	(center red) Not meat, blood dripping down.	D	Bl		Cm
		3. Thing over here looks like meat too.	(side red) Long bone and red meat on it. (insists shape more important than color)	D	Meat		FC
IV. 20"	9"	1. Like a skin, this looks like. That's all. This looks like the skin of an animal.	Shape and the darkness. Some prehistoric animal.	W	A Obj		FC'
V. 30"	4"	1. This looks like a bat. This is the thing what I said looked like a mouse last time. That's all.	These feet, when it flies always stick out this way.	W	A	P	FM
VI. 34"	5"	1. This looks like something made by the Indians—a skin. They cut it out in this feature.	Cut out that way so he can wear it. Different colors make it look like fur.	W	A Obj	P	Fc
VII. 62"	∧∨25"	1. Top looks like a butterfly.	(lower third) Shape of a butterfly body and wings.	D	A		F+
		2. Bottom looks like part of a moun-	(usual head) Shape of it, cold mountain,	D	N		FC'

Card	Loc	Determinant	Content	P	Response	Inquiry
VIII. 60"	W	F−	At		1. Whew, definitely looks like a body.	Shaped like it, the meat, the bones coming out and holding it there. (denies color)
	D	CF	Rock		2. Rock.	(lower center pink) Color and shape, I have a rock the same color.
	D	F+	A	P	3. Mouse.	(usual animals) Feet head, body—rats.
	d	FC'	At		4. Part of an animal's body, the main bone.	(midline) Just the main bone of the body shaped and darkened.
	d	F+	Ad		5. Fox's neck.	(center of top detail) Think it's shape of fox's neck.
IX. 62"	D	FC−	A		1. Top looks like an insect.	(pink) An insect that eats bushes—a red insect. I was bit by a dog once.
	(Denial) (D	F+	Ad)		2. Green looks like some bushes. (Add. I changed my mind, looks like a hippo's head.)	
	D	cCF	Meat		3. Down here is some meat and bones.	(orange) Bones sticking out, the redness and the lightness.
	D	F+	At		4. Inside of an animal.	(midline) Main bone.
X. 68"					4″ Whew, the last one is certainly hard.	
	D	F+	A		12″ 1. These gray things look like insects.	(top gray) The way they are shaped. Here's the feelers and the things they grab their prey with.
	D	F±	Pl		2. Seaweed under the ocean.	(side blue) Shape and all the stuff coming out.
	(Denial) (D	CF	At)		3. Front part of an animal. (Add. I think I saw the inside of an animal, the redness. [pink])	
	D	FC'−	At		4. Bone of an animal's head.	(top gray) The way the bone comes out, the grayness.
	D	FM	A		5. Bug eating stuff.	(side brown) Shape of a bug.
	D	F+,CF	A & Pl		6. Looks like a frog caught in green seaweed.	(lower center) Feet of frog and greenness.

R   25 + 2

W	4 ⎫ 5	F+	5 ⎫	A	7 ⎫ 10 + 1	P 3
W̶	1 ⎭	F±	3 ⎬ 9 + 1	Ad	3 ⎭	
		F−	1 ⎭	H	(1)	
D	18 + 2			Bl	1	
				At	5	
d	2	FM	2	Meat	2	
		Fm	1	A Obj	2	
				Map	1	
		FC	2 (1−)	Rock	1	
		CF	2 + 2	N	1	
		cCF	1	Pl	1 + 1	
		Cm	1			
		Fc	1			
		FC′	6 (1−)			

W	20%	F	36%	A	40%
D	72%	F+	56%		
d	8%				

$$M \ : \ C$$
$$0 \ : \ 5\tfrac{1}{2}$$

$$Fm + FM \ : \ C' + c$$
$$4 \ : \ 4\tfrac{1}{2}$$

$$VIII + IX + X = 52\%$$

Seventeen months after the previous record was taken, during which time this boy had psychotherapy one hour a week, the test was repeated. The picture is now a strikingly different one. Taken by itself rather than in conjunction with his earlier performance, this protocol reveals a highly unstable, disturbed personality. However, when compared to the earlier productions, it can be seen that changes of a positive order have taken place. Most conspicuous is the subject's shift in emphasis. He no longer focuses his energy on his fantasy life but uses it to make contact with the world about him. The one M and 7 FM that appeared in the first record have now practically disappeared (only 2 FM), and a color sum of 5½ appears in contrast to the previous total lack of any color response. It is true that much of the time his affect lacks control and is of an impulsive, demanding order, marked by aggression and brutality, yet there are occasions when he does bring his feelings under control. His desire to relate to the world and his responsiveness to it are reflected not only in the sharp increase in color answers but in the fact that he now gives 52 per cent of his responses on the last three cards, whereas formerly they brought forth only 33 per cent of his answers.

It should be noted that, with the increase of color responses, there is also an increase in the number of times he responds to the black attribute of the blots. His contacts with the environment and his therapy have by no means dispelled the unpleasant and disturbing feelings that the world arouses in him. In fact his sense of disappointment and unhappiness has increased. At the same time he is willing to go ahead and contact that environment and seek for satisfaction and reassurance in it. The therapy has apparently built up his need for social contacts and has strengthened his confidence in himself and his ability to make such contacts, but it has not relieved much of the anxiety he experiences when he makes them. As part of his changed approach, the subject no longer strains to encompass total situations. Rather he definitely delimits the sphere of his activity and picks from his experiences those aspects which he feels he can handle.

The morbidity of this boy's concepts and the aggressive nature of his thoughts are reflected in his repeated interpretation of "raw meat" and "insides." Fear and hostility are concomitants of these reactions, and reveal the unwholesome nature of this boy's perception of social and interpersonal relationships. For him they are bloody, unpleasant, dangerous experiences.

Right now this subject is so busy dealing with his social relationships and responding to his environment that there is no energy available for fantasy activity. Rather, the things that were previously internalized are now, to a large extent, worked out in his social and interpersonal contacts. With this expansion into the outer environment, there goes a definite broadening of interests and a reduction in stereotypy. The concentration on animals (78 per cent A) which he showed earlier now is reduced considerably (40 per cent A). Unfortunately, human responses have not taken over as yet but, instead, evidences of aggression and anxiety rather than good interpersonal relationships are suggested by the content.

The oral aggression and the intellectual pretentiousness that were noted earlier are still present, though to a somewhat lesser degree. The disturbed relationship with the mother has not been resolved but is being handled in less aggressive fashion. Instead of fighting with her, he now "puts her at a distance" ("mountain," "cold mountain").

What therapy has done for this boy is to bring him out of his fantasy world and encourage him to work out his problems in relation to others. While he has by no means reached the point where he can do this constructively, it is evident that he is working in that direction. At the same time, his handling of his maternal relations have acquired a certain maturity through emphasis on detachment rather than counteraggression.

During this period this boy began making friends in the neighborhood. In fact, at one time he carried this to such extremes that the mother complained about the children that came into her house all day long. He also joined the Cub Scouts. In his social contacts he had many stormy experiences, friendships were broken up, battles took place, but the direction was a social one. The tall tales that had characterized his early contacts with the therapist and the constant demand for pets instead of friends almost completely disappeared. He also learned to disregard much of the unpleasantness he experienced at the hands of the mother, and turned to the therapist for the response he did not receive from her.

RECORD No. 12

Behavior Problem, Neurotic Traits, Girl, Age 8 Years 5 Months, I.Q. 141

					Response	Inquiry
I. 15″	W	FM	A & Arch	5″	1. Look like two bears holding on to the top of a building, putting their nose up in the air.	(side details are bears because of shape, center detail is building)
II. 47″	W	MC	H P	10″	1. Two clowns dancing with each other.	Head, mouth, hat, holding hands together. Never heard of anyone with a red face, except a clown.
	D	CF	N		2. Sun's going down.	(lower center red) These things (points coming out) and it's red.
III. 54″	W	M	H P	7″	1. Two people like picking up jugs from a mouth of something.	(lower center is mouth) Like a monster's mouth (?). Women, have skirt.
	D	CF−	N		2. Two pieces of sun.	(side red) Because red.
IV. 38″	W	F+	A	6″	1. Looks like a monster, face and hands.	Like a big monster. (points out parts)
V. 30″	W	F+	A P	4″	1. Like a vampire bat.	Shape of wings and feet.
VI. 72″	W	M	H	∧∨19″	1. Looks like two people holding on to a stick so they shouldn't get burned.	(all but feathers which are fire) Have arm and leg.
	D	Fm	Fire		2. Here's a fire.	Things come out of it. (usual)
	d	F+	Ad		3. Cat whiskers.	
VII. 44″	W	M	H & Rock	12″	1. Two Indians making faces at each other. They're on a rock.	Have feather in head, sticking out their tongues.

RECORD No. 12—*continued*

VIII. 59″	6″	This is a nice one.		
	19″	1. Looks like a Christmas tree.	(top gray) Shaped like it.	D } CF Pl
		2. And under it kind of colored snow.	(lower center)	W{ D C N
		3. And two frogs hanging down from the Christmas tree.	(Usual animals) Salamanders.	D } FM A P
IX. 37″		This is a nice one too.		
	14″	1. Looks like a guitar with decorations over it.	Shaped like a guitar in the middle, rest is decorations.	D→W F. C/F Obj
X. 30″		Even nicer.		
	14″	1. Looks like a design.	Different colors and shapes.	W C/F Design

R   16

W	6⎫		F+	3⎫		A	4⎫		P 4
W	2⎬9		F+. C/F	1⎬4		Ad	1⎬5		
D→W	1⎭					H	4		
			M	3		N	3		
D	6		MC	1		Fire	1		
			FM	2		Obj	1		
d	1		Fm	1		Design	1		
						Pl	1		
			CF	3(1−)		Arch	0 + 1		
			C/F	1		Rock	0 + 1		
			C	1					
W	56%		F	25%		A	31%		
D	38%		F+	100%					
d	6%								

$$M : C$$
$$4 : 6\tfrac{1}{2}$$

$$Fm + FM : C' + c$$
$$3 : 0$$

$$VIII + IX + X = 31\%$$

This child's insecurity manifests itself primarily through her inability to deal in reasonably adequate fashion with her emotional experiences (as evidenced on Cards IX and X), and also in her strong efforts to treat with every situation in its entirety, to leave no aspect of any circumstance unaccounted for, even if she has to force issues to achieve this (again most evident on VIII, IX, X). It is this forcing which explains her poor responses on Card III ("two pieces of sun") and also her inadequate and infantile reactions to the last three cards. It is when called upon to set up emotional contact with the environment that this girl becomes disturbed, and it follows that, in emotionally colored circumstances, she is bound to act less acceptably and maturely than she could. Her emotional inadequacy (2 C, 1 C/F) are in sharp contradistinction to the control and maturity she manifests when she is not affectively involved and when she can deal with her emotions on a fantasy basis (4 M responses).

Despite her emotional disturbance, it is clear that this girl has had some positive emotional experiences (the Christmas tree, the dancing clowns). Because of these she is not altogether lacking in emotional spontaneity and she apparently still hopes for support and reassurance from the environment (high color sum). As it is, she is dependent upon emotional response from the environment and is so open to emotional stimulation, that practically all her experiences have strong affective coloring. She seems unable to defend herself against emotional pressure, and instead gets repeatedly carried away by her feelings. Formal, objective attitudes are only infrequently attained (only 25 per cent form answers).

The subject's emotional dependency is paralleled by a generally passive dependent orientation (nature of M and FM interpretations). The experience of "holding" and "hanging on to" things is a frequent one, and reflects her own sense of precarious balance and need for support. Her response on Card VI is particularly significant in this connection. It would seem from her reaction here that there is some recognition of the fact that the thing to which she clings is being consumed by the same fires or emotions that are destroying her.

Conflict with the mother (Card VII) is certainly one of this girl's major problems. It is not definite whether the mother is also the monster on Card IV, though it seems very likely, or whether the father too constitutes a disturbance and a threat.

This is the kind of child who wants desperately to feel that those on whom she depends are positively oriented toward her. To this end she adopts passive roles and tries to please, to do what she feels is expected but, despite her efforts, she cannot succeed when any emotional factors come into consideration. Instead, when emotional demands are made on her, that is, in crucial relationships, she is compelled to react much less adequately and acceptably than she does on other occasions. There is a certain self-punitive quality in the way she defeats her own purposes and reacts to the push of her own needs regardless of the nature of the external circumstances.

The initial complaint in this case was thumb-sucking, but it quickly became apparent that there were many other problems. This child apparently gets along relatively well with every one except her mother. With the mother she lies and is obstinate and spiteful. The mother is afraid that the child will "grow up to be like her husband and his family," especially her mother-in-law whom she despises. The relationship between the parents has not been a good one and the mother lets out much of her disappointment and her rage on this child. There is a younger sister who is more like the mother's family and is therefore favored by the mother. The cause for the child's deviant behavior clearly lies in the home situation and especially her relationship to her mother. The diagnosis was behavior problem, neurotic traits.

RECORD No. 13

Boy with Family Problems, Age 10 Years 5 Months, I.Q. 120

				Response	Inquiry
I. 16"	W	FC'	A P	∧∨∧ 1. Vampire, with spots around it.	Look at the wings of it and the points and it's black. (Spots?) Just little feathers from it.
II. 21"	W	F+	A Obj	∧∨∧ 1. Skin.	(black area) Looks like an animal skin, a small animal, it looks like a skunk.
	DW	F−	A	2. Butterfly.	Put it together and the tail looks like a butterfly's tail. Get the thing together close it up, it looks like a butterfly.
III. 41"	D	F−	At	∧∨∧ 1. It looks like a body, a skeleton.	(lower center) Shaped like around the stomach.
	D	C	Bl	2. Blood all around.	(all red) This red is blood.
	W	M	H P	3. Two gentlemen, they are trying to walk into a bar.	(all black) They just look like men.
	D	F−	Obj	4. Umbrella.	(outside red) Long handle.
IV. 6"	DW	F−	A	∧∨∧ 1. Looks like some sort of an animal. (makes face and sounds as if he were disturbed)	Face looks like a horse or a dragon. (lower center D is face)
V. 4"	W	F+	A P	∧∨∧ 1. Butterfly.	Tail, head, wings.
VI. 15"				∧∨∧ 5" What's this? Which is the right side.	
	W	FC'	A Obj P	9" 1. Looks like skin of an animal.	Like the body opened out, no head, no tail, maybe the top is the tail, and it's brown, no black, like a bear.

RECORD No. 13—*continued*

					Response
VII. 12"	∧∨∧	1. Outside of the body.	W	F−	At	Shaped something like a body. Insides should be in here. (in space) Man just fits himself in there.
		2. Or a coat.	W	F−	Clo	
VIII. 71"	∧∨∧	1. Insides of a person.	W	C/F−	At	Look at the bones and everything. Person is colored inside.
		2. Two animals climbing up a mountain, hunting for food.	D	FM	A P	(usual) Head, long body, four legs.
IX. 23"	∧∨∧	1. Two animals breathing fire.	D	FM.CFm	A & Fire	(orange) Strange animal, like dragon—it's fire because it's orange coming out on the ends.
X. 52"	∧∨∧	1. Couple of spiders.	D	F+	A P	(side blue) Look like it in every way, legs and everything.
		2. All kinds of animals.	D	F+	A	(top green and top gray) like a sheep maybe, sort of fat.
		3. Pole.	D	F+	Obj	(top gray) Shaped straight.
		4. Rabbit's head.	D	F+	Ad P	(usual) Mostly the long ears and the pointy chin.
		5. Two green things are worms.	D	F+	A	(bottom green) Look at the long tails.

R   20

W	6 }		F+	7 } 13	A	8 }		P 7
W	2 } 10		F−	6 }	A & Fire 1 } 10			
DW	2 }				Ad	1 }		
			M	1	H	1		
D	10		FM	1	At	3		
			FM.CFm	1	Bl	1		
					A Obj	2		
			C/F	1	Obj	2		
			C	1	Clo	1		
			FC'	2				

W	50%	F	65%	A	50%
D	50%	F+	54%		

M : C
1 : 3½

Fm + FM : C' + c
3 : 1

VIII + IX + X = 40%

One of the most striking features in this record—and one which has not appeared in any of the previous protocols—is the subject's need to alter situations rather than accept them as they are given to him. This shows itself in the fact that he immediately turns each card the instant it is offered to him. Even though he returns it in each case to the upright position before he begins interpretation, it is necessary for him first to express his negativism and defiance. The turning is his way of saying in effect "I'll change it the way I want." Further indication of this type of resistance to circumstances as he finds them is found in his second interpretation on Card II. Here he says on the inquiry "Put it together and the tail looks like a butterfly's tail. Get the thing together, close it up, it looks like a butterfly."

The overall picture presented by the subject's responses indicates that his dissatisfaction with the environment and his aggressive efforts at altering it are caused by his basic unhappiness. There are two responses which employ the black aspects of the blot (Cards I and VI) and point to experiences of a frustrating order. It is these which have made him see the world as dangerous, aggressive and predatory ("vampire," "skeleton with blood around it"). His own impulses are also of an aggressive, destructive order ("animals hunting for food" on Card VIII, "animals breathing fire" on Card IX). He tries to keep these impulses in check; witness the 63 per cent form responses and the attempts to immobilize aggression and hostility ("animal skins" on Cards II and VI, as well as the "gentlemen" response on Card III, following the disorganized emotional answer just preceding). This sequence on Card III and the sequence of interpretations on Card II are especially interesting and important. The association to the parental figures is obviously not a pleasant one—a skunk—but he again tries to immobilize it and minimize its offensiveness by reducing it to something inanimate, something socially acceptable and useful, an animal skin. However, it can be inferred that the very absence of activity on the part of these animals, the fact that they cannot get together, is disturbing to him. His next response therefore deals intensely with this need to "get things together," to fill up any gaps in the environment. In fact the need is so strong that he must find expression for it at this point, even if in doing so he distorts his perceptions and ends with a poor form response. (This boy comes from a broken home and has reacted badly to the fact that the mother has ejected an alcoholic father from the house.)

The disturbance on Card II, which is so closely associated with his special problems that it interferes with his control and judgment, carries over into Card III and results in the production of a disorganized answer as his initial reaction to this card. The cold, detached, frightening reactions he gives to stimuli intended to evoke his associations to people in general become even more intense as he attempts to deal with the emotional facets of the situation ("blood all around"). It takes some time for him to recover sufficiently to give a well organized response and the content of this again highlights his own problems ("trying to walk into a bar"); the disturbance caused by this association is probably responsible for the inadequacy he manifests in the following answer ("umbrella," scored $F-$).

This boy's relations with his mother are obviously very disturbed. Both responses on Card VII are poor ones, showing an absence of control and objectivity in this connection. Both responses deal with things which might serve as covering and protection, "outsides of a body" and a "coat." Indeed, the fact that he begins the second response with "or" rather than "and" indicates that both responses have much the same meaning for him. That this covering is not adequate is reflected not only in the poor form, but in the sense of emptiness conveyed by the first interpretation and his comment on inquiry "the insides should be in there." The need for shelter and warmth are strong but he certainly does not feel they are forthcoming. Rather the "animals hunting food" on Card VIII points up his own unsatisfied oral need and consequent affect hunger.

The eventual inadequacy and passivity which he experiences find reflection in the type of animals he sees on Card X. He begins with the spider, the symbol of the aggressive, all absorbing, destroying mother, and then follows this with sheep, rabbits, worms—small, mild, relatively ineffectual figures. The fire-breathing, food-hunting activities give way to gentle, supine ones.

One other factor in this record merits discussion, and that is the sex shock this boy shows on Card VI. At this age this need not necessarily be considered indicative of anything but the disturbance that most children would show when first aware of sexual implications for which they have no backlog of experience. They therefore cannot react smoothly and readily, but rather become blocked. The fact that after a short time lapse this boy can pull himself together and give a good response indicates that sexual problems, per se, are not pressing at this time.

As has already been indicated, this boy is the product of a broken home. His father is an alcoholic and throughout the child's lifetime the relationship between the parents has been an unhappy conflicted one. The boy is well aware of this and of his father's alcoholism. However, he has also many positive feelings for the father and has identified with him. When the father was forcibly ejected from the home about a year before the record was taken, this boy had very mixed feelings about the matter. The fact that through much of his life the mother has worked and that she vents much of her frustration on him when she is home has not led him to see her in a positive light or to feel warmly toward her. His very identification with the father causes him to fear that he too may be ejected unless he adopts passive conforming attitudes. Thus he vacillates between this passivity and conformity and sporadic aggressive outbursts. He also has gone in for petty thieving. Diagnostically he is considered a behavior problem with neurotic traits.

CHAPTER X

The Emotionally Disturbed Child (continued)

THE CHILD WHO SHOWS primarily neurotic disturbances and is diagnosed accordingly is the child whose disturbances in equilibrium produce behavior which can be best described as exaggeratedly infantile and dependent. This is the child who, as the result of his interpersonal relationships, has come to see himself as inadequate, unacceptable, unloved, and "bad." He has developed patterns of response which, for him, best serve to allay the discomfort associated with these disturbing perceptions of himself. These habit patterns are of a self-defeating order in that they preserve and even enhance the very attributes which are responsible for his negative self-concept. Nevertheless, he feels that these must be maintained at all cost, and any experience, impulse, or feeling which threatens to disturb the status quo is warded off.

The following records are those which have been obtained from children who present primarily neurotic pictures, though some behavioral deviations are also manifested. The personality structure in these cases is in many instances similar to the type found in the preceding chapter, and differentiation between the so-called neurotic child and the behavior problem child on the basis of his Rorschach productions is frequently not possible. In some instances the violence of the emotional experiences and the absence of control indicate that the conflicts will be acted out in a way that will be unacceptable, but in other cases the nature of the overt behavior is less evident. In all cases, however, it is clear that conflicts are not being effectively handled.

Boy in Anxiety State, Age 5 Years 3 Months, I.Q. 110

	Response				Inquiry
I. 19"	1. He seems like a wicked man.	WS	M	Hd	He looks terrible, he's going to eat something up. This is his mouth (lower space), here are his eyes (upper spaces).
II. 20"	1. This is a fire.	W	CC'	Fire	Smoke and fire, red and black.
III. 20"	1. They're pulling apart a crab. That's all.	W	M	H P	(Who?) Mr. Jack, it's a man, they're fighting.
IV. 24"	1. That's a turtle it looks to me.	W	F+	A	Legs sticking out and little head.
	2. Raccoon.	D	FC'	Ad	(top detail) Just the head, black stripes.
V. 20"	1. Snail.	D	FM	A	(top detail) Sticking his feelers out.
	2. Bird.	W	F+	A	With big wings.
VI. 26"	1. That's a bird, an insect, a praying mantis I think.	DW	F−	A	Two feet, fighting claws and a head.
VII. 56"	1. That looks like a map. That's all.	W	F±	Map	All different shapes.
VIII. 35"	1. All different kinds of leaves.	W	C/F−	Pl	All different colors and shapes.
IX. 18"	1. Looks like many leaves. (seems preoccupied)	W	C/F−	Pl	Different colors and shapes.
X. 57"	1. Looks like all leaves, purple leaves and everything.	W	C/F−	Pl	(points to different parts)
	2. Skinny crab.	D	F+	A P	(side blue) Lots of legs.

R   13

W	7 } 10	F+	3 } 5	A	5 } 6	P	2
W	1	F±	1	Ad	1		
WS	1	F−	1	H	1		
DW	1			Hd	1		
		M	2	Pl	3		
D	3	FM	1	Fire	1		
				Map	1		
		C/F	3−				
		CC'	1				
		FC'	1				
W	77%	F	38%	A	46%		
D	23%	F+	60%				

$$M : C$$
$$2 : 4\tfrac{1}{2}$$

$$Fm + FM : C' + c$$
$$1 : 2$$

$$VIII + IX + X = 31\%$$

The contrast between the maturity this child is able to achieve in his inner life (two good human movement responses) and the disorganization in his emotional life is extreme. In his contacts with the environment this boy evidently tends to fall apart (CC' on Card II, perseveration on Cards VIII, IX, X). His emotional disturbance apparently centers about his own position and security ("leaf" interpretations) and about his aggressive impulses in relation to the parents. It is primarily his concern about his own security that has hampered his emotional development and produced responses more typical of a younger child.

His anxiety is so extreme it has invaded his fantasy life, and here too he is conflicted and threatened both by others and by his own impulses (Cards I and III). His identifications appear to have been with these evil and aggressive figures and his efforts are directed toward repressing, denying and minimizing the impulses associated with these identifications and fantasies. These impulses must be vigorously denied and ascribed to somebody else ("Mr. Jack," Card III) and controlled righteous attitudes adopted. He is the "snail with feelers sticking out," hesitantly testing out a world in which he finds no security and to which he tries to adjust by exercising control and striving for a maturity that is beyond him.

He tries to react in formal detached fashion ("map" on VII) and his entire manner, as well as the time he takes for most of his responses, points to his efforts at careful deliberation. There is something of a "little old man" about this boy, a certain righteousness in his "wicked man" and other expressions.

His treatment of Card VII suggests that he does not feel any great warmth in the mother figure, and can only respond to her on a formal level. His time delay here points to blocking and uncertainty which he resolves by seeking for a detached, intellectual relationship. As reflected in Card IV, he shows a more positive reaction to male authority. There are primarily pleasant associations in this area, though some disturbance is reflected in his use of black. He does not appear unhappy in his relation with the parents yet, on the other hand, his concept of people which can only come from his experiences with the parents are anything but pleasant ones (Card I, "wicked man, going to eat something up," Card III, "pulling apart a crab").

This boy's history throws considerable light on his rather strange attitudes. He is an only child, born while his father was overseas. He was taught by the mother to recognize the father's picture and to think of the father as everything that is good and desirable in a man. The father returned about eight months before this record was taken, and the relations between the parents very quickly became stormy. The child was a constant witness to their bickerings and actual fights. A few months ago the father left and the child has developed anxiety attacks since then, is afraid to go to sleep or to be left by the mother, who leaves him with a neighbor each morning because she has to go to work. The neighbor reports that the child is very quiet, withdrawn and sad, and as the time for the mother's return approaches, he becomes obviously anxious. His response to Card VII points up his uncertainty about the mother who first built up in him a strong positive attitude toward the father, only to destroy it before the child actually had a chance to test it out. His identification with the father who is "wicked" undoubtedly causes him to wonder whether the mother will also reject him and force him to leave the home.

RECORD No. 15

Anxiety Reaction with Somatization, Girl, 6 Years 9 Months, I.Q. 106

I. 52"	W	FM	A	1. It's a bird but I don't know the name.	Has wings and it's up in the air.
II. 25"	W	CC'	Fire	1. Like a fire, burned.	All the red is fire and the smoke is black.
III. 34"	D	F+	A P	1. Like a butterfly.	(center red) Has wings.
	W	FM–, C'F	A & Germ	2. I think these are worms.	(all black is worm) They both have mouths. They are putting some germs on the floor. Like you put your fingers in your mouth from the floor. (lower center black is germ) Germ is black.
IV. 14"	W	FM–	A	1. Like a spider.	Spider has hands like that and he crawls. This (lower center detail) helps him crawl and he has two feet.
V. 20"	W	FM	A P	1. I know, this flies but what is it?	Which way? Now it looks like a butterfly.
VI. 19"	D→W	FM	A & Ground	1. Like a snake.	I think it's a poison one, because it doesn't go into water. Water snakes are not poison but all the others are poison. My teacher told me and I heard it on TV. This (top detail is snake, all the rest is the ground), he's coming out from something or going in or out.

VII.
41"   W   C'   Snow or Smoke

6" 1. Like ice or snow.

Or smoke, somebody burned something, makes smoke, black. Or dirty ice.

VIII.
20"   (D FM A P)

(looks at back) Nothing.
(Add. Mice going up or a bear going up.)

IX.
40"   ......
      (D F− A)
      (D F+ Food)

16" Doesn't look like anything. I never saw these.
(Add. Looks like a lion. [pink] Has a big head.)
(Add. [midline and pink] A little ice stick.)

X.
31"   W   mCF− Pl

17" 1. These look like leaves falling down. I don't even know who knows it.

Top (gray) is tree and rest is leaves.

R   9 + 3

W	6)		F+	1 + 1)		A	6 + 2	P	2 + 1
W	1 }8		F−	0 + 1) 1 + 2		Pl	1		
D→W	1)					Fire	1		
			FM	5(2−) + 1		Snow	1		
D	1 + 3					Food	0 + 1		
			mCF	1−		Ground	0 + 1		
			CC'	1		Germ	0 + 1		
			C'	1					
			C'F	0 + 1					
W	89%		F	11%		A	67%		
D	11%		F+	100%					

M : C
0 : 2½

Fm + FM : C' + c
6 : 3

VIII + IX + X = 11%

The unpleasant nature of this girl's relations with her environment are clearly brought out in her marked tendency to react to the black aspects of the test stimuli. There is a strong "burnt child" aspect to her responses, and it is evident that she has had difficulties with those who are important to her, namely, the parental figures. In consequence, contact with the world about her is tension producing and disrupting (mCF, CC', C'). At the same time she has little capacity for defending herself against emotional onslaught. Rather, she is repeatedly swept away by her feelings in helpless, disorganizing fashion. (All responses except one have emotional coloring of one kind or another.) In particular, she finds it practically impossible to deal with the more exciting affects, as represented by all the colored cards, in reasonably objective fashion. Her disturbed emotional and interpersonal relations leave her paralyzed under such circumstances. She simply does not know how to relate to others and share her feelings with them. For her, the environment is a place where threatening, dangerous and anxiety provoking experiences take place. The impression obtained from her many C' responses is that, for her, life has been sad, that she does not feel loved and cannot get close to others. She actually has only one color response that is not associated with a black response, and that tells a story all its own: "looks like leaves falling down," is the subject's way of symbolizing her deep insecurity, her sense of being without anything solid to which to hold. Her added statement "I don't even know who knows it" has all the pathos of a child who feels herself completely alone and rejected.

Certainly the subject does not see the mother as a warm, reassuring, accepting figure, but rather as someone who is cold and anxiety producing (Card VII, "ice," "snow," "smoke"). It is quite obvious that her relations with her mother have been of an order which stresses health and cleanliness rather than love. People are constantly assailed by danger, and any satisfaction carries with it the possibility of harm ("worms that have mouths" and "these worms are putting germs on the floor"—just like the child who puts dirty fingers in the mouth).

There would seem to be some sexual concern reflected in her response to Card VI. The response suggests that she strongly feels that men ("snake") in their sexual role are dangerous and she calls on authority to back her up in this conviction. In view of this girl's history, it seems very possible that she has been warned against men, the harm they can do. The same dangers she ascribes to "dirt" and oral pleasures are also being attributed to any sexual contact, and probably to contact with men in general.

This girl has few adequate defenses and seems to be repeatedly overwhelmed by her impulses and feelings. Reality is not well perceived and objectivity only infrequently maintained. The frequency of this child's disorganization is such as to make for a very guarded prognosis. She has few defenses and, unless these are soon developed, it is possible that she may develop schizophrenia.

It is particularly interesting in this case that the response toward IV is a "spider," the symbol of the all-encompassing destroying mother. For this child, then, the mother is the authority figure, rather than the father. The history definitely bears this out: the father left the home when the subject was three weeks old and she has actually never seen him. He is mentally ill, and has been institutionalized twice. The mother works and the child is left with a grandmother much of the time. The mother has very mixed feelings about this child. She certainly resents her, feels she makes life unduly difficult for her, possibly stands in the way of a second marriage. She also has a great deal of guilt because of this rejection and apparently compensates for it by stressing the child's physical well being. The grandmother with whom the child spends much time is also overconcerned about her physical welfare. She was brought for treatment because she has a cough in the morning, sneezes a great deal, has eczema and bronchial asthma. She was diagnosed as an anxiety reaction with somatization.

RECORD No. 16

Tics (Mouth Stretching and Lip Sucking) in a 7 Year 8 Month Boy, I.Q. 102

					Response	Inquiry
I. 50"	W	FM (Denial)	A	P	1. A bat.	Right here, flying. (denies)
	D	F+	(H)		2. A bird, a special bird. I don't know what kind.	
					3. Looks like a witch except for the head.	(center detail) Sometimes a witch turns into a bat. Take the wings off and you have a witch.
II. 25"	W	M	H		1. Looks like two ladies dancing. No head on them people.	(all but upper red) Legs together and the hands, like two fat ladies, hitting their hands together.
	D	F+	Obj		2. Two knives.	(top center detail) Attached together. Like maybe the ladies would start a fight. Two ladies are going to use them. Dancing first but going to start a fight because something happened.
III. 40"	W	F+	H	P	1. Looks like somebody all cut up. Hands down here.	Clothes all ripped up.
	D	F+	Clo	P	2. And a bowtie.	(usual) Belongs to the man that's all cut up.
	d	F+	Ad		3. Teeth of a tiger.	(small lower center details) Sharp like a tiger, if they closed they would eat you up.
	W	F+	(H)		4. Ghosts with a pointy nose.	Ghost because not stuck together.
	D	C	Bl		5. Blood because sometimes ghosts bleed all red and everything.	(all red) All red and everything.
	D	FM—	A		6. And two fishes.	(head and torso of usual men) Some kind dive like that before they go in the water.

IV. 52"	Dr	M	(Hd)	1. This looks like a ghost. — (usual arms, head and spine but nothing else, not really connected) Hands of a ghost are shaped like that, like when they choke people—and a ghost spine.
	W	Fc	(H)	2. Snowman with big feet. — No head, and a stool. The feet look like snow all over. (rubs card in a way that indicates awareness of shading)
	D	F+	Obj	3. Stool. — (lower center detail) Stool made of ice because it all sticks out.
	D	F+	Ad	4. Top looks like a crab. — (top center detail) Do crabs ever put their heads inside shell? Head is chopped off and the legs. (shell-like shape)
V. 40"	W	F+	A P	1. Looks like a bat. — Wings look like a bat and the head. Looks like a man bat. Legs looks like they belong to a man bat, without the wings looks like a man with a helmet on.
	(D / D	F / FC'–	H) / A	2. Animal that has bone horns. — (center) Just a giraffe. Horns and legs, giraffes have two like legs, body all black, long neck.
	DW	C'F	A & Dirt	3. Two animals buried. — Like a tender animal. His legs are sticking out. He's buried beneath the dirt, black dirt.
VI. 25"	W	F+	A Obj	1. This looks like a flat cat, like a rug too. A cat rug with whiskers. — Like a car ran over it and took all the hair off and used it for a rug.
VII. 40"	D	F+	Obj	1. Crooked stool like a chair, back of a chair. — (top two thirds) Top is crooked and bottom is crooked.
	V	D	F+	A	2. An elephant. — (top two thirds) Trunk and legs and head.
	<	D	F+	Rock	3. Little rock. — (lower third) All humpy and sharp.

RECORD No. 16—continued

		Loc.	Det.	Cont.	P
VIII. 69"	1. It looks like them crocodiles.	D	FM–	A	
	2. Up here it looks like a ghost without a head.	D	MC'	(H)	
	3. Bones.	D	F+	At	
	4. Big mountain.	D	F+	N	
IX. 52"	1. Buffalo.	D	F+	A	
	2. Witch.	D	M	(H)	
	3. Monster dog.	D	FM	A	
X. 31"	1. Spider.	D	F+	A	P
	2. Bee.	D	FM	A	
	3. Frog.	D	F+	A	
	4. Bunny.	D	F+	Ad	P
	5. Two little tiny giraffes.	d	F+	Ad	O
	6. Reindeer.	D	FM	A	
	7. Sand.	D	CF	Sand	
	8. Chair.	D	F–	Obj	

Inquiry:

1. (usual animal) Two feet, tail and head, looking down. A monster crocodile.
2. (top gray) Ghost like pushing down the crocodile. He don't want them to get up. All gray, old fat ghost.
3. (middle riblike area) Skinny like a spine.
4. (lower center) Shaped like it.

1. (pink) Head looks like it.
2. (orange) High hats on them. Their faces and their hands touching something. Got electric in them so when they touch somebody they kill them.
3. (green) Like standing on a rock. Tail in wrong place.

1. (side blue) Shaped like it. If they ever took a bite out of you you get sick.
2. (top gray) Fighting. Don't know what fighting about. Two sharp things on them.
3. (side brown) Legs looks like it. Can't see head, I don't think he has any.
4. (usual) Just the head.
5. (small detail on lower green) Shaped like it.
6. (side brown) Like jumping.
7. (side lower orange) See how it's brown? Somebody dug it up and shaped it like that, making mudpies.
8. (center yellow) Back and seat.

R   36 + 1

W	4 ⎤	F+	20 ⎤ 21 +1	A	13 ⎤ 17	P	7
W	3 ⎬8	F−	1 ⎦	Ad	4 ⎦	O	1
DW	1 ⎦			H	7(5) + 1		
		M	3	Hd	1(1)		
D	25 + 1	MC′	1	Bl	1		
Dr	1 ⎤3	FM	6 (2−)	At	1		
d	2 ⎦			Clo	1		
		CF	1	Obj	4		
		C	1	Sand	1		
		FC′	1	A Obj	1		
		C′F	1	N	1		
		Fc	1	Rock	1		
				Dirt	0 + 1		

W	22%	F	58%	A	47%
D	70%	F+	95%		
Dr→d	8%				

$$M : C$$
$$4 : 2\tfrac{1}{2}$$

$$Fm + FM : C' + c$$
$$6 : 3$$

$$VIII + IX + X = 42\%$$

This boy seems torn between his aggressive impulses and his need to control these drives. There is marked vacillation between identification with destructive forces and controlled ones. In other words, in this case the battle between the id and the superego is unusually intense. His anxiety is in large measure due to his conviction that he is not adequate (repeated interpretation of "people without heads," "heads chopped off," "ghosts not together"). This is to say he does not feel he has the head, the adequacy, to deal with his experiences effectively. It is his inadequacy which will make it impossible for him to effect a constructive adjustment, and keep down the drives that will devour and destroy him (Card VIII, response 2).

His adjustive efforts consist in large measure of recourse to fantasy. It is in his inner life that he battles with the conflicts that threaten to overwhelm him. It is in this fantasy world that he attempts to cope with the "evil" and destructive forces that assail him from within.

The formal aspects of this personality are not too deviant. Beside the fact that there is slightly more emphasis on detail responses than might be expected in a boy of this age, along with three responses that involve black, there is nothing of especial significance in the psychogram. In other words, this boy seems to be functioning at a reasonably adequate level.

His disturbances manifest themselves primarily in the content of his interpretations, the fact that in every situation for this boy there is symbolization of conflict, oral aggression and castration threats. He seems to be constantly anticipating destruction at the hands of forces within and without which are too much for him. Authority is certainly a frightening figure, and the mother not a reassuring object ("crooked chair," "little rock" and "elephant" on VII).

While there is no complaint regarding the boy's behavior, he has developed a number of neurotic symptoms. Chief among these is a sucking of the lip and stretching of the mouth which is so extreme that it leaves his mouth encrusted with sores all the time.

This boy is the second of three boys, his older brother being 20 and his younger brother seven. The patient is in the third grade. The mother is a rigid, righteous kind of person who will not allow her boys to play on the street because she does not approve of the children in the neighborhood. The child is expected to obey implicitly. The father is 57 years old, and is described as a hard worker and a stern yet kindly person.

The subject gets along reasonably well in school except for poor reading. In fact he is practically a nonreader. In addition to his lip-sucking, mouth-stretching symptom, he also occasionally has mild asthmatic attacks and vague stomach complaints.

RECORD No. 17

Stutterer, Boy, Age 8 Years 9 Months, I.Q. 95

I. 29"	W	F+	A	11" I got these before. 13" Mm, it's kind of hard. 16" 1. Bug. — Body in center, wings on side, I saw them in school.
	W	F+	A P	(Urged to find more) 2. Or butterfly. — Could be that too, wings and body.
II. 16"	D	C	At	2" 1. Tonsils. (responses always made in questioning voice) — (points to all red details) I don't 'know, because red. (denies shape)
	WS	F−	Hd	2. Mouth. — Shaped like one.
III. 12"	W	M	H P	3" 1. Two men. — They are dragging something. A pot or something. (Why men?) I don't know, have pants.
	D	FM	A	2. And those are monkeys. — (side red) See tail, head, hanging, playing.
IV. 14"	W	F+	(H)	4" 1. Giant, giant feet. — Half of a giant, no head.
V. 23"	W	F+	A P	15" 1. Bat, it's an animal, looks like one. — Wings and body, the way it's shaped, I saw one around our school, wings are big, the body is small.
VI. 22"		......		6" Mm—what's this? 13" 1. I don't know what this is. 22" I don't know.
	(W	F−	A)	(Add. Could be a mouse, I don't know.)
VII. 10"	W	F+	H	3" 1. Is it two Indians? — Body, head, legs and feathers.

RECORD No. 17—*continued*

VIII. 8"	W	C/F±	Design	1. Design.	(omit bears) All colors on it.
	D	F+	A P	2. And two bears.	(usual) Shaped like a bear.
IX. 9"	W	C/F±	Design	1. Another design.	By its colors and shapes.
	(D	F+ Ad)		(Add. [orange] Deer, these are deer things.)	
	(D	F+ A)		(Add. [pink] And these are pigs.) Shaped like pigs.)	
X. 30"	W	C/F±	Design	1. Another design.	Colors and shaped like it.
	D	F–	A	2. Has animals in it.	(blue center) Maybe a bear, I don't know.
	D	F+	A P	3. Crab.	(side blue) Lots of legs.
				That's all.	

R   15 + 3

W	7 ⎫	F+	7 ⎫	A	7 + 2 ⎫	P 5
W	2 ⎬ 10 + 1	F−	2 ⎭ 9 + 3(1−)	Ad	0 + 1 ⎭ 7 + 3	
WS	1 ⎭			H	3(1)	
		M	1	Hd	1	
D	5 + 2	FM	1	At	1	
				Design	3	
		C/F	3±			
		C	1			
W	67%	F	60%	A	47%	
D	33%	F+	78%			

$$M : C$$
$$1 : 4\tfrac{1}{2}$$

$$Fm + FM : C' + c$$
$$1 : 0$$

$$VIII + IX + X = 40\%$$

Much of the rigidity, stiltedness and stereotypy described by Krugman and his coworkers[41] as characteristic of stutterers is reflected in this Rorschach record. There is little flexibility and little alteration of behavior despite the changing nature of the circumstances in which the subject finds himself. His interests and his resources are very limited, his outlook constricted.

Although he gives repeated evidence that he feels uncertain and inadequate (Card I, "Mm, they're hard," rejection of VI, question on VII) he forces himself to encompass everything that comes within his frame of reference. Despite the difficulties involved, he gives a whole response on every card, even though it is obvious that it is well beyond his capacity to do this effectively. This forced emphasis on whole interpretations also reveals his general lack of practicality. It would seem as though this boy felt he must take account of everything, and in his way control all his experiences.

Control is certainly emphasized in this case, at the expense of emotional spontaneity and development. This boy's affective development is of a most inadequate order. His emotional reactions are either highly forced and arbitrary (designs on Cards VIII, IX, X) or completely disorganizing (C on Card II). Emotional release through fantasy is permitted only minimal expression and fantasy productions receive little acceptance (only one M and one FM). Under pressure, emotional regression takes place (perseveration on Cards VIII, IX, X).

This boy's exaggerated need for control comes from his perception of authority as large and overwhelming (Card IV) and possibly aggressive (Card VII), in comparison with his own helplessness and inadequacy. It is through the exercise of control that he can give conformity (high F+ per cent, 5 adult popular answers) and so avoid conflict with the environment. To this end he inhibits emotional response and strives to maintain strict intellectual control. While he apparently achieves this control much of the time, he pays a severe price for it in terms of total personality development.

The oral emphasis on Card II is especially significant. His own oral tensions and possible perception of the parents as oral figures undoubtedly play a part in his particular disturbance.

The presenting complaint in this case was stuttering. The subject, who is the older of two boys, is unhappy about his stuttering because the children in school and on the street make fun of him. Developmental history is uneventful aside from the fact that he was born while the father was overseas and he did not know the father until he was three years old. He started stuttering when he began school, but at the present time the stuttering is largely in relation to the mother who also stutters when she is upset. She is a tense woman who felt nervous and inadequate about bringing up this child during her husband's absence. The boy has no complaints aside from his unhappiness about his stuttering, but states that he "hates to fight" and that he does not like to play games with his father because his father "always wins."

RECORD No. 18

Enuretic Boy, 10 Years 6 Months, I.Q. 106

				Response	Inquiry
I. 40"	W	F+	A P	1. Could be a bat or a butterfly.	More of a bat without the holes. Like hands up here.
II. 45"	WS	mCF	Blast	1. Blast out of a rock, dynamites rock.	Hole in the middle, they want to blast it out bigger. Put dynamite in so they blast both sides out. It makes a noise and all the rock comes out red.
III. 45"	DWS	F−	H→Clo	1. Could be a man, looks like a bowtie.	Like a suit or something on a man. (all but side red)
	D	kF	X-ray	2. Could be bones of a person through an x-ray.	(lower center detail) Gray and black like.
IV. 87"	W	F+	A	1. Looks like an animal.	Legs, horns, big animal.
	W	F+	Pl	2. Looks like part of a tree if it didn't have the these. I thought you had to look at the whole thing. I could have taken it apart and seen lots of things.	(omit side details, usual arms) Goes up to a point.
V.	W	F+	A	1. Looks like a bat in a way or a bird.	Wings look too bumpy for a bat. Mouth could be a stork's mouth.
61"	......			Don't think I can think of anything for that.	
VI. 48"	(D	F+	Ad)	(Add. [top detail] Could be feathers how it's made, shaped just like feathers.)	

RECORD No. 18—continued

Card	Loc.	Det.	Content	P	Response	Inquiry
VII. 76"	WS	F−	H		1. Could look like a person but the parts are missing to it. (Add. Looks like a girl, could be a boy. Pants wouldn't be that short.)	Could look like a person. Awful fat, legs face. Could be two people because of the line, it separates them.
	(W	F+	H)			
	S	F+	N		2. Or could be caravan. (Means cavern.)	Nature made, like a tunnel.
VIII. 64"	D	FM	A	P	1. These two look like animals climbing like a rock.	(usual) (Asked what animal) A raccoon maybe, way it's shaped.
IX. 91"	D	F+	Rock		1. Could be a rock with a fossil in it.	(usual camel's head) Way it's shaped.
	D	F+	(Ad)		2. Looks like a face, dragon's face.	(same as 1) See eyes and head.
	D	CF	Pl		3. Could be a tree.	(green and midline) Green part and bark.
	D	C	N		4. Could be the earth. (Add. [pink] Top part could be like a burst, atomic bomb over Japan.)	(green) Earth is sometimes green.
	(D	Fm	Bomb)			
X. 80"	DS	F−	(A)		1. Looks like another fossil, animal that lived thousands of years ago.	(top gray) Mouth, eyes.
	D	CF	N		2. Lake or a river connecting with another.	(center blue) Water is blue and it's connected.
	D	F+	Pl		3. Tree branch.	(top gray) Long like tree.
	DS	F+	Geog		4. And islands.	All pieces with water around them. (side orange)

R   18 + 3

W	3		F+	9		A	5(1)		P	0
W	1	} 7 + 1	F−	3	} 12 + 2	Ad	(1) + 1	} 6(2) + 1		
WS	2					H	1 + 1			
DWS	1		FM	1		H→Clo	1			
			Fm	0 + 1		X-ray	1			
D	8	} 10 + 2				Blast	1			
DS	2		mCF	1		Pl	3			
			CF	2		N	3			
S	1		C	1		Geog	1			
			kF	1		Rock	1			
						Bomb	0 + 1			

W	39%		F	67%		A	33%
D	56%		F+	75%			
S	5%						

$$M : C$$
$$0 : 4\tfrac{1}{2}$$

$$Fm + FM : C' + c$$
$$2 : 0$$

$$VIII + IX + X = 50\%$$

This is definitely a very disturbed boy. Outstanding is his immaturity which manifests itself in all areas—social, emotional, interpersonal. His inability to control his emotions and the impulsive, demanding, disorganized nature of his affective reactions are clearly evident in the nature of his color responses (2 CF, 1 mCF, 1 C). He cannot relate to others in controlled, acceptable fashion, but rather as a very young child might. It is also evident both from the nature and the content of his emotional responses that this boy is very dependent upon his environment, that it is almost entirely to the environment that he looks for satisfaction and security, while his inner promptings and fantasy activities are repressed. This emotional dependency naturally keeps him at an infantile level of development and his repression of his inner life precludes resolution of his problems. In other words, he simply inhibits his own drives and cuts off whole areas of experience that would be advantageous to him in working out his problems. Such a resolution of the conflict between inner and outer pressures is obviously seriously crippling.

The emotional relationships that this boy has established between himself and his environment have evidently not fulfilled their function, have not afforded him the stability he seeks. Instead, he manifests a deep sense of insecurity and apparently sees himself as a weak individual, badly in need of protection and shelter (preoccupation with "caves," "island," "tree," "rock," in other words, with concepts which are most frequently found in the records of very young children who are still strongly tied to the protective figure of the mother). It was undoubtedly this sense of inadequacy that produced the original repression of inner life and the exaggerated recourse to dependency on the world about him, but an increased sense of security has certainly not been forthcoming as a result of the subject's adjustive efforts. Instead, he has only hampered his development and ruled out the possibility of becoming a self-sufficient mature individual. His sense of inadequacy and his search for support and shelter show themselves repeatedly in the content of his responses, his "caves," his "islands" and "trees," responses typical of the three and four year old.

The subject's efforts to inhibit his inner life are indicated not only by the absence of movement responses (no M, only one FM) but also by the fossilization of at least two of his animals. This occurs on the last two colored cards, where the impact of emotional demands probably makes inhibitory efforts especially difficult.

His inability to achieve any sense of security and self-sufficiency in the emotional area is somewhat feebly compensated for by the subject's attempts to prove himself intellectually. His very use of the word "fossils," his "x-ray" interpretation, his use of the word "caravan" all point in such a direction. Similarly, his effort at justifying his meager productivity by claiming that he did not know he could take parts of the card (Card IV), yet continuing to give whole responses after he definitely knows it is permissible to break up the blot, also reflects his strivings to impress and the essential futility of these strivings.

His disturbance in relation to the mother figure finds expression in his response to Card VII. Negative attitudes toward her are apparent. It is also evident from this and from his response on Card III that he has little real understanding of people or of the attributes that are ordinarily ascribed to men and women. Clothes and superficial trapping are all that people mean to him, and they are the only way he can distinguish between men and women. His own lack of substance, of real individuality, is reflected in his perception of others.

The subject's negative attitude toward his environment, despite his dependence on it, comes through in his numerous space responses. That his negativism is a function of his feelings of inadequacy, and reflects his desire to disrupt (explosion on II) and alter a world in which he is not happy, in no way alters the intensity of that negativism. Certainly it is his sense of insufficiency, of being lacking, that produces his hostile impulses, his feelings of insecurity and his tensions.

It is important in this case to recognize that while the emotional experiences this boy has are disorganizing, they are only occasionally explosive and destructive ("dynamites rock"). As often as not, they reflect an extreme passivity. The negative reactions are essentially on an intellectual level, and only infrequently are they invested with emotional energy.

It is obvious that this boy is a long way from being ready for the problems that will soon present themselves as he enters the prepuberty period. He cannot possibly experiment with roles, settle on his attitudes and orientation when he is in a sense not at all sure that he really is a person in his own right. Rather, he is the sort of individual who will remain tied throughout his adulthood to the authority figures on whom he is so dependent.

This ten year old boy has never stopped wetting his bed. He also cries easily and seems generally tense and high strung. Although able to do his school work, his teachers claim that he does not concentrate. When pressure is brought to bear on him to perform more adequately he "closes up," according to one teacher, and cries and insists he cannot do what is expected of him.

He is the older of two boys, his brother being five. He is overweight, lisps, and gives an immature and somewhat feminine impression. The mother is a tense, anxious woman, who cannot understand why he is not a "regular boy." The father is apparently a passive individual. The subject is friendly and cooperative during interview and testing but makes a very passive impression.

CHAPTER XI

The Emotionally Disturbed Child (continued)

EMOTIONAL CONFLICTS carry with them disturbances in bodily functioning. At times the individual is aware of these disturbances: for example, when there is a sharp acceleration in the heartbeat, when there is urinary frequency, contractions of the stomach muscles, etc. Other disruptions in bodily functions are not perceived by the individual, but nevertheless constitute part of his total reaction to the disturbing stimulus. It is obvious that emotional conflicts can interfere with normal bodily functioning, and if these disturbances are frequent and sufficiently intense, they may eventually cause structural changes. Visceral and respiratory disturbances are prominent in this connection, but other systems also manifest the adverse effects of emotional turmoil and conflict. In particular, the individual who is in a constant state of anxiety, with accompanying bodily tensions, is likely to show psychosomatic disorders.

The four records which are presented in this chapter were taken from children who were suffering from somatic disorders—asthma, eczema and colitis. The long duration of their illness and its failure to respond to treatment led to their referral to psychiatry. In all of these cases the emphasis on control, conformity and compliance is marked. The need to repress aggression and accept the dictates of authority is unusually strong in most of these children, producing marked constriction and inhibition in emotional development.

Record No. 19

Asthmatic Boy, Age 4 Years 4 Months, I.Q. 115

An inkblotter, a picture on a blotter.

	Location	Determinant	Content	Response	Inquiry
I.	WS	F+	Obj	1. Looks like a pumpkin.	A big one, with eyes.
II.	W	C	Fire	1. Fire.	When you turn it around it's red.
III.	D	F+	Clo P	1. Tie.	(center red) I see a tie, man wears a tie.
IV.	W	F−	A	1. That's part of a dog.	(asked what the dog was doing) He's turning. He wants to see what's in the kitchen to eat.
V.	W	F+	A	1. Bird.	(what kind of a bird?) A parlor bird. (polly?)
VI.	W	F+ (C Projection)	Pl	∧∨ 1. Tree.	Big and it's colored like that color. (points to something green in room)
VII.	W	C′	Fire	1. Part of fire.	Black.
VIII.	D→W	FM	A & Pl P	1. Animal—tiger.	Climbing up on a tree, lion, two lions.
IX.	W	CF	Pl	1. Tree too.	It's same like other one, green. (points correctly) Has lot of leaves on it.
X.	W	CF−	Pl	1. Tree.	Same as there (points to where Card IX is lying)

R   10

W	7⎫	F+	4⎫5	A	3	P 2
WS	1⎬9	F−	1⎭	Pl	3 + 1	
D→W 1	⎭			Fire	2	
		FM	1	Clo	1	
D	1			Obj	1	
		CF	2(1−)			
		C	1			
		(C Projection 1)				
		C′	1			
W	90%	F	50%	A	30%	
D	10%	F+	80%			

M : C
0 : 3½

Fm + FM : C′ + c
1 : 1½

VIII + IX + X = 30%

The striking feature in this record is the disparity that exists between this child's intellectual and his emotional control. His ability to handle his experiences objectively is good and is reflected in his capacity for responding in discriminating fashion. This is in marked contrast to the emotional disorganization that occurs when he is confronted with affectively charged circumstances. While his reactions in this respect are not so unusual for his age, that is, a child of his age can be expected to give 1 C and 2 CF responses, they are conspicuous when compared with his ability and control in other areas.

His many tree responses and the dependency implied in these is also typical for his age. That he is still much concerned with the security he can get from the family ties is obvious and natural. The color which he projects into the tree on Card VI probably does not have the significance that color projection has when given by adults. It rather gives evidence of the arbitrary kind of reasoning that can be expected from children of this age.

In general this boy's test productions show that on the whole he is developing in line with expectancy, although his emotional development appears to be lagging a bit when contrasted with his intellectual development. If he continues in this manner some emotional instability can be anticipated. However, at this time it is difficult on the basis of the test findings alone to predict what his subsequent development will be.

This child has been suffering from asthma since he was an infant. He has been overprotected as a result, and is "spoiled" and definitely a behavior problem.

Record No. 20

Severe Eczema in a Girl, Age 7 Years 4 Months, I.Q. 111

Card / Time	Loc.	Det.	Cont.	Response	Inquiry
I. 47"	WS	FM	A	20" 1. Looks like an eagle, with two holes here.	Has wings, looks like he could bend his wing.
II. 77"		(Descript.)		5" A white spot is here, it's dark here in the middle and red is down here.	
	d	F+	Ad	18" 1. Looks like lobster's foot. They have little things here, they clack together like a lobster's foot.	(small projections on top red)
III. 87"	D	F+	Clo P	4" 1. This looks like a bow tie.	(center red) It's like a ribbon, just like a bow tie to me.
	D	F+	Pl	2. This looks like sort of a branch, a leaf.	(usual leg) Looks like a branch on a tree I saw once.
	D	F+	Pl	V∧ 3. It looks like two bushes here, big leaf with strings on the end.	(lower center detail) Just looks like a bush to me.
	(Denial)	F+	Pd	4. Big bush except here.	(can't find)
	D			5. These look like people to me.	(side red) Could be man or lady.
IV. 36"	W	F+	(H)→A	5" 1. Looks like a giant to me with a tail in back of him. His arms look like a loop, you can jump through it.	A gorilla has a tail, a big one, a gorilla is that fat, and he has some kind of a head, only bigger.
V. 34"	W	FM	A	5" 1. Looks like some kind of an animal that flies in the air. Has two horns, not a bee, some kind of an animal that flies in the air.	That's the eagle.

RECORD No. 20—*continued*

				Response	Inquiry
VI. 19"	W	FC'—	(H)	Wow! 1. That looks like a witch, that's all it looks like, dark in the middle and light here.	That's her hair.
VII. 27"	D	F±	Pl	Who made these? 1. Looks like a couple of bushes.	(top two thirds) Just looks like it to me.
	D	F+	Clo	2. But down here it looks like a pair of pants.	(lower third) A pair of pants are shaped that way. Through here and here. Here like pants because it has a line in the middle.
VIII. 49"	W	FC	H	1. Looks like a girl with long hair, part of her dress.	A queen has something like that, a blue jacket and an orange dress. (top gray is hair, rest is clothing)
∧>	D	F+	A P	2. Here it looks like a bear and here it looks like a bear. A queen with two bears on the side of her. Only got two more left.	The bear is this way. (usual)
IX. 44"				I don't know what this is.	
7" 34"	d	Fm	Pl	1. Looks like some kind of a branch, a little branch reaches across.	(orange projection)
	D	CF—	Sky	2. Orange sky.	(orange) That's the way the sky is shaped.
	dS	F+	Obj	3. The green a little loop.	(space in green and some of surrounding area) You could jump through.
	d	C	Sky	4. Here a sort of sky.	(pale blue in center)
	D	CF	Cl	5. Pink clouds.	Some clouds are pink and like that.

X.
152″

10″	D	F+	Obj	1. This looks like a tool, you pull nails out of the wall. (lower center detail) Good to pull.
	D	F+	A P	2. This looks like a crab. (side blue) Just looks like it.
	dS	F+	Obj	3. Over here sort of a loop again. (space between pink and center blue)
	D	F±	Sky	4. Here the pink looks like a sky, a skinny sky. (Just looks like it.)
	D	F−	N	5. Over here looks like some part of a mountain. (side brown) Just looks like it.
	D	CF	Food	6. This over here looks like potato croquettes. (orange) Color and looks like it.
	D	F+	Obj	7. Pair of glasses. (center blue) two things and a middle.
	d	F+	Food	8. Peanut in the middle of this yellow. (brown in center of yellow) Look like it.
	D	F+	A & Obj	9. This looks like an animal with a stick. (top gray) Got a head like an animal has.

R   27

W	4 ⎫ 5	F+	15 ⎫	A	5 ⎫ 6	P	3
WS	1 ⎭	F±	2 ⎬ 18	Ad	1 ⎭		
		F−	1 ⎭	H	2(1)		
D	16			H→A	(1)		
		FM	2	Hd	1		
d	4 ⎫ 6	Fm	1	Clo	2		
ds	2 ⎭			Food	2		
		FC	1	Sky	3		
		CF	3(1−)	Pl	4		
		C	1	Cl	1		
		FC'	1	Obj	4 + 1		
				N	1		

W	19%	F	67%	A	22%
D	59%	F+	83%		
d	22%				

$$M : C$$
$$0 : 5$$

$$Fm + FM : C' + c$$
$$3 : \tfrac{1}{2}$$

$$VIII + IX + X = 59\%$$

This is an unusually long record for a child of this age. The length is function of her emphasis on large detail responses (59 per cent) which, in conjunction with the repression and control she manifests (67 per cent F, 83 per cent F+), presents a picture very like that found in certain adult neurotics. Certainly this child manifests an exaggerated need to select out from her experiences limited aspects of them, as though in so doing she could achieve a greater sense of stability than she would otherwise. What she is apparently blocking is her own fantasies (no M, only 2 FM). What little fantasy there is suggests that her tendency to identify with aggressive, predatory figures ("eagle"), "an animal, not a bee, has two horns," frightens her, and she can defend herself against the anxiety such impulses arouse by repressing the promptings that come from within. So she focuses her energy on control and on response to the environment.

The subject's repeated response to the white spaces raises questions as to her own sense of adequacy as well as her basic acceptance of the conforming type of behavior which, by means of her repressive efforts, she has so well attained. Two of these space responses refer to "loops," something to jump through, and one cannot help speculating about the meaning of this for the child. Does she have to jump through loops in order to achieve the type of adjustment she feels is necessary?

The disturbances in identification and her marked dependency needs which the content of her responses reflect go a long way toward explaining why she is so insecure and tries so hard to accept environmental pressure. The branch and the leaf are found a number of times in this protocol, pointing to an immature concept of the self symbolized in highly infantile dependent roles. The food responses also suggest oral tensions and probable affect hunger. However, she dare not be too vigorous and aggressive in her efforts to find emotional satisfaction. She must be the little "queen" (Card VIII), flanked by two "bears" (parents?).

There is a sense of being small, lost and alone in the reactions given to Card IX. Despite her need for and dependence on emotional response from the environment, there certainly are times when she gets disorganized by these emotional involvements. Thus on this card there is first the blocking as shown by the long delay in time, followed by a small detail response which presents the picture of something little and dependent, silhouetted against an overwhelming expanse.

It can be inferred from her efforts at control and compliance that this girl has developed a strong superego, and would probably experience marked guilt if she opposed the precepts laid down for her in any way. She has accepted and internalized these and devotes much of her energy to maintaining attitudes which will in no way upset the equilibrium she has established through her recourse to repression and dependency. That there is such a danger is something that she seems well aware of and something that must be strenuously guarded against.

This is an only child of first generation Italian parents. The father is a skilled laborer, the mother does not work outside of the home. The parents have set very high standards for themselves and this child and they expect complete obedience from her. For several years she has suffered from severe eczema which at times completely covers her face.

RECORD No. 21

Chronic Eczema in a Girl, Age 9 Years 1 Month, I.Q. 88

		Response	Inquiry	Location	Determinant	Content	P
I. 20″	1.	Looks like a person's hands.	(top center projections) Like gloves on them.	D	F+	Hd	
	2.	And looks like a person from the back, their feet.	(lower center small detail) Shaped that way.	d	F+	Hd	
	3.	And looks like bunny's ears.	(top center humps)	d	F−	Ad	
II. 23″	1.	Looks like, I don't know, looks like somebody waltzing.	I didn't see anything in that. (urged to try and find people) Going up steps. I don't know. I don't think it looks like anything.	W	M−	H	
III. 19″	1.	Like monkeys picking up something.	Looks like that. I don't know. It looks funny. They have a round head.	W	FM	A	
	2.	Butterfly.	(center red) Some of them look like that. Has a thing in middle and the shape.	D	F+	A	P
IV. 59″		I don't know.					
23″	1.	Looks like the limb of a tree down here.	(center lower detail) When they're old they're like that. When they die they're underground.	D	F+	Pl	
	2.	Looks like people's feet right here, like big feet.	(usual) Shaped like feet.	D	F+	Hd	P
V. 23″	1.	Looks like a bunny here.	(center detail) Black stuff hides the body. Yeah I see the body and head and feet.	D	F+	A	
	2.	And dust.	(everything but bunny) Black stuff.	D	C′	Dust	
VI. 26″	5″	Don't know what that looks like.					
	17″	Nothing. (Add. Like whiskers on pussy cat.)		…… (d	F+	Ad)	

					Response	Inquiry
VII. 71"	D	F+	Arch	5"	1. Looks like a door down there.	(lower center detail) Shaped like that.
	D	M	(H)		2. I don't know what—something standing up, funny people.	(top two thirds) Funny people, like people from Mars.
	D	F+	Pl		3. Like bushes around here.	(lower third) Shaped like bushes.
VIII. 25"	D	FM	A P	7"	1. Like bears.	(usual) Look like they're climbing.
IX. 34"	d	F+	Hd	15"	1. Like a person's fingers.	(small lines between pink and green) Thumb and fingers.
X. 21"	D	F−	Obj	8"	1. Candle.	(usual rabbit's face) Cause those things stick up.
					No more.	

R   16 + 1

W	1⎱2	F+	9⎱11 + 1	A	4⎱5 + 1		P 3
W	1⎰	F−	2⎰	Ad	1⎰		
				H	2(1)		
D	11	M	2(1−)	Hd	4		
		FM	2	Pl	2		
d	3 + 1			Obj	1		
		C′	1	Arch	1		
				Dust	1		

W	13%	F	69%	A	31%
D	69%	F+	82%		
d	18%				

M : C
2 : 0

Fm + FM : C′ + c
2 : 1½

VIII + IX + X = 18%

This girl's energy is being largely absorbed by her efforts at control. To this end she sharply limits the scope of her activity, rarely facing a total situation, but rather skirting its edges or picking from it aspects that she feels she can manage (only 13 per cent W). Her avoidance techniques also take the form of severe emotional inhibition (no color responses, 69 per cent form responses). These adjustive efforts have left her with a very skewed perception of the world. She finds in it no warmth or spontaneity and no emotional reassurance or stimulation (no color answers, only 18 per cent of the responses on Cards VIII, IX, X). It follows then that her relationships with others cannot be pleasurable or reassuring. Rather, her interpretations indicate that people seem strange and remote to her ("dancing people" on Card II who are promptly denied, "people from Mars" on VII being her only human or near-human responses). Only in her fantasy does she permit herself any emotional release, and even this is of a relatively limited and unsatisfying order.

Deep feelings of inadequacy underly her exaggerated need for control, as well as her withdrawal. She has no confidence in herself and often gives direct expression to this (Cards II, IV, VI, VII). Her treatment of Card I also reveals how cautious she feels she must be in any unfamiliar experience, how little faith she has in her capacity for meeting such experiences effectively.

The uncertainty, the inadequacy, the remoteness from people which are so integral a part of all this girl's experiences appear to be tied in with her perception of herself as "bad." The "black stuff (which) covers the body" on Card V proves to be dust, something unwanted, something dirty, something evil. It may well have been this train of associations that produced the blocking on Card VI, as much as the qualities of the card itself. That her feelings of unworthiness, of being evil, are in part at least tied in with sexual disturbances appears indicated by certain other of her answers, particularly those on Card VII. The door surrounded by bushes strongly suggests sexual symbolism. The nature of her attempts to control, repress, and deny her unacceptable thoughts and impulses are indicative of a strong, punitive superego. Apparently her experiences with her immediate world have led her to see herself as "bad," "dirty," and in need of constant, overwhelming restraint.

The response on Card IV is of interest in that it points up the possibility of a dead or missing parental figure. This girl's father has been out of the home for the past three years, and she has not seen him during that time.

This patient has been suffering from eczema since she was an infant. Her father was overseas when she was born and she did not know him until she was four. Shortly after his return she also began to suffer from asthma. When the father came home, she slept in the bedroom with the parents, and it would seem most probable that she witnessed considerable sexual activity on their parts. When she was six the father left and she has not had any contact with him. During the short time that he was home her relations with him were varied. Initially he was very kind to her and she responded to this kindness after a short period of shyness. As his relations with the mother became increasingly disturbed, he also frequently vented his irritability on the child. About a year after the father's return a baby boy was born and this added to the general stress, created by crowded quarters and personality conflicts.

RECORD No. 22

Chronic Colitis in a Girl, Age 9 Years 1 Month, I.Q. 117

	Response	Inquiry				
I. 40"	1. Looks like two people dancing around a pole.	(points out hands, head feet) (?) Ladies, have dresses.	W	M	H	
II. 30"	1. Looks like two people clapping hands and dancing.	(points out heads, hat hands clapping) (?) Ladies.	W	M	H	P
III. 27"	1. Two men.	Just standing, heads, hands—there's a stove.	W	M	H	P
	2. Butterfly in the middle.	(center red) Way it's shaped.	D	F+	A	P
IV. 30"	Oh...... Can I turn it upside down?					
V 17"	1. This way it looks like an eagle.	Head, feet, wings.	W	F+	A	
V. 10"	1. Looks like a butterfly.	Shaped like it, head, feet, wings.	W	F+	A	P
VI. 55"	1. Looks like a mountain with a totem pole on top.	The rugged shape and the top is like an Indian totem pole.	W	F—	N & Obj	
VII. 40"	1. Looks like two little lambs, lambs upside down.	Standing on a rock.	D→W	FM—	A	
	2. Looks like dwarfs.	Two old dwarfs, hat and head. (top two thirds)	D	F+	(H)	
VIII. 12"	Pretty colors.					
7"	1. Looks like a Christmas tree.	Top is shaped like a tree, rest is decorations hanging down. Looks like cotton animals the way they're hooked on the tree.	D→W	CFm	Obj	

IX. 20"	D	M−	H	1. Looks like two ladies dancing.	(orange is ladies, green is dresses) Because of shape.
X. 85"	D	F+	N	1. Looks like mountains.	(pink) Looks like a cliff, the way it's separated.
	D	FM−	A	2. Looks like a horse crossing them.	(top gray) Crossing.
	D	F+	A P	3. Looks like a crab.	(side blue) So many legs.
	D	F+	A	4. A mouse.	(top green) Head, tail paws of mouse.

R   15

W	5 $\rbrace$8	F+	7 $\rbrace$8	A	7	P 5
W	1	F−	1	H	5(1)	
D→W	2			N	2	
		M	4(1−)	Obj	1 + 1	
D	7	FM	2−			
		CFm	1			

W	53%	F	53%	A	47%
D	47%	F+	88%		

$$M : C$$
$$4 : 1$$

$$Fm + FM : C' + c$$
$$3 : 0$$

$$VIII + IX + X = 40\%$$

This is an uncertain child who manifests exaggerated concern about her security and stability. This concern finds expression in her constant reference to "two." Such an emphasis reflects the same awareness of balance, the same anxiety about balance, as is found when the subject becomes preoccupied with the symmetry of the cards. Her withdrawal into fantasy (4 M, 1 CF) is therefore probably a function both of her beginning prepuberty concern about herself and her role, and of her efforts to maintain her equilibrium.

The threat to her equilibrium seems caused primarily by the difficulties she has in dealing with her primitive impulses. Both her FM interpretations are poor ones, in each instance being distorted by the impact of her own special needs. Thus on Card VII the "upside-down lambs" suggest severe maternal disturbances and the "horse crossing" on Card X may well reflect her forced efforts to bridge the gaps and uncertainties in her life. In view of the disturbance that exists in these elemental fantasies, the relatively superficial nature of her M responses points to a kind of "whistling in the dark" attitude as far as her concept of herself or her relations with others are concerned.

The powerful, predatory quality that she ascribes to authority (Card IV, "eagle") may well account for the distortions that appear in her instinctual reactions. That she is "shocked" by authority is apparent from the way she responds to this card (begins with an exclamation, asks if she may turn— this is the only card that is turned). Furthermore, in her relations to the familial figures, it would seem that her own impulses have been given practically no opportunity for expression, but rather have been completely immobilized (Card VIII, "looked like cotton animals, the way they are hooked on the tree"). The tension this situation induces is reflected in the m.

Although she tries to overcome the effects of the repressive experiences she has had, largely through indulgence in pseudohappy fantasy, these efforts are not sustained. All but one of her M responses come at the outset of the record, actually constitute the first three interpretations, and then disappear. It may well be that the shock induced by Card IV disrupted her, and made such recourse to fantasy impossible. She attempts it once more, after the production of the immobilized, stuffed animals, but her attempts at this point are too forced to be successful and so end in an M—.

The overall picture is that of a child who is experiencing considerable insecurity and is concerned about herself and her ability to maintain her equilibrium. Her difficulties focus about her relations to authority. As she sees it, she has apparently been permitted little opportunity for spontaneous expression, but rather been held in considerable restraint by her family. Her only escape from this has been in fantasy, and this has not been of too meaningful or satisfying an order. Thus, while she begins with two ladies dancing—an interpretation that may well symbolize her hopes and desires— she ends with a "mouse," giving superficial conformity (5 adult populars out of 15 responses).

This child has been suffering from colitis for many years. She is an only child from a middle class family. The atmosphere in the home is a somewhat rigid, puritanical one and, while the child is loved, she is subjected to much criticism and restraint.

CHAPTER XII

Schizophrenia

THE CONCEPT OF CHILDHOOD schizophrenia is a relatively recent one. In fact, as short a time as 15 years ago very few children were so diagnosed, and many psychiatrists in institutions and in private practice did not feel that such a diagnosis was applicable to children. To Dr. Lauretta Bender more than to any other psychiatrist goes the credit for formulating the concepts underlying the entity now known as childhood schizophrenia, and for setting the criteria for such a diagnosis.

According to Bender[6] the diagnosis of childhood schizophrenia can only be made when "it is possible to demonstrate characteristic disturbances in every patterned, functioning field of behavior." Included in this formulation are disturbances in the vasovegetative system; in the physiological rhythms with resulting disorders in sleeping, eating and elimination; in growth; in motor patterns and in postural reflexes; in affective development; in perception; in thought and language. The disturbances, which cut across every system of the growing organism, seriously interfere with the child's ability to deal with the usual problems of childhood, namely, the problem of identification, the establishment of adequate reality concepts and the formation of object relations.

Mahler, Ross and De Fries[45] state that these children suffer "from an early defection in ego development." They point out that, whereas in adolescents and adults, the personality has already been structured before the onset of illness, this is not the case with children, and that it is this which makes the psychotic process a different one in the growing child than in the adult. They postulate six primary symptoms characteristic of psychosis in children: psychotic panic reactions; diffusion of erotic and aggressive instinctual forces; fusion of the orbit of the self with the nonself; inability to differentiate between animate and inanimate reality; strong, spurious, clinging but nonspecific attachments to adults; direct manifestations of the primary processes appearing on the surface of behavior.

The way in which the child will react to his illness, the mechanisms he will develop for handling his disturbances, as well as for dealing with all the problems that confront him as a growing organism, will naturally vary from child to child, depending upon the age, abilities, resources, and past experiences in each individual case. It follows that overt behavior and symptomatology will vary from one child to another. One child may be excessively aggressive and destructive, another markedly withdrawn; one may indulge in ideation dealing with grandiose, cosmic concepts, while another may perform at a defective level. However in all of these children there will be a severe disturbance in connection with the development of an adequate and stable self-concept; they will have marked difficulties in identification, and so will be unable to find themselves and relate to the environment in stable and usual fashion. Associated with all this goes marked anxiety which further hampers the child's adjustment.

The Rorschach records of the schizophrenic child will not only reveal the disturbances produced by the disease, but also the mechanisms the child has developed for dealing with all his problems, those typical of his age and those produced by the illness. Thus the protocols will vary considerably. However, certain manifestations must be present, without which the diagnosis of schizophrenia cannot be made. These are the aforementioned disturbances in identification, disorganizing anxiety, defects and distortions in reality testing far beyond what could be ascribed solely to general immaturity, and an inability to establish object relations that are satisfying and reassuring. In addition, the child's test productions frequently give evidence of disturbances in his concepts of time and space. They are also likely to show a tendency toward hyperideationalism, because of the child's concern with abstractions, with scientific and cosmic problems far beyond his understanding, no matter how bright he may be. Sexual interests and preoccupation, more typical for the prepuberty and puberty child, are found with relative frequency in these children's productions, manifesting themselves in crude and atypical fashion.

Disturbances in identification are indicated by 1) the child's complete inability to identify with human figures, with the result that there are no human movement responses and often no human or human detail answers whatsoever; 2) exaggerated efforts at finding the self as reflected in an exceptionally large number of human movement responses which are out of line with what most children of similar age produce, and which are inappropriate to the general developmental level of the child, and which therefore cannot be integrated into his experiences in meaningful fashion; 3) indications of highly distorted bizarre identifications.

In the first instance, where no identification is made, there is often a complete, or almost complete, lack of the capacity for any emotional experience. In these cases the content of the responses consists almost entirely of animals, objects and nature, offered in crude, unelaborated and poorly perceived fashion. Furthermore, the child's uncertainty about everything, combined with his compulsive efforts at establishing reality concepts, often leads him to deal with these responses in most unusual fashion. He begins by giving an interpretation which may or may not bear some recognizable relationship to the blot and then proceeds to play with the concept in a semiperseverative fashion. For example, the child may interpret Card I as a "bird" and follow this up with "It's a blackbird," "It's a bluebird," "It's an eagle," "It's a hawk," etc. If uninterrupted, this word play can go on indefinitely. Sometimes it moves away from the original generic concept, either because something in the environment has distracted the child or because his own productions have aroused some new association. When another card is presented to him he may continue with the associations he had on the previous blot or start off with a new category and treat it in the same fashion (see Record No. 25).

In these cases the child's inability to come to terms with his environment is clearly indicated by this compulsivelike activity. He attempts to deal with the anxiety thus aroused by a kind of intellectual play on his own creations. It is apparent from his disturbed reality concepts and his general lack of emotional reactions that he cannot establish any satisfactory interpersonal relationships.

In contrast to the child who makes no attempt at identifying with the human objects in his environment, there is the child who expends most of his energy trying to find himself through others. This child takes on the roles of the adults he encounters, going from one to the other, much like an actor running off a series of imitations. The Rorschach records of these children will have a large number of M responses. However, the fact that these identifications lack emotional investment will be manifest by the fact that the color responses will be few or completely lacking; and where they do occur they will be of a most immature, impulsive, disorganized order (CF−, C), all out of line with the maturity ordinarily indicated by the capacity to give M answers. Furthermore, and more important, the forced, artificial nature of these identifications is shown by the absence of any evidence that these identifications form part of a normal developmental process. Unlike the healthy child who goes from primitive, immature identifications to more mature ones, the schizophrenic child makes only forced superficial attempts at getting close to people and understanding them by indulging in a kind of meaningless role playing. In the records of the schizophrenic child with many M responses, there will therefore be few or no FM answers, a complete reversal of the usual findings for children. Driven by his desperate need to understand what it is to be a "person," the schizophrenic child tries to act as he see others act, tries to imitate the behavioral experiences and emotions of others. At the moment that he does this, the child may present a fleeting picture of maturity and insight, all out of line with his general developmental level. Such adjustment lacks any solid foundation in reality, and his failure to achieve any sense of security from this activity only adds to his marked anxiety and pushes him on to attempt ever new roles. These are the children who can momentarily relate to anyone, even a complete stranger, who will rush up to passers-by and cling to them, but who have no real feeling to offer anyone.

Finally there are those children who make most primitive infantile identifications, whose records, again like the records of the three year olds, are replete with flowers, plants, and natural forces such as rain, snow, etc.; or who identify with the very objects and forces against which the healthy child attempts to defend himself. Their defective understanding of reality prevents them from discriminating between the forces that lead to healthy living and those that lead to destruction. Thus, in the records of schizophrenic children it is not unusual to find that what weak and unstable identifications they do achieve are with morbid, gruesome figures, with dead and deteriorating objects (Record No. 29, page 214). Responses like "This is a man with three red eyes, a tree on his head and holes in his body" are typical.

Similarly, his inability to establish his own limits, his distorted preception of his own size and importance, sometimes leads the child to make identification on a grandiose scale. In such cases the figures he sees are not only likely to be frightening but of cosmic significance and importance. These records will be replete with responses like the following one given to Card IX: "These are two gods, standing on top of the universe, plotting the destruction of mankind. They are pregnant with their own ideas with which they will people the new world." (Given by a ten and a half year old schizophrenic with an I.Q. of 142.) It is important to bear in mind, though, that the current trend in comics emphasizes cosmic characters, space cadets and men from Mars. However, responses of this order, when produced by a schizophrenic child, are part of a generalized distortion of reality, and found along with other very crude, bizarre and poorly formulated answers (F—, possibly M—). In the schizophrenic child such responses are an intregal part of his generalized distortion of reality, and are accompanied by disorganizing anxiety.

Sexual interests and preoccupations which are atypical for the child's age may find expression in the Rorschach in the form of sexual interpretations, the naming of sexual parts and sometimes of excretory activity. By themselves such responses are certainly not indicative of schizophrenia, since many children show such interests at different ages, depending upon their experiences with their environment. However, when found in conjunction with the other disturbances characteristic of schizophrenia, this sexual preoccupation is one more indication of the child's deviant ways of seeking to understand and find himself. In his abortive efforts at achieving identification, he adopts all kinds of roles, many of which are all out of line with his age and experience. In some instances, the sexual aspects of these roles are emphasized and it is through them that he tries to find an answer to his conflicts and uncertainty. This may lead to overt sexual contact, investigation and activity, as well as preoccupation with these matters. Frequently the sexual interest is tied in with a need to know about birth, where one comes from, thus possibly shedding light on the perpetual problem of who one is and what his place in the environment is.

In a research which is not yet completed, an attempt to establish the nature and consistency of a subject's attitudes toward himself is being made by classifying each individual response under certain specific headings. These include such categories as: adequate-inadequate, passive-aggressive, and accepted-rejected. The assumption underlying this investigation is that with the achievement of identification, the attitudes toward the self should become more consistent and stabilized. To date, the results indicate that the schizophrenic children tend to cluster at the extremes of the distribution, that is, they show either highly variable, inconsistent attitudes which make for unpredictable behavior, or they adhere rigidly to one stereotyped way of perceiving themselves, and are thus unable to act in reasonably flexible, adjusted fashion.

The schizophrenic child's failure to make identification, to grasp the nature of inner and outer reality, and to structure his own experiences accordingly, leaves him in a state of uncertainty and disorganization which is accompanied by much anxiety. The anxiety of the schizophrenic child far outweighs that of the normal or even the disturbed, but nonpsychotic child.[26] This anxiety can manifest itself in a number of ways. As has already been indicated, it drives the child into the compulsive, stereotyped behavior he manifests in his efforts at making identification. It also reveals itself in the content of his interpretations which so often is of a gruesome, brutal, bizarre order. Such interpretations give indication of the horrifying experiences the child is constantly undergoing because of his inability to organize and integrate his ideas and his feelings and relate them to his experiences in meaningful fashion.

As was pointed out earlier, anxiety in children rarely manifests itself in the Rorschach through shading responses. Certainly, the more mature, controlled forms of reacting to anxiety, as reflected in Fc and FK answers, will be absent. However, the confusion and disorganization which are so intimately tied in with the schizophrenic child's anxiety may find expression in responses calling for the scoring of K or KF and c or cF.

Other ways that anxiety will manifest itself is through extreme loss of intellectual and emotional control, exaggerated shock reactions, constant indications of feelings of inadequacy given both in direct and in symbolic form, and in the nature of the child's fantasies.

Anxiety is responsible for the fact that many of these children cannot come to grips with the circumstances that confront them, cannot analyze them and deal with them in practical fashion. Instead they approach them in a crude, sweeping, high-handed, undifferentiated manner. Their Rorschach records therefore contain more whole responses than is compatible with common sense adjustment.

In many instances the records are so shot through with evidences of anxiety that they fairly crackle with it, and a simple reading of the protocol reveals the intensity of the agitation the subject is experiencing. In other cases, the extremity of the defenses that are being mobilized gives a measure of intensity of the subject's anxiety (see Record No. 28).

In addition to the manifestations of anxiety given in his test productions, the behavior of the schizophrenic child throughout the examination also reveals his intense disturbance. There is the child who cannot sit down and take the test until he has opened every door and examined every nook and cranny in the office. This is not just bad training or "orneriness." Such a child is afraid, and he must reassure himself about the place in which he finds himself. Having once settled what is behind each and every door, the child can give his attention to other matters. However, even when his anxiety about the nature of the room or the office is relieved and a relatively good relationship has been established with the examiner, the child gives constant signs of tension and agitation. He generally cannot sit still for any great period of time, but finds he must pace about and handle everything within reach. He also is likely to ask what other children do on the test, where his mother has gone, if the examiner is married, has children, and so on. Some make attempts to conceal the fact that they are disturbed, others try to laugh off the disturbance by ridiculing the blots, the examiner, their own responses. They often act in a "smart-alecky" fashion or seek to impress their audience by giving interpretations that have a scientific or pseudoscientific flavor, and also by displaying any other assets they think they possess.

In addition to all the aforementioned ways in which the child's poor relationship to reality can manifest itself, there is the matter of reality testing. In the records of many schizophrenic children, the number of poor form responses will be far in excess of what is ordinarily encountered at the child's particular age and mental level. Not only are his autistically determined perceptions poorly organized and deviant, but they often are of such a vague order that he cannot formulate them a second time. Thus, in the short period that elapses between the giving of a response on the Rorschach card, and the discussion of that response in the inquiry, the child has lost his concept and is unable to recapture it. While this occurs occasionally to almost any subject, especially if the record is a relatively long one, it happens with great frequency in schizophrenics. Many of these children defend themselves against the implication of inadequacy which the loss of the response entails by denying that they ever gave such a response and vigorously asserting that it is the examiner who has made the mistake. Others simply act in anxious or hopeless fashion. Still others are completely indifferent to the whole matter.

Sometimes the reality concepts are not so poor, as far as organization is concerned, but they are deviant, bizarre and morbid. What objects the child does recognize and respond to in his environment are not those ordinarily perceived by his age group or those which might have adjustive value. Instead, they are reflections of the highly deviant world he has created and in which he lives. This type of perception has already received some consideration in in the discussion on identification (see p. 185).

Similarly, the earlier discussion (see p. 187) on the relationship between the whole and the detail responses in the records of schizophrenic children is also relevant in connection with the disturbances they manifest in the development of sound reality concepts. Prevented by their extreme anxiety from getting really involved in any situation, pushed by the necessity to deal with all their experiences in a sweeping grandiose fashion, they fail to recognize the usual, practical, concrete, everyday aspects of many matters.

The disturbed interpersonal relationships of the schizophrenic child show themselves in a number of ways. Primary, of course, is the disturbance in relation to the self, the inability to find and establish a concept of the self. This failure makes the development of any kind of object relationship impossible. Because of this basic weakness or defect, there is often no capacity whatsoever to bridge the gap that exists between the child and the world about him. Actually he may not be aware of the necessity for bridging the gap, since he is often not aware of the difference between the self and the nonself. In these cases the Rorschach records may have no color responses whatsoever. They reveal either a complete lack of the capacity for emotional sharing at any level, or what emotional responses exist are rare and of a disorganized, infantile order (CF−, C). Finally there are those whose interpersonal relationships are forced and artificial, without emotional investment. These subjects have been discussed in relation to the problems of identification (see p. 185). They are the children who give human movement responses without accompanying animal movement answers and with few if any color interpretations.

The schizophrenic child's preoccupation with time and space is not too frequently reflected in the Rorschach record, but there are instances when it is very apparent. There are the children who make comments about the amount of time they have used to give a response, and have a compulsive need to keep it identical for each card. There are those who bring time concepts into the interpretations. Similarly, there are the children who are concerned about space relationships and these are also reflected in the protocols. Responses like "standing on top of the world," "hanging down from the sky," not only have a grandiose note, but also emphasize the whole question of spatial relationships. There are other disturbances in spatial relationships which may well be a reflection of the child's inability to establish limits to his concepts and to formulate integrated concepts in line with objective reality. Such deviations manifest themselves in the child's inability to differentiate between the immediate circumstances and unrelated matters. These are the children who, in interpreting the white space around a given blot, carry their use of the white area to the very edge of the card. This type of response has been seen only in schizophrenics. The same is true of the child who interprets an accidental mark which appears in the white areas—a small ink blot, dirt spot, etc.

One of the most significant aspects of the schizophrenic child's functioning is the gross unevenness of development that it reflects. The disease process which interferes with the development of all systems does this with varied emphasis. Moreover, this interference does not always take the form of a lag, but can also manifest itself in gross acceleration. Again, as Bender has indicated, in discussing growth discrepancies, "the children are too big or too little."[6] Similarly she points out that while the onset of schizophrenia in the first few years of life may retard, inhibit or block speech, other children who have already mastered language "may show an increased activity in the field of language and in thinking processes." In other words, it is extremes of behavior that are likely to distinguish the performance of the schizophrenic child in any area of functioning whether emotional, ideational, verbal.

In the Rorschach records these extremes will manifest themselves in persistent, gross retardation, all out of line with the child's age and endowment (see Record No. 30), and in the acceleration of the personality development as indicated by the presence of a too well crystallized personality structure at a very early age, generally a personality structure not unlike that found in adult compulsives. This neuroticlike personality structure will not be consistently maintained, however, but will show breaks in control and shifts in the whole adjustive pattern.

The gross retardation shown by some schizophrenic children makes it difficult at times to differentiate them from mental defectives. Their Rorschach records are generally meager, and have many poor form responses. The schizophrenic features usually consist of unexpected concern about matters which the defective child does not consider, such as the preoccupation with time and space mentioned above, or a compulsive absorption in numbers or words.

The behavior in these cases is also not like that of the defective child, but rather shows a complete detachment from the situation. These children somehow convey an impression of being completely apart from their surroundings, of being in another world, whereas the defective child produces no such impression.

The hypertrophy reflected in the presence of a well crystallized, compulsive-obsessivelike personality structure which is typical for some schizophrenic children, is the product of their efforts to handle their illness. However, the impact of the disease process produces breaks in their neurotic defenses which are both severe and unexpected. Thus for example it is likely to be Card V, the easiest card, that will be rejected, or produce an unexpected poor form answer. Unlike the true neurotic, the obsessive-compulsive pattern will sporadically alter and break. In their discussion of these children, Des Lauriers and Halpern[11] indicate that:

"... the Rorschach records generally have a large number of responses, the form perception is comparatively good, there will be a fair range of interests, a reasonable capacity for adaptability, and often rich intellectual and emotional resources. The main difference between these records and those of non-schizophrenic children is the sudden appearance of a poor form response on cards where they are least expected ... a tendency to confabulation, sudden and unexpected refusals of a plate, and extremes of emotional expression after periods of flatness."

In summary, then, it can be said that childhood schizophrenia, like adult schizophrenia, manifests itself in a variety of ways with the result that no one form of test pattern can be considered typical for all schizophrenics. However, the common factors in all instances of the disease are the extreme anxiety the child manifests, the disturbances in identification that he experiences, the fluidity of his concepts, his disturbances in reality testing, and the variable nature of his functioning.

RECORD No. 23

Schizophrenic Girl, Age 4 Years 7 Months, I.Q. 93

I.	W	F–(?)	War	4″ 1. War.	(questioned) In Germany. (nothing more could be obtained)
II.	W	F–	War	3″ 1. War.	A man was in Germany, just is.
III.	W	F–	War	3″ 1. More war.	(nothing further could be obtained)
IV.	W	F–	War	4″ 1. More war.	(nothing further could be obtained)
V.	W	F–	War	6″ 1. More war.	(nothing further could be obtained)
	W	F–	Arch	2. House.	
VI.	W	F–	Arch	2″ 1. House.	(nothing further could be obtained)
VII.	W	F–	Arch	2″ 1. Another house.	(nothing further could be obtained)
VIII.	W	F–	War	2″ 1. Another war.	(nothing further could be obtained)
IX.	W	F–	War	2″ 1. Another war.	(nothing further could be obtained)
X.	W	F–	War	2″ 1. Another war.	(nothing further could be obtained)

R 11

W 11   F   11 (all minus) War   8   P   0
                                      Arch 3

W 100%   F   100%   A   0%
                F−   100%

                          M : C
                          0 : 0

                      Fm + FM : C′ + c
                          0 : 0

                    VIII + IX + X = 30%

This record is more typical for a two and a half to three year old than for a child of four years and seven months. The test reactions give absolutely no indication that this child has any understanding whatsoever of objective reality. She has no awareness that reality has a meaning of its own and is not simply whatever she chooses to make it. Not only is every one of her responses a poor form response but the content of these, while limited to two categories, is, in the main, atypical: the response, "war," is not often obtained from four year olds.

The subject's failure to develop adequate reality concepts is paralleled by the absence of all forms of emotional experience. Since no separation of the self from the rest of the environment has taken place, since no self has actually been as yet developed, there is no need for such emotional responses or for any sharing or internalizing of feeling. The subject is actually, then, at a most elementary or primitive stage of development.

Without knowing what "war" means to this child, it is not possible to interpret the limited content that the record offers. War might stand for conflict, for the absence of the father, or for any number of other experiences. The only thing that the interpretation does indicate is a decided atypicality in thinking, while the whole record points to a gross deviation in development. This girl is definitely not progressing in line with expectancy.

The subject is the older of two girls, her sister being about two and a half years old. The parents do not have a good relationship and have separated twice during this child's lifetime. At the time the record was taken, they were living together, but not happily. The mother complains that the subject is completely unmanageable, has violent temper tantrums and constantly upsets the routine of the whole household. The possibility of schizophrenia was suggested by the psychological tests, especially the drawing and some of her reactions to the Stanford Binet. What the Rorschach contributes is confirmation of lags and deviations in development

RECORD No. 24

Repeat Rorschach (See Record No. 23), Age 6 Years 0 Months, I.Q. 105

Card	Loc.	Determinant	Content	Response	Inquiry
I.	WS	F–	Hd	10" 1. Looks like a body.	(usual wings are hands, upper spaces are eyes, left lower space is mouth, right lower is nose)
II.	D	F+, FC	Hd	17" 1. A pair of feet, two pair of feet.	(upper red) Just two, with red socks, red blood, black blood.
	D	CF–	At	2. A red heart.	(lower red) Heart because it has a splash (sings *Jingle Bells*)
	W	F–	Ad	3. A black body. Give me a scissors so I can cut. (touches examiner's hair and clothing)	(black area) Body of some kind of animal. I don't know.
III.				I had this two times already.	
	D	F–	Sex	30" 1. Looks like a flush here. (points to breast area on self and examiner)	(lower dark center area) A big pair of flush on you. (touches examiner in breast area)
	D	F–	Hd	2. Two pair of feet.	(all red) Just feet.
IV.	D	F+	Hd P	45" 1. Feet here, two pair.	(usual) Just feet.
	D→W	F+	H	2. Body here, feet, feet, leg, leg, feet, feet, neck, body.	Of a man.
V.	D	F–	Clo	6" 1. I see underpants, dirty.	(upper center detail) (licks card) That's where the blood is.
	D (C Projection)	F–	Clo	2. A hankerchief, all in blue.	(all projections)
VI.	W	F+	Pl	5" 1. Tree.	Tree, tree, tree, tree, etc.
	D	FM	A	2. Spider where you can cut. You are asking questions?	(top detail) Hanging on the tree.

RECORD No. 24—*continued*

VII. 10″   1. I see somebody's underpants, maybe white, maybe pink, boy oh boy, do they stink.

     D→W   F—   Clo   (lower third is pants, rest is body)

VIII. 5″   1. Blue, blue, pink, pink, orange, white.

     Cn

     (Denial)

     2. Pair of pants.   No pair of pants.

     D→W   CF—, Position   At & N

     3. Bunch of hearts.   (lower center is heart, side is body, upper is sky)

IX. 13″   1. Grass.

     D   C   N

     (D→W   C   N)   (Add. [green] Really a pink sky, a green sky, an orange sky.)

     2. Dress, an orange dress.

     D   C/F—   Clo   (orange)

X. 10″   1. Looks like the sun.

     D   C   N   (All blue is sky, all yellow is sun)

R   17 + 1

W	1⎫		F+	4⎫		A	1⎫2		P	0
W	1⎬6 + 1		F−	7⎭11		Ad	1⎭			
D→W	3					H	1			
WS	1⎭		FM	1		Hd	4			
						At	2			
D	11		CF	2−		Sex	1			
			C/F	1−		Clo	4			
			C	2 + 1		N	2 + 2			
			(Cn	1)		Pl	1			
			(C Projection 1)							
			(Position	1)						

W	35%		F	65%		A	12%
D	65%		F+	36%			

M : C
0 : 6

Fm + FM : C′ + c
1 : 1

VIII + IX + X = 24%

Marked changes have taken place in this child in the 17 months that have passed since the first record (see Record 23) was taken. She has now developed the capacity for selecting from her experiences certain limited aspects of them, she can give emotional responses, and she even makes an occasional attempt to internalize her feelings. However, despite this progress, she is anything but healthy and well adjusted. All the capacities which she now possesses are used in a deviant manner and only serve to emphasize the distortions that are present in her thinking and in her feeling reactions.

The self which she has managed to develop is perceived in most unusual fashion. Apparently her efforts at trying to find a self have led this girl to focus on her physical aspects, have made her "body conscious" to the neglect of all other forms of experience. Thus there is a constant preoccupation with bodies, with their genital and sexual features and even with clothing as an extension of the body. All her energy is focused in this area. The self then is a very limited one, developed only along specific and unusual lines, with no understanding of broader, deeper and richer relationships and experiences. It is this concern with the self, this endless seeking to find and maintain the self through this atypical emphasis, that accounts for the unusual content found in this record, the constant references to breasts, blood, pants, feet, bodies, clothes.

The ego in this case is very weak, and frequently unable to maintain contact with reality, or to differentiate between reality and autistic projection. At times this loss of control is reflected not only in the responses but in the child's overt reactions (licking the blood on Card V). Much of the time reality is dealt with in most arbitrary fashion and there are occasional flights of ideas (Card II, "red socks," "red blood," "black blood"; Card IX, "really a pink sky," "a green sky," "an orange sky"). What routinization there is in her thinking is certainly not comparable to that found in most children. It does not take the form of high animal per cent, but is focused around her bodily concerns.

Her color responses point to efforts at relating to the environment, but these are of a most arbitrary and uncontrolled order (C/F, C, Cn and Color projection). There seems to be no understanding whatsoever of what is involved in an emotional exchange. The color projection in this case does not seem to be associated with depressive trends as it is in adults, but is rather an extension of this girl's complete indifference to the demands of reality. The essential quality of her reactions, emotional and nonemotional, is the indifference toward reality and objectivity that they reflect. Whatever occurs to this child, whatever she feels, is immediately expressed without any consideration of what is acceptable and what is expected of her. This arbitrariness is not only indicated by her poor form responses but also by her loss of distance, and her recourse to position responses.

RECORD No. 25

Schizophrenic Boy, Age 6 Years 7 Months, I.Q. 80 (?)

			Inquiry	Loc.	Det.	Cont.
I.	7"	1. Gingerbread.	Just does. (vaguely indicates whole blot)	W	F−	Food
		2. Leaf.	(shrugs)	W	F−	Pl
		3. Tree.	(points arbitrarily)	W	F−	Pl
		4. Farm.	Looks like it.	W	F−	Arch
		5. Cow.	(just stares at examiner)	W	F−	A
		6. Lion.	(no response to inquiry)	W	F−	A
		7. Tiger.	(no response)	W	F−	A
		(at this point card was removed)				
II.	4"	1. Looks like a shoe.	(sweeps finger rapidly all around)	W	F−	Clo
		2. Like tiger.	(same as 1)	W	F−	A
		3. Like a crocodile.	(same as 1)	W	F−	A
		4. Lion.	(same as 1)	W	F−	A
		5. Alligator.	(same as 1)	W	F−	A
		6. Horse.	(same as 1)	W	F−	A
		7. Cow.	(same as 1)	W	F−	A
		(card removed)				
III.	10"	1. Gingerbread.	(points arbitrarily)	W	F−	Food
		2. School.	(same as 1)	W	F−	A
		3. Tiger.	(same as 1)	W	F−	A
		4. Lion.	(same as 1)	W	F−	A
		(puts card in mouth, flops it around; card removed)				
IV.	4"					
	10"	(looks at back)				
		Did you paint this?				
	13"	1. Christmas tree.	(vaguely indicates outline)	W	F+	Pl

RECORD No. 25—*continued*

V.	W	F+	A	P	19" 1. Butterfly.	(much turning and edging) Looks like it.
VI.	W	F—	Food		2" 1. Ice cream.	Here (top D) is cone, rest is ice cream.
VII.	D	F—	A		4" 1. Look like bears.	(top two thirds) Just look like bears.
	D	F—	Arch		2. Two houses.	(lower third) Because.
VIII.	W	F±	Obj		3" 1. Ship.	Has a point on top and I want it to be a ship.
IX.	W	F—	Food		2" 1. Ice cream cone.	(shrugs)
X.	DS	F—	A		2" 1. Butterfly.	(pink and space between) Long wing.
	D	F+	A	P	2. Crab, I guess it looks like a crab.	(side blue)

R   27

W   23   F+   3⎫
                     F±   1⎬27   A   16   P   2
D   3⎫   F−   23⎭   Clo   1
DS   1⎭⁴   Food   4
                                           Pl   3
                                           Arch   2
                                           Obj   1

W   85%   F   100%   A   59%
D   15%   F+   11%

                          M   :   C
                          0   :   0

                     Fm + FM   :   C' + c
                          0   :   0

                     VIII + IX + X = 15%

This record provides an excellent example of the kind of thinking and associations found in some cases of schizophrenia. Responses are triggered off by inner needs (Card I, response one), or by vaguely perceived aspects of the blot, and then followed by a series of responses which are stimulated not by the test material, but by the subject's associations to his original answer. Thus he goes from "leaf" to "tree," to "farm," to "cow," from "cow" to other four-legged animals such as "lion" and "tiger."

This subjective type of association continues until Card IV when it is suddenly replaced by a well perceived concept, a "Christmas tree." After much manipulation of the stimulus, response is made to Card V and this too is an acceptable interpretation. If from no other evidence than these two answers, it is possible to state that this boy can handle his experiences on a reality basis. This contention receives further substantiation from his. "ship" response on Card VIII and the "crab" interpretation on Card X. However, his abilities are variably applied and easily disturbed: in a new and unstructured situation it takes him a long time, actually the total time spent on the first three cards, to get organized, and his efforts in this connection are not sustained. As soon as the situation becomes difficult he again reacts in most subjective arbitrary fashion (Cards VI, VII).

It is evident that the ego structure in this case is of a very weak order. In addition to this boy's repeated failure to appreciate the nature of the reality that confronts him, there is the marked immaturity of the formulations that he does achieve. His "leaf" response on Card I and his "Christmas tree" on Card IV are more typical of three and four year olds than of a boy his age. Likewise, the very limited indication that he gives for any selective judgment (85 per cent whole responses, only 15 per cent good form answers) and his failure to develop any capacity for emotional experience (no movement or color answers of any kind) point to serious lags and deviations in personality development. This cannot be accounted for on the basis of limited endowment, since his performance on the Rorschach, as well as on the intelligence test, is too erratic to permit of such explanation. In fact his functioning on the intelligence test is so erratic as to cast serious doubt on the validity of the obtained I.Q. of 80.

This child is the son of a mechanical engineer, the second of three children. The mental level of all the members of the family is in the bright-normal-to-superior range. Shortly before this protocol was obtained, this boy showed a sudden change in behavior, became extremely restless and distractible, attacked people most aggressively without warning or provocation, in one instance actually seriously hurting another child. All his former routines were disrupted, and it became increasingly difficult to handle him. School was out of the question, and his active nights, his strange nonconforming behavior at all times, finally made it impossible to keep him at home, and hospitalization became necessary. The diagnosis was childhood schizophrenia.

RECORD No. 26

Schizophrenic Boy, Age 7 Years 0 Months, I.Q. 119

	Response	Loc.	Det.	Content	Inquiry
I. 67"	20" It's nothing, is it?				
	30" 1. Mountain.	W	F—	N	Just looks like one, high and smooth.
	2. Tunnel under the mountain.	S	FK	Arch	(spaces) Shaped like tunnels and it looks like you could go through.
II. 32"	3" 1. Oh, fire.	D	C	Fire	(all red) Well, it's red.
	2. And a house on fire.	WS	F—	Arch	(black is house, space is chimney) The part that's been burned out of the chimney.
III. 17"	2" 1. Oh, two people.	W	F—	H	Bottom leg, front leg, the head. (black with usual arm as bottom leg)
	2. And a bow tie.	D	F+	Clo P	(center red) Has a knot.
IV. 15"	3" 1. Two tunnels.	S	F→FK—	Arch	(spaces on either side of lower center detail) One over an express highway, one over a brook with water.
	2. And a flower on top.	D	F+	Pl	(top center) Just looks like a real flower, how it's opened.
	I want to make blots, they look nice.				
V. 33"	13" 1. New flower, just come out.	D	F+	Pl	(top projections) How a flower opens.
	2. Roots of a tree.	D	F+	Pl	(lower projections) Sticks down.
	3. Wolf's mouth.	D	F+	Ad	(side projections) Long and bad.
	4. Camel's humps.	d	F+	Ad	(bumps on top of usual wing four camel bumps)
VI. 31"	17" 1. Four kitten's whiskers.	d	F+	Ad	(little lines on top detail)
	2. And a mountain.	W	F—	N	So high.

RECORD No. 26—*continued*

VII. 15″		Oh, this is gonna be hard. I think I better put this away.					
	√10″	1. Tunnel.	S	F→FK	Arch		(space) Just like you go in on express highway.
VIII. 37″	6″						
	10″	This ain't very hard. 1. Two bears. How many color inks do you have?	D	F+	A	P	(usual) Four legs and a bear's head.
		2. And a flower.	D	F+	Pl		(lower center detail) Shape like a flower. (denies color)
IX. 20″	6″	1. Oh God, a mountain.	W	F−	N		Round here and the side.
		2. Tunnel under it.	DS	F→FK	Arch		(center area) Go in.
		3. Roots of tree.	d	F+	Pl		(orange projections) Lot of sticks.
X. 27″	4″						
	14″	Oh God, this one's hard. 1. A tree with flowers.	D	F+	Pl		(top gray) Here are the flowers, like little dots.
		2. Bunny's face.	D	F+	Ad	P	(usual) I saw some long ears and a pointed face.
		3. Roots of tree, two roots of a tree.	D	Fm	Pl		(side blue) Lots of different sticks hanging and the middle a full body.

R 23

W	3 ⎫	F+	12 ⎫	A	1 ⎫	P	3		
W	1 ⎬5	F→FK	3(1−) ⎬20	Ad	4 ⎬5				
WS	1 ⎭	F−	5 ⎭	H	1				
				Arch	5				
D	11 ⎫12	Fm	1	Fire	1				
DS	1 ⎭	FK	1	Clo	1				
				Pl	7				
d	3 ⎫6	C	1	N	3				
S	3 ⎭								

W	22%	F	87%	A	22%
D	52%	F+	60%		
d + S	26%				

$$M : C$$
$$0 : 1\frac{1}{2}$$

$$Fm + FM : C' + c$$
$$1 : 0$$

$$VIII + IX + X = 35\%$$

This is the first of three records obtained from the same child at approximately one year intervals. The presenting complaints were manifold, including very poor relations with the parents and intense sibling rivalry with a younger sister. He was beset with strange ideas which he often verbalized, both at home and at school. The school authorities had decided that he could no longer come to class because he so seriously disturbed other children with his conversation and his behavior. During the test he talked almost constantly in a loud, unmodulated tone of voice. He asked innumerable questions—why he had to take the tests, who else took them, how were they scored, etc. Right after Card IV he insisted on making inkblots of his own, and refused to go on unless permitted to do so. His challenge to authority, as represented by the examiner, was probably stimulated by his associations to Card IV.

Analysis of the Rorschach findings indicates that this boy experiences deep feelings of inadequacy and suffers from overwhelming, disorganizing anxiety (tendency to vista responses, the numerous tunnel interpretations which usually symbolize the child's need for shelter, the comments preceding interpretation, such as "this is gonna be hard" on Card VII). Emotional experiences other than anxiety are rare and then are of a very infantile, destructive order (only one color answer, a C, on Card II).

Despite his anxiety, the subject is able to deal with his experiences in a differentiated fashion and maintain some objectivity (52 per cent large detail answers, 60 per cent good form answers). He also attempts to control his anxiety and put it at a distance from himself (3 tendencies toward FK, 1 FK). Along with the absence of emotional release (only 1 C, no M or FM) and the exaggerated emphasis on form (87 per cent F), the picture strongly suggests a compulsive type of adjustment. That these adjustive efforts are not meeting with success is apparent in the frequency with which objectivity is lost (seven poor form interpretations) and in the extremely regressive, perseverative, "sticky" kind of thinking the subject reveals in the content. Moreover, the nature of this content reflects primitive, infantile identification (many trees, flowers, roots). There is, then, a marked disparity between the goals this boy sets for himself in his adjustive efforts and what he achieves. In consequence, he appears to be in a constant state of tension, as he strives to maintain whatever stability he can.

The repeated interpretation of "flowers"—four in all—requires special consideration. Flowers as a rule symbolize grace, beauty, delicacy, fragility, tenderness. They are much more likely to be used to express the needs and desires of girls and women than of a boy of seven. Seven is a time when boys are very definitely "rough and tumble." The subject's repeated recourse to such an interpretation points to a striking deviation in identification and a passivity frequently encountered in the records of schizophrenic boys. His deviations in this connection are especially strongly indicated by his flower interpretation on Card IV where one would expect him to find and identify with strength and virility.

In general this boy's concepts of people are limited and confused. His only human response comes on Card III, and he then spoils the answer by describing the people as though they were animals with a "bottom leg and a front leg."

The significant features in this record which point to the diagnosis of schizophrenia are the failure of the compulsive mechanisms to ward off regressive and disorganized reactions, and the marked passivity with which this boy appears to identify. The way he does this reveals not only his confusions in identification but the extremely infantile level at which he is struggling with this whole problem.

RECORD No. 27

Repeat Rorschach (See Record No. 26), Age 7 Years 11 Months, I.Q. 128

Card / Time	Response	Loc.	Det.	Content	Inquiry
I. 25"	See what I saw the last time.				
2" 8"	1. I see two bears with wings, no with paws.	D	FM	A	(side details) Face like a bear.
	2. In between they're both carrying some wolf, both dragging it different ways.	D	F+	A	(center detail) See the bottom of the face. (asked to tell more about wolf) He's dead, they'll tear him.
II. 15"					
3"	1. Two elephants are fighting.	W	FM	A P	Head and trunk looks like an elephant.
	2. And the red stuff is blood.	D	C	Bl	Where did I get the red stuff from?
III. 20"					
2"	Oh well this is so easy, no wonder it took so long.				
6"	1. Two men both fighting over...	W	M	H P	Heads looks like men.
	2. ...Bowtie.	D	F+	Clo P	(center red) Formed like a bow tie.
	3. And blood in back of each one.	D	C	Bl	(side red)
IV. 8"					
2"	This one's going to take a long time.				
6"	1. Giant, a big giant.	W	M	(H)	This (lower center) could be a stool he's sitting on. (asked what kind of a giant?) Unfriendly. I want him to be unfriendly. He doesn't talk to anybody.
V. 19"					
3"	1. This is wings.	D	F+	Ad	(each side detail) Like butterfly wings.
	2. No, this is wolves, no not two wolves, two crocodiles.	D	F+	Ad	(side projections) I saw the heads and I made them crocodile heads, because crocodiles are thinner than wolves.
VI. 9"					
2"	This looks pretty hard.				
6"	1. Looks like a cat.	D	F+	Ad	Looks like a cat's head with whiskers.

RECORD NO. 27—*continued*

		Loc		Content	P	Inquiry
VII. 8"						
5"	1. Two boy's arguing.	W	M	H		One hand out, Indian boys.
VIII. 10"						
1"	Oh, this one of course.					
4"	1. Two bears climbing a mountain.	D	FM, F/C	A	P	(usual) Red bears. Face, legs, body.
IX. 10"						
3"	This is hard.					
V5"	1. This is a tree, an apple tree.	W	FC	Pl		Apples because it's red. Has a trunk in the middle.
X. 12"						
5"	1. This is a lot of crabs.	D	F+	A	P	(side blue) Legs and body.
	2. With turtles and fish.	D	F−	A		(brown and orange side details) Looks that way.
	3. And two crocodiles.	D	F+	A		(pink) They're long.

R   17

W	3 }5	F+	7 }8	A	7 }10	P	5
W	2	F−	1	Ad	3		
				H	3(1)		
D	12	M	3	Bl	2		
		FM	3	Clo	1		
				Pl	1		
		FC	1				
		C	2				
		F/C	0 + 1				

| W | 29% | F | 47% | A | 59% |
| D | 71% | F+ | 88% | | |

$$M : C$$
$$3 : 3\tfrac{1}{2}$$

$$Fm + FM : C' + c$$
$$3 : 0$$

$$VIII + IX + X = 29\%$$

This Rorschach record was obtained after the patient had had about 11 months of intensive psychotherapy. Radical changes have taken place in the formal structure of this personality and in the way this boy now symbolizes his problems. The changes are definitely in a positive direction.

The subject now gives repeated expression to his aggressive, hostile impulses and identifies with aggressive, strong, battling figures (Card I "bears dragging a wolf different ways"; Card II, "two elephants fighting"; Card III, "two men fighting"; Card VII, "two boys arguing"). This acceptance of his aggression suggests a diminution in anxiety and a more constructive attack on his problems. He no longer needs to seek the shelter provided by tunnels or the passivity of flowers. Similarly he can now give expression to his fantasies and accept them (3 M, 3 FM), and more frequent emotional responses to the environment also occur (2 C, 1 FC). Actually, aside from the fact that he has 2 C responses and no CF responses, there is nothing in the formal aspects of the psychogram to indicate how sick this boy is. The distribution of his color answers certainly points to efforts at control (1 FC), but these efforts are overshadowed by the disturbing impact that emotional involvements have for him (2 "blood" answers).

The fact that this boy is still anxious and confused is best indicated by the content of his responses, the conflicted nature of his interpretations, plus the behavior he showed and the comments he made throughout the testing. Ambivalence, uncertainty and futile efforts at laughing off deep anxiety are evident. For example, on Card II he says "The red stuff is blood," but on the inqiury tries to deny the intensity of the experience by asking "Where did I get the red stuff from?" Similarly he makes a number of contradictory statements, such as on Card III, "Oh, this is so easy, no wonder it took so long," or Card IV, "Oh, this one's going to take a long time," and then he responds immediately.

Extreme concreteness is reflected in the subject's need to find the exact response that he feels meets the demands of the situation and his inability to accept the possibility of more than one such solution. Thus on Card V he does not say "This could be two wolves or maybe two crocodiles," but rather first interprets "wolves" and then rules them out completely, substituting the "crocodiles." No area of any blot is therefore interpreted more than once.

Compulsive concern with time was manifested by the subject's behavior during the testing. He tried throughout to watch the time, to note the recording of it and to gear his interpretations so that they would not take more than one minute. There is also his comment after Card VIII, "Make sure it's just one minute."

Arbitrary treatment of his experiences is reflected in the patient's statement that the giant on Card IV is unfriendly "Because I want him to be unfriendly," and further justification is not considered necessary.

At this time the subject was definitely less tense and agitated, and although he certainly presented seriously disturbed behavior, he was not as autistic and "different" from the other children as had formerly been the case. He now possessed ways of dealing with his disturbances other than regression or direct acting out.

RECORD No. 28

Repeat Rorschach (See Record Nos. 26 and 27), Age 9 Years 1 Month, I.Q. 130

I. 52″	D	F+	Ad	12″	1. Mm—could be two bears, heads are like bears.	(top side) Just look like bears' heads.
	D	F+	A		2. And this little part here looks like a crab.	(top center) Because of clawlike part.
	D	F+	Ad		3. These are wings, but what do they belong to? That's all. The crab is really good, you know, looks like a crab.	(side projections)
II. 53″	D	F+	Obj	9″	1. Oh, looks like two revolvers two guns. These sort of look like guns here.	(top red) Shaped like a gun sort of. Should be a trigger.
	D	F+	Ad		2. Two elephants' heads without trunks.	(upper half of black) Shaped like it.
III. 69″				2″	I remember this one from last time.	
	W	F+	H P	8″	1. Two men. Each man has only leg and one hand.	Just look like it.
	D	F+	Clo P		2. And a bowtie, a nice bowtie. It doesn't look like an ink-print, just looks like you made a bowtie. I don't know what that is. (points to side red)	(center red) Just in every way. The shape of it.

RECORD No. 28—*continued*

IV. 24"	1"	Oh, God.			
	7"	I don't think it's anything.			
	14"	1. Could be the back of a gorilla.	(omit lower center detail) Look at the back of the head and the big feet.	W F+	A
		That's all I can get. What could you make out of that?			
V. 62	16"	I see something here. I guess I can't make it out.			
	25"	You could say......			
	38"	1. Body and legs of a man without hands and without head. There are legs, there are body, no hands, no head.	(side detail) Just see the body.	D F+	Hd
VI. 65"	6"	Oh, not too good either. I'll get it yet. I wonder what are you writing down. From this—from this way it looks like it might be something. (makes faces) Oh yes.	Naw, nothing on that. I can't find nothing, when there's nothing to find.	......	
VII. 71"	3"				
	8"	1. Two elephants with only one leg. Yes, two elephants with only one leg. What are you writing down? Oh, I forgot I could always use that too.	(top two thirds) Head, trunk, body. A good one if it had the rest of the legs.	D F+	A

D	F+	A	><V <	2. Butterfly, this side is a butterfly. Its a pretty nice butterfly too. The elephants I saw from this direction.	(lower third) Two wings.

VIII.
52"

D	F+	A P	7"	1. Perfect animals but I don't know what kind they are—two lambs.	The animals are perfect, but not really like any kind—stuffed animals.
D	F+	Pl		2. And a pine tree, a pine tree.	(top center detail) Way it's pointed and slants down.

IX.
60"

4" It's gonna be hard.

W (DS	C/F± F+	Design Rock)	21"	1. Nice designs but that's all. (whispers) I think I can see something. No.	Just shapes and colors. (Add. Rock with two holes in it.)

X.
58"

3" It better be good, I can't make it bad on this.

D	F+	A P	12"	1. Crab, two crabs, two cras.	(side blue) Legs.
D	F+	A		2. Two sandcrabs, two sandcrabs. Got to find something else. Such a big thing. Nothing more.	(side brown) Easy to identify.

R   16 + 1

W   1⎫3   F+   15⎫15 + 1   A   7⎫10   P 4
W   2⎭   F−   0⎭   Ad   3⎭
                                          H   1
D   13   C/F   1±   Hd   1
                                          Pl   1
DS   0 + 1   Clo   1
                                          Obj   1
                                          Design 1
                                          Rock   0 + 1

W   19%   F   94%   A   63%
D   81%   F+ 100%

M : C
0 : 1

Fm + FM : C' + c
0 : 0

VIII + IX + X = 31%

Fourteen months after the last record was obtained and about 25 months after therapy was instituted the Rorschach was given again. Once more there are marked changes in the personality picture. Energy is now directed toward the maintenance of severe control (94 per cent F, 100 per cent F+). All the emotional spontaneity and recourse to fantasy that were present earlier are now once more severely repressed. Caution is conspicuous as this boy carefully picks from each situation certain limited, circumscribed aspects of it that he can manage to respond to in controlled, circumspect fashion.

A strong sense of inadequacy appears to be responsible for this boy's need to be so careful and controlled. This sense of inadequacy finds both symbolic and direct expression. There is the "I don't know" in connection with the first response on Card VIII, the failure on Card VI and the comments scattered throughout the protocol. Symbolically, there is an over-awareness of objects with parts lacking (Card II, "two elephant heads without trunks"; Card III, "two men with only one leg and one hand"; Card V, "body of a man without hands and without head"; Card VII, "two elephants with only one leg"). This sense of being lacking, incomplete, inadequate, is what causes the subject to move in circumscribed, cautious, overcontrolled fashion. He dares not take chances.

It is very possible that the exaggerated need for control that this boy now manifests is tied in with prepuberty problems. For a child who has had so much difficulty finding and asserting himself, the changes that take place at this time, physical and psychological, the need to reevaluate the self, would be unusually tension producing. He therefore emphasizes constriction rather than permit himself the indulgence in fantasy that is so typical for this age group. That he is capable of maintaining his control despite the obvious shocks he is experiencing (especially Cards IV, VI, IX) points up the efficacy of his therapy.

Again it is the behavioral responses rather than the test interpretations that give indication of the seriousness of this boy's underlying disturbance. In particular his remark on Card VI, "I wonder what you are writing down," reveals the latent paranoid quality of this boy's outlook. Confronted with concrete evidence of his inadequacy, he becomes most suspicious. Similarly, on Card IX, the awareness of failure produces whispered comments.

In summary, this boy is a schizophrenic who, at the age of seven, was presenting such seriously disturbed behavior as to be unable to attend school or get along at home. With therapy he made definite gains, becoming less anxious and more able to accept his fantasies. With the coming of prepuberty he once more resorted to overcontrol, presenting a picture not unlike that seen in severe obsessive-compulsives. At this time, his control efforts were successful and, although they curtailed spontaneity, they also enabled him to maintain good contact with reality, despite paranoid trends.

RECORD No. 29

Schizophrenic Boy, Age 7 Years 10 Months, I.Q. 96

Card	Response	Inquiry	Location	Determinant	Content	P
I. 16"	1. Looks like somebody dead and all bloody, a monster.	Like a cat's face. Phew! Doesn't it look like blood all scattered around? (dots are blood)	WS	F−	Ad	
II. 22"	1. Two feet.	(top red) Not feet. It's inside of somebody.	D	F−	Hd	
	Λ V 2. His bottom where he makes bowels, place where all the bowels are.	(space and top center detail) Just looks like it.	DS	F−	At	
	3. Like a seashell.	(lower red) All pointy.	D	F+	A Obj	
III. 15"	Ugh!					
	1. Partly a butterfly.	(center red) Looks more like a butterfly.	D	F+	A	P
	2. Partly a mouse, two mice.	(side red) Cause it has like a tail.	D	F+	A	P
	3. Two men with kettles.	They look like ladies, they have long noses like Jimmy Durante.	W	M	H	
IV. 11"	1. This looks like a man that doesn't have any head, only a little head.	See his arms and his legs and his scarecrow.(?) (scarecrow is lower center detail)	W	F+	H	
V. 13"	Ugh!					
	1. Bat. (throws down card) Who made these blots?	Look at the wings.	W	F+	A	P
VI. 18"	1. This part looks like a butterfly.	(top detail) It's a moth, has cracked up wings.	D	F+	A	
	2. Otherwise it looks like a coat, some kind of skin.	Just made it up. Looks like paws, an opened up skin.	W	F+	Clo	

VII. 11"	D	F+	A	1. Bug.	(lower center detail) Long and thin.
	W	F+	N	2. Like a steep precipice.	All bumps, where he is gonna fall.
VIII. 16"	d	F+	Obj	1. Like an arrow stuck in somebody, you know.	(smaller center midline) Just stuck.
	(D	FM A	P)	(Hey doesn't this look like rat climbing?)	(usual animal)
IX. 16"	W	F–	Ad	1. Looks like a butterfly wing I can't make that out.	When it's dead it's often cracked up and stuff.
X. 40"				(Looks around room, plays with reflection of sun on his hand, etc.)	
	D	F+	Pl	1. This doesn't look like anything but a half chopped down tree—and its root all ready to fall down the cliff.	(top gray) Ready to fall.
	(D	F+ A)		(Add. This looks like a seahorse.)	(lower green) Long with a curved head.

R   16 + 2

W	4 ⎫		F+	11 ⎫ 15 + 1	A	5 ⎫ 7 + 2	P	3 + 1
W	2 ⎬ 7		F−	4 ⎭	Ad	2 ⎭		
WS	1 ⎭				H	2		
			M	1	Hd	1		
D	7 ⎫ 8 + 2		FM	0 + 1	At	1		
DS	1 ⎭				Clo	1		
					A Obj	1		
d	1				Obj	1		
					Pl	1		
					N	1		

W	44%		F	94%	A	44%
D	50%		F+	73%		
d	6%					

$$M : C$$
$$1 : 0$$

$$Fm + FM : C' + c$$
$$0 : 0$$

$$VIII + IX + X = 18\%$$

This record contains a number of features frequently found in the protocols of schizophrenic children. Outstanding is this boy's anxiety which is reflected in his many responses dealing with horrifying, morbid concepts (Cards I, VIII, IX, X), his fear of losing his balance (especially Cards VII and X), and his preoccupation with his body (Card II). His initial "Ugh" on Cards III and V suggests that even on those cards which do not appear to evoke disturbance he is nevertheless experiencing some discomfort. In fact, practically all stimuli and all circumstances produce marked anxiety and tension in this subject.

The fact that his first three responses are all poor form points up the extremity of the impact that new and unexpected experiences have on this boy. In unfamiliar and unstructured situations, it is most likely that this child will lose control altogether and become seriously disorganized. The unexpected mobilizes all his fears and distorts all his perceptions. While this type of initial disorganization is not necessarily confined to schizophrenics, it is a frequent phenomenon for these subjects.

Along with this boy's extreme anxiety there goes a striking lack of personality resources. This subject has almost no channels through which to drain off his feelings and impulses. Affect and impulse therefore find outlets in direct, overt behavior. The fears, the horrors and the aggression revealed in his interpretations are therefore something very real, something this boy lives with, not feelings or ideas that find expression in fantasy, conscious and unconscious. This barrenness of personality is part of this boy's sharp emotional withdrawal which manifests itself not only in his failure to give any color answers, but in the fact that only 18 per cent of his responses occur on the last three cards. On the other hand, the fact that his approach to the first all-colored card takes the form of a small detail strongly suggests that he is not as emotionally blunted as he appears, that he is aware of emotional stimuli though unable to respond positively to them.

The very quick initial reaction time which this boy shows to every card except one (and the delay on X seemed determined more by matters extraneous to the test stimulus than by any need or effort to avoid the blot) is typical of the behavior of certain schizophrenic children. Since all situations are perceived almost exclusively in subjective terms and little differentiation is made among them, they are all responded to in about the same time. Again, since the subject is sure that all experiences are of a disturbing and horrifying order, and also since he has no ways of warding this off, does not have to select among a variety of ways for dealing with these experiences and actually cannot defend himself against the anxiety thus mobilized, his reactions come forth without any delay.

The very obvious symbolism of this boy's responses, along with his failure even to attempt symbolization in some instances (Card I especially), is again a frequent finding among some schizophrenic children. In these cases the disturbances are close to consciousness, or actually in consciousness, with little effort made to repress or disguise them. In this case it is very evident that it is his masculinity and the impulses that derive from this masculinity that frighten this boy. (Card IV, the lower center detail, the usual "penis," is what makes the man a scarecrow, particularly since he has only a small head, or limited control.) Again, the tree about to fall on Card X and the precipice "where he is gonna fall" on Card VII give direct evidence of this subject's extremely precarious balance. His first response furthermore is a direct statement of his morbid, frightening preoccupations. That he is capable of more controlled and objective perceptions is indicated by the fact that his two additional responses are quite adequate, and in line with commonly accepted reactions. On the inquiry, even his first formulation to Card I—"the cat's face"—shows a capacity to share in fairly usual concepts. In other words, when his anxiety is even momentarily allayed, he is capable of more acceptable forms of response. He thus gives indication that there is no impairment in his visual perceptions nor in his organizing capacities. His difficulties and deviations are all the result of the atypical associations that he brings to his experiences. This is characteristic of all schizophrenics.

Another typically schizophrenic disturbance is found in this boy's confusion as to what is inside and what is outside. Thus, on Card II he first saw "feet," but later insisted it was not feet, but something inside the body. He could not elaborate this concept further, but his shift here suggests that he is not sure what is inside and what is outside. In other words there appears to be some confusion in his body image concept, again of a type found in schizophrenics.

The first two responses to Card III also show some atypicalities. The usual butterfly was first interpreted as "partly a butterfly" and the side red as "partly a mouse." The subject was unable to explain why he had said "partly," but it may be inferred that the use of "partly" was caused by the fact that he was responding to the red areas as if they were one stimulus. If this inference is correct it points to a highly deviant approach to affective stimuli.

In general the findings of this protocol point to gross disturbances and deviations in all areas of functioning. This child sees the world as a morbid, frightening place and he therefore withdraws sharply from it. In particular he views the family as unstable and nonsupporting, the mother as cold, hard and threatening, the father as frightening and uncontrolled. He cannot handle the anxiety which he experiences, has no means of repressing, sublimating or otherwise dealing with this, and so probably acts out his distorted and aggressive impulses and feelings in unacceptable fashion.

This child was so disturbed that the school would no longer put up with him. Similarly, the parents were at their wits' ends as to how to handle him at home. He walked about the house talking to himself, threatening everyone, insisting that his food was poisoned and that strangers were lurking about waiting to kill him. He rarely slept at night and kept his whole family awake, as well as the neighbors. After a short period of therapy, he calmed down a bit, and at present seems to be making relatively good progress. He recently returned to school and is managing to get along. The Rorschach record was taken before the child started therapy, at the time when his anxiety was at its peak.

Record No. 30

Schizophrenic Boy, Age 8 Years 4 Months, I.Q. 192

					Response	Inquiry
I. 67"	W	F+	At	13"	1. I should say that it might be—can't exactly be—the bone structure of an animal. Except that bone structure is solid. (urged) As a matter of fact, inkblots never get this size or as symmetrical as this.	It's hard to say of what animal, a bird maybe.
II. 65"	W	F±	Design	18"	Doesn't look like anything familiar particularly, but if I can think for a few minutes......	
				28"	1. Nothing except a design of unusual shape.	(asked design of what?) Nothing in particular.
III. 40"	W	M	H P	16"	1. Not counting the red it would look somewhat like two people tugging at the outsides of a pot.	(asked if the people were men or women?) One is male and one is female.
	D	F+	Obj P		2. Looks like a bowtie.	(usual) A red bowtie.
IV. 40"	DW	Fc±	A	18"	1. I'd say it looks somewhat like the shape of some animal, the head suggests a raccoon but there is a slight exaggeration in the rest of it, especially the thick tail.	The coloring over here is like fur.

RECORD No. 30—*continued*

					Response	Inquiry
V. 18"	Dr	F+	A		1. Without these parts it might be a moth or butterfly—with the end it doesn't look like anything.	(center and a small unusual portion of the wings) Form of it.
VI. 40"					Laughs. Doesn't suggest anything but an inkblot. Can I turn it?	
∧∨38"	W	F±	Emblem		1. Can't see anything in particular except perhaps an emblem of something.	(emblem of what?) Nothing in particular.
VII. 20"	W	F+	A & Rocks		1. Well it looks something like two rabbits or other small animals on rocks.	Shape, pointed ear. (why rocks?) No reason I can think of, just a high spot on the earth.
VIII. 20"	D	FM	A	P	1. All I can see is two buffalo like animals climbing up this, whatever it is.	(usual animals)
	W	C/F±	Design		2. Say this is a multicolored design.	Many colors and shapes.
IX. 26"		......			I can't see anything in this.	Seems to suggest certain things one way and not another.
X. 59"	W	C/F±	Design		1. That's a pretty design.	All the colors and shapes.
	D	F+	A		2. All I can see is two snakes of some kind, I can't find anything else.	(lower green) curved and snakelike head.

R   12

W	6⎫	F⁺	5⎫	A	5	P	3	
W	1⎬8	F±	2⎬7	H	1			
DW	1⎭	F−	0⎭	At	1			
		M	1	Design	3			
D	3	FM	1	Emblem	1			
				Obj	1			
Dr	1	C/F	2±	Rocks	0 + 1			
		Fc	1±					
W	67%	F	58%	A	42%			
D	25%	F+	71%					
Dr	8%							

$$M : C$$
$$1 : 2$$

$$Fm + FM : C' + c$$
$$1 : \tfrac{1}{2}$$

$$VIII + IX + X = 33\%$$

This record is included primarily because of the unusually high I.Q. this subject attained. This boy's mental capacities are in marked contradistinction to his emotional immaturity and his general personality development and integration. Actually, he appears to be employing his extraordinary intellectual assets in critical, destructive fashion (especially Cards I, IV, V), rather than in a way that would indicate a positive, accepting attitude toward himself and others. This critical, nonconforming approach to the environment is not simply the result of this subject's excellent capacities which enable him to perceive his experiences differently from others. Rather, it stems from insecurity and anxiety which make him overly cautious and unwilling to commit himself. If he were less able he would probably simply block on most of the cards, or deny his responses to them more directly. As it is, he certainly avoids committing himself in many circumstances.

This boy is extremely rigid and stimulus-bound. He cannot enter into any experience in easy, comfortable manner Neither does he permit himself any ready flow of fantasy or feeling. Rather, he tries to handle all his experiences in highly rational, overcontrolled fashion. As a result, despite his resources, he shows relatively few interests and he certainly has not developed his personality assets. These are only hinted at, but never brought to fruition.

Most conspicuous is the subject's inability to deal effectively with emotional experiences. In practically every instance where affective stimuli are introduced, he shows most inadequate behavior, either blocking completely or regressing sharply (Cards II, VIII, IX, X). The best he can do when confronted with emotional demands is to resort to concepts which were acceptable when he was much younger, but which certainly are not appropriate now (perseveration of "design"). Again, this emotional inadequacy is all out of line with the indication he gives of sensitivity and maturity, the effort he makes to bind his anxiety and deal with it in adult fashion (Fc±). Even though his constant doubting and carping foil this effort, the ability to respond to nuances is certainly present.

The subject's rigidity not only makes it impossible for him to disregard nonessentials in any situation and respond to it as most people do, but by the same token curtails a free flow of associations. For a child of his capacities, his content is extremely meager and undiversified. Yet at the same time there is a need to deal with his experiences in a high-handed, all encompassing fashion (8 whole interpretations), which is markedly at variance with the inadequacies and avoidance efforts he shows. Similarly, despite his caution and over-criticalness, he frequently shows a very arbitrary attitude and deals indiscriminately with reality (decides that one of the figures on Card III is a man and one a woman; Card VIII, "Say, this is a multicolored design").

The conflicts and deviations in personality functioning which this child manifests cannot be attributed solely to his exceptional mental abilities. Subjects with such exceptionally high I.Q.'s do tend to meet their experiences on a somewhat detached, formal level. However, all other things being equal, they do not show the conflicts and regression found in this instance.

This child shows seriously disorganized behavior both in school and at home. He is apparently unable to achieve any sort of emotional adaptation, and is remote from everyone. His thinking has a highly deviant coloring, at times becoming almost bizarre. Psychiatric diagnosis was childhood schizophrenia.

RECORD No. 31

Schizophrenic Boy, Age 9 Years 0 Months, I.Q. 128

Card	Time	Response	Inquiry	Loc.	Det.	Content	P
I. 43"	2"	1. Looks like a dragon, a face, I don't know, a devil. All things that are bad, something ferocious, it has ears, horns, a beard and it stares.	This is the face. (indicates entire blot—the spaces are the eyes, the usual wings the ears, the mittened hand the horns) It has horns and ears and looks ferocious.	WS	F+	(Ad)→(Hd)	
II. 20"	4"	1. Looks like a cat, looks like an animal, just the face.	(center space is a mouth, but can point out no other parts) I don't know what the rest of it is.	WS	F−	Ad	
III. 18"	3"	1. These are all practically the same, all mouths, face.	(the mouth is the space between the legs of the usual human figures) All have mouths, mouth of a person.	WS	F+	Hd	
	∧∨	2. Looks like a man, the face part of him.	(lower center detail and center red which is the mouth) Mouth is red.	DS	FC−	Hd	
IV. 18"	6"	Shrugs—I don't know anything about these.					
	13"	1. Looks like a beaver skin, it has fur. (Add. Spider, lots of legs.)	Just feels like fur, (runs hand over card) and a head. (lower center detail)	D (W	cF F− A)	A Obj	
V. 8"	3"	1. A fly, I mean a butterfly.	A bat, it has wings and legs.	W	F+	A	P
VI. 10"	5"	1. Well, it looks somewhat like a fish.	Like a blowfish, the round of it. (indicates shape with his hands)	W	F+	A	

RECORD No. 31—*continued*

Card	Response	Loc.	Det.	Content	Inquiry
VII. 9"	1. Design	W	F±	Design	It doesn't have any character on this one, it's just like a design.
	(Add. No people, but a spider, and an elephant's head.) (middle third)	(W	F−	A)	
		(D	F+	Ad)	
VIII. 15"	1. Design too.	W	C/F±	Design	Colors altogether. (usual animals) (asked what animals they might be he says) Lizards. (asked what they might be doing he replies) Crawling up the design.
	2. And there's some animals on it.	D	F+	A P	
IX. 15"	Shrugs				Combination of colors. Colors and form somewhat.
10"	1. Design combination.	W	C/F±	Design	
	2. Looks like coral somewhat. (Add. Could be a spider, I don't know.) (orange area with extensions as legs)	W	C/F±	N	
		(D	F−	A)	
X. 18"	1. Design.	W	C/F±	Design	Combination of colors.
	2. Painting.		(Denial)		I didn't say that, you got it wrong.
	3. Looks like leaves in it.	D	FC−	Pl	(top green and orange) Shape and color.
	4. Birds.	D	F−	A	(side brown) They have the characteristics.
	5. Lobsters.	D	F+	A	(side blue) Have claws.

R   16 + 4

W	7		F+	6		A	5		P 2
WS	3	10 + 2	F±	1	9 + 4	Ad	1	7 + 4	
			F−	2		(Ad) → (Hd)	1		
D	5		FC	2−		Hd	2		
DS	1	6 + 2	C/F	4±		Design	4		
			cF	1		A Obj	1		
						N	1		
						Pl	1		

W	63%		F	56%		A	44%
D	37%		F+	67%			

$$M : C$$
$$0 : 5$$

$$Fm + FM : C' + c$$
$$0 : 1$$

$$VIII + IX + X = 50\%$$

It is evident from the nature of this boy's reactions to the Rorschach test that he is not adjusting in line with expectancy nor performing at a level commensurate with the potentialities reflected in his I.Q. of 128. Rather, there is repeated evidence that his perceptions are distorted and inadequate, his control and objectivity poor. Conspicuous are the "stickness" of his thinking and his lack of flexibility. The former is reflected in his rather considerable perseveration, the latter in the rigidity of his approach to all circumstances. Even when the situation is a complex one, this boy cannot alter his method of tackling it. In every instance he feels compelled to give a whole response as his first answer, and only then can he attempt more practical and better methods of dealing with the matter confronting him. There is something ritualistic in the way he goes about this. That this ritualistic approach does not in any way facilitate his adjustment but rather results in inadequate and inappropriate reactions does not serve to deter him.

The threats against which he feels he must defend himself by recourse to ritual would seem to be primarily his own oral aggressive impulses which are reflected in his oral and aggressive responses. His handling of Cards VII and IV indicates that this disturbance leads back to and is closely associated with disturbances in his relationship with the mother. Initially he finds the diffuseness of Card VII too much. His response to it is indicative of his way of reacting to his own inadequacies and confusion—recourse to intellectualization of a highly superficial, infantile order. His subsequent interpretation of "spider," the symbol for the aggressive, all-absorbing mother figure, followed by the "elephant's head," suggests a train of associations which goes from a "spider-mother" to a "phallic" mother. Again, the additional interpretation of Card IV as "spider" may well indicate that the mother is the primary authority figure in this boy's life.

The many "face" responses, especially the quality of some of these interpretations (Card I), indicate that this boy perceives the world as a frightening, threatening place. Thus his very first interpretation is that of a "dragon," a mysterious, unreal figure which soon evokes association with the devil and with evil. He says quite spontaneously "Things that are bad, something ferocious, it has ears, horns and a beard and it stares." That he experiences guilt and anxiety in relation to evil and ferocity is obvious. Yet judging by the nature of all his productions, the only identifications this boy can make are with characters who possess "other world" qualities and are conspicuous for the fact that they symbolize evil, danger and aggression. Certainly the distinction between human, animal and supernatural is not clear to this child. (Card I changes from "dragon" to "face" to "devil"; Card III starts by remarking on the similarity of the cards, then interprets a man's face whereas the response to the previous card had been an animal's face.)

In the emotional area this boy shows serious defects. Practically all his efforts to relate to the environment on an emotional basis are of a forced, arbitrary order (4 C/F±) and, when he does attempt more mature and integrated forms of response, his control and understanding are not adequate to the circumstances (2 FC−). Despite the inadequacy of his emotional contacts with the outside world, it is evident that this boy is extremely dependent upon that world (50 per cent of his responses on Cards VIII, IX, X). This dependency is the greater because the subject apparently has no capacity for dealing with his emotional experiences on a fantasy level. Rather, the absence of M and FM responses, in conjunction with the weird nature of his interpretations, strongly suggests that much of what in others would be internalized is, in this case, permitted to come directly into consciousness and is responded to on that level.

Feelings of inadequacy and negativism are reflected in the subject's persistent use of white spaces on the first three cards. However, this emphasis on spaces stops at this point and does not reappear. It may therefore be indicative primarily of the anxiety and concomitant resistance that the test situation, or any unfamiliar situation, would evoke in this child.

The subject's failure to recall his second response on Card X has considerable significance. This response, which is very similar to the "design" response which precedes it, is followed by the interpretation "leaves." Leaves are among the most primitive identifications the child can make, pointing to inability to develop a self-concept beyond this primitive level, and to great concern about himself and his identification. The response "painting" was probably introduced to ward off the anxiety that flooded him in relation to the "leaf" interpretation and, when the situation reappeared, he could no longer remember that he had used this device to delay his approach to an anxiety-evoking stimulus.

In summary, this is a well endowed but seriously disturbed child. He is unable to develop any sort of stable, integrated self-concept nor establish meaningful and reassuring emotional and interpersonal relationships. Rather, his emotional experiences are characterized by arbitrariness and weak control. Reality concepts are inadequate, distorted by his own autistic needs. His disturbed perceptions and relationships find expression in his reactions to the mother. He sees her as an overwhelming, devouring figure who has not permitted him to develop on his own or in any way helped him to find the "self." The anxiety that his lack of integration and structure produces makes for rather marked regression in all areas.

Despite the severity of this boy's difficulties, there are certain positive features here, and from the therapeutic point of view the outlook is reasonably good. Conspicuous in this respect are the following: the strong efforts to meet each situation, rather than withdrawing from it, and the dependence on the environment, especially as it manifests itself in the attempts to achieve mature emotional relationships (FC).

The subject is the only child of intelligent, well educated parents. They have tried to bring this child up in a way that would provide him with considerable opportunity for spontaneity and self-expression. Nevertheless, the child states that he is pushed about and dominated, especially by the mother. His overt behavior during the past few years has been characterized by agitation, aggression and tension. This is more marked when he is home, but is also noted in school. He is like so many of these children who can neither find themselves nor set up self-limits, and who perform best in the purely formal, well structured areas where no emotional demands are made on them. Psychiatric diagnosis was childhood schizophrenia.

CHAPTER XIII

Organic Disorders of the Central Nervous System

ISORDERS of the central nervous system include such conditions as postencephalitis, birth injury and brain injury as a result of trauma. Children suffering from such conditions generally have difficulty in controlling their impulses and in developing patterned concepts in all areas, intellectual, social, emotional, perceptual and motor, with the result that their experiences tend to be weakly organized and lacking in stability. They frequently have learning difficulties, and are generally less mature and self-sufficient than they should be. Instead, the weakness of their personality organization makes for easy disorganization and regression. Disruptive behavior, emotional, social and motor, is therefore frequent. Because of the difficulties they experience and the anxiety that their inadequate control and ready disruption mobilizes, they are on the whole more dependent than the average child in their age group.

The child with an organic disorder has all the problems that other children are called upon to face, plus the problems associated with his disturbances in perception and his easy disorganization. His failure to achieve at levels commensurate with the standards he has set for himself in various areas of experience produces multiple frustrations and thus increases the anxiety which he can so poorly control. In his efforts at adjusting, he adopts the behavioral patterns which give him the greatest sense of security and satisfaction. In some instances this leads to exaggerated withdrawal and dependency, in others to compulsive efforts at reinforcing control and still in others to repeated and rapid indulgence in impulse satisfaction.

Disorders of the central nervous system manifest themselves iu Rorschach protocols only when the disturbances are located in the cortical and subcortical areas. The way in which they are reflected varies from child to child, depending upon the nature and extent of the damage that has been sustained, the age of the child, his assets, his past experiences and the type of adjustment he had made up to the time of illness or injury.

In most instances of organic disorder in children, difficulties in control and perception can be readily detected in their records. The number of poor form responses is generally in excess of that obtained from healthy children of similar age and ability. The difficulties they encounter in attempting to handle their experiences adequately frequently lead to emotional outbursts or sharp regression or both. Thus the records are likely to be of a perseverative order and to contain responses which indicate emotional disorganization and primitive infantile attitudes and interests (inclusion of many responses characteristic of the very young child, such as "leaf," "water," "fire").

That the child is aware of his inadequacy and is concerned about it produces one of two extremes of behavior. The child is likely to protest constantly concerning his inability to deal with the given circumstances, or he will try to compensate for his keenly felt limitations by rushing into his experiences in ill considered, impulsive fashion with resulting inappropriate reactions. In the first instance the child will make innumerable statements about his inability, will constantly insist that he does not know how or cannot do it. These protestations will far exceed those ordinarily obtained from children and will be accompanied by requests for help, reassurance and guidance.

That his inadequacies are very real and hampering to him is demonstrated not only by the poor form responses and perseveration so characteristic of his records, but also by the frequency with which he will fail to interpret altogether and lapse into description. Color naming and color description are usual in the records of these children, but this ineffectual way of dealing with his experiences is not limited to the color cards alone. In many cases other cards are also met on this inadequate level. In such instances, interpretation is sometimes also achieved, but in some cases it is never effected.

The severe anxiety these children suffer adds to their difficulties and increases their ineffectiveness. In the Rorschach records, this anxiety often shows itself in considerable midline emphasis; in symmetry awareness; in frequent production of responses using "black"; in recourse to compulsive efforts at handling situations, covering all aspects of them or going over and over them and, finally, in direct expression of this anxiety.

As compensation for the deep inadequacy these children experience, one frequently finds considerable intellectual pretentiousness—interpretations dealing with geography, anatomy and other concepts which the child is not really equipped to handle and which he deals with very poorly. In some instances there is also evidence of considerable self-assertiveness accompanied by a kind of "whistling in the dark" attitude. The child will make a statement about the card in a tone of finality which brooks of no argument or contradiction, and yet go on discussing it or strongly asserting that, "That's right, it has to be that way," in his infantile efforts to reassure himself and bolster his self-esteem. While other children also resort to such a mechanism, it is not usual to find it in the face of the really overwhelming ineffectualness manifested by the organically disturbed child.

As part of his general disturbance in organization, there are certain responses which may be considered pathognomonic for the "organic" subject. These are the responses which specifically point up the disturbance in the patient's body image. For example, a subject gave the interpretation of a face on Card II, using the white space between the top red and the black as the eyes, the large center white space as the nose and the detail *above* the space as the mouth. When asked how the mouth could possibly be above the nose the subject looked confused and distressed but had no explanation of his deviant perception.

In some children suffering from an organic disorder, there is a sharp contrast between the way, they handle the chromatic and achromatic cards. They find great difficulty in interpreting the black cards, seem unable to analyze them or organize them adequately. Confronted with the colored blots, they are able to make distinctions among the different areas because of the sharp differentiations provided by the colors. Thus they can handle these situations more effectively than the others. It cannot be assumed in such cases that it is the emotional factors that help these children, but simply the visual aid provided by the color contrasts.

Differentiation between the productions of the schizophrenic and the organically disturbed child is often difficult to make. In both instances, inability to deal successfully with the stimuli, disturbed perceptions, regression and disorganization are marked. However, in the "organic" child there is likely to be little negativism, even in those extreme cases where the child has difficulty complying with the requirements of the situation because of the push of his impulses and his consequent inability to sit quietly and attend to the demands being made on him. Likewise the "organic" child strives to do something about the assignment, even if the best he can offer is enumeration of color or description of blot.

In many instances the personality structure is so primitive that little control or delay of impulse can take place. However, in those cases where the structure is more complex, the child's struggle to keep his drives in hand, the tension that is evoked by the dangers implicit in the release of his drives and the energy he puts into checking them are manifested in the emphasis on animal movement responses. In most instances where any internalization of conflict and fantasy takes place, it will be of a childlike order and there will be only FM interpretations, in contrast to the schizophrenic child (see p. 184), who acts out his primitive impulses without making much effort at checking them, yet is at the same time absorbed in fantasy about his problems in identification. In his case there are likely to be M responses without FM responses—the reverse of what occurs in the organically disturbed child.

RECORD No. 32

Boy with Convulsions, Age 3 Years 5 Months, I.Q. 95

				Response	Inquiry
I.	W	F –	Obj	1. It's a lamp.	That's dark black. Is it heavy? A big lamp.
II.	W	F –	Obj	1. Another lamp.	Because it has to be a lamp.
III.	W	F –	Obj	1. Lamp is in it.	
IV.	W	F –	Obj	1. Lamp is in it.	
	DW	F –	A	2. Its a "turkel."	Because of this. (usual arm) (means a turkey and side projection seen as neck and head)
V.	W	F –	A	1. A turkel is in it.	See? (holds up blot for Examiner to see)
VI.	W	F –	A	1. Turkel's in it.	
VII.	W	F –	A	1. Turkel's in it.	(turns around, back and forth) Cause it wants to be.
VIII.	W	F –	A	1. Turkel's in it.	
IX.	W	F –	A	1. Turkel's in it.	
X.	W	F –	A	1. Turkel's in it.	

R   11

W	10⎫		F+	0⎫		A	7		P	0
DW	1⎭10		F−	11⎭		Obj	4			

W	100%		F	100%		A	64%
			F+	0%			

M : C
0 : 0

Fm + FM : C′ + c
0 : 0

VIII + IX + X = 27%

This child's inability to give even one good form response suggests some lag in his development, some inability to achieve even the simplest concept of reality on an adequate basis. Not only are his reactions indicative of an extremely arbitrary approach to his experiences, but there is no evidence of any richer potential.

On the basis of the test findings, nothing more can be determined about this boy. At best, it can be suspected that his personality development is not keeping pace with his chronological age and mental growth.

Record No. 33

Boy with Convulsions, Age 6 Years 1 Month, I.Q. 107

	Loc.	Det.	Content	P	Response	Inquiry
I. 28"	W	F–	Map (Descript.)		1. Looks like a map. I see something, looks the same over here and here (symmetry awareness), but has a line down the middle.	It's a map of America, the biggest map.
II. 31"	S	F–	Arch		1. This could be I think a lighthouse, but has this jumping on it—I don't know what it is.	(space) Round like a light house.
	WS	CF–	Map		2. If you turn it this way it could be New York.	Sometimes they're red and white.
III. 48"	W	F–	H		1. Kind of a man like, so silly, he has his hand on his jacket.	Can't shake hands because the hands are over here. (usual legs—organization of men all confused)
	D	F+	Clo	P	2. Bowtie.	(usual) Just like a bowtie.
	D	F–	Arch		3. Like a lighthouse.	(lower center) Shaped round.
IV. 26"	DW	F–	A		1. Ox it must be.	(lower center detail is head, becomes all confused in accounting for rest)
	W	F+	H		2. King you got here.	Big king, and that's his chair.
V. 19"	W	F+	A	P	1. Looks like a butterfly.	I know.
	W	F+	A		2. Like a bird.	It's a big bird.
	W	F–	A		3. Like a bumblebee.	Got stingers.
VI 33"	DW	F–	Arch		1. Kind of a lighthouse, I think.	Got a big thing sticking out on top.
	W	F–	A		2. Think it's an octopus. I think I don't know what it is, ink spilled.	(large lower section) Lots of arms.

RECORD No. 33—*continued*

VII. 17"	S	3"	1. Sort of like an open cave or tunnel.	Just a big empty place.	F+	Cave
VIII. 15"	W	5"	1. I think it looks like a sailboat.	Round like and a point on top.	F+	Obj
IX. 16"	DS	4"	1. Looks like a little place where you can—a place like a nest—where you can dig out of.	(pumpkinlike detail in center) All round like.	F+	Obj
X. 15"	D	2"	1. I know what this is, it's different colored clouds, so silly, one is pulling the other.	(picks out various details as clouds) All colors and round like clouds.	CmF	Cl

R   17

W	6⎤		F+	7⎤15		A	5		P	2
W	2⎱11		F−	8⎦		H	2			
DW	2					Map	2			
WS	1⎦		CF	1		Arch	3			
			CmF	1		Clo	1			
D	3⎱4					Cave	1			
DS	1⎦					Obj	2			
						Cl	1			
S	2									

W	64%		F	88%		A	29%
D	24%		F+	47%			
S	12%						

$$M : C$$
$$0 : 2$$

$$Fm + FM : C' + c$$
$$1 : 0$$

$$VIII + IX + X = 18\%$$

This boy's efforts to achieve equilibrium are definitely hampered by his inability to organize his experiences at a level commensurate with his age and mental ability (only 47 per cent F+). His lags and deviations are indicated not only by his poor form percentage, but by his failure to develop a capacity for internalization (no M or FM), and by his perseverative tendencies.

The subject expresses his sense of instability almost immediately (symmetry awareness on Card I), as well as his feelings of inadequacy. It is evident that there are many moments of stress when he feels especially lacking, and it is then in particular that he falls back on methods of adjustment which are no longer appropriate (utilizing responses already given because of inability to develop any better formulations).

His special need for shelter and security finds very obvious reflections in his "cave" and "nest" responses (Cards VII and IX), and there are some aspects of his performance that suggest he is not getting as much comfort and reassurance from the environment as he needs and seeks. One such indication is the inability of the men to shake hands (Card III). It is true that his organic disorder, his inability to organize a human body in usual fashion (suggesting disturbances in body image), is probably responsible for his distorted perception here. However, his stress on the social and interpersonal disturbances involved in this production must stem from his own problems, his own failure to find human contact.

There is a pretentiousness in the way this boy resorts to map responses and tries to justify them. This pretentiousness is probably induced by efforts to overcompensate for his inadequacies and his need to impress others and win approbation from them.

The overall picture is clearly one of lag and deviation in development. The nature of some of the productions suggests that this lag is probably caused by some organic disorder of the central nervous system which interferes particularly with the subject's ability to organize an adequate body image and self-concept. However, on the basis of the Rorschach findings alone, such a diagnosis would be most tentative. Other tests, however, also pointed strongly to such a finding.

This boy is an only child of lower middle class parents. They are very ambitious for him and push him a great deal, socially and intellectually. A few months before this record was taken, he entered the first grade and, according to the teacher, has not made a good adjustment or progressed as well as the other children. The mother was disturbed by this report and spoke to the family physician about it, particularly since this child has been on medication for a number of years because he had had seizures when he was two and three. The seizures have been well controlled—in fact there have been none for sometime—but psychological test findings certainly indicate the presence of some organic disturbance. In addition, this child does not seem to be receiving as much emotional support as he should.

RECORD No. 34

Postencephalitis in a Girl, Age 7 Years 10 Months, I.Q. 87

				Response	Inquiry
I. 23"	W	F± (Descript.)	Map	1. A map. (urged) I see holes, has lines over it.	Shaped like it.
II. 20"	D	C	Fire	1. Fire.	(all red) Cause it's red.
	W	F±	Map	2. Map.	Looks like it.
III. 13"	D	C	Fire	1. Fire.	(all red) Cause it's red.
	WS	F±	Map	2. With half a map with water.	(white is water) Looks like it.
IV. 38"	DW	Fm	Pl	I don't know. 1. A tree.	Has this on it. (lower center detail)
	W	F−	N	2. With mountains all around. Something hanging from tree, leaves, huh?	Big. (side, armlike details)
V. 29"	W	F−	A	I never saw it. 1. A deer, it has wings, feet on the wings.	I don't know, I never saw it.
VI. 62"	W	MC'−	(H) & Dirt	What's that? I never saw it. 1. Like a giant. I never saw it, a magic giant. What does he want to do, give you silver and gold? Dirt on a face with whiskers.	It's big—a giant so mad. I don't know what he's doing, putting dirt on his face.
VII. 17"	W	C'F	Smoke & Arch	1. Smoke of a house.	Here's the house. (lower center detail) Black all over house, that's smoke.

RECORD No. 34—*continued*

					Inquiry
VIII. 56"				I never heard of it.	
	D	C	Water	4" 1. Blue water.	(blue area) Nice color.
	D	C/F±	N	2. Pink sea.	(lower center) Nice color.
	D	C/F−	Obj	3. Orange dresser.	(lower center) I don't know.
	D	C'F±	Dirt	4. Gray thing is a piece of dirt.	(top detail) (tells story about gray squirrel)
IX. 41"				I told you this one.	
	D	C	Fire	5" 1. Fire.	(pink) Cause it's red.
	D	C/F−	Paper	2. Piece of paper.	(green) Green paper.
	D	C'	smoke	3. Dirty smoke.	(midline) Black.
X. 64"					(side blue)
	D	C	Water	3" 1. Water.	(side yellow) Just a yellow dress.
	D	C/F−	Clo	2. Wearing a yellow dress.	(top gray) Cause it's black.
	D	C'	Smoke	3. Smoke, smoke.	(lower green) Green rug.
	D	C/F−	Obj	4. Rug.	

R   21

W	5		F+	0		A	1		P	0
W	1	8	F±	3	5	H	(1)			
WS	1		F−	2		Map	3			
DW	1					Fire	3			
			MC′	1−		Pl	1			
D	13		Fm	1		N	2			
						Obj	2			
			C/F	5 (4−, 1±)		Clo	1			
			C	5		Water	2			
						Smoke	3			
			C′F	2 (1−)		Paper	1			
			C′	2		Dirt	1 + 1			
						Arch	0 + 1			

W	38%	F	24%	A	5%
D	62%	F+	0%		

$$M : C$$
$$1 : 12\tfrac{1}{2}$$

$$Fm + FM : C' + c$$
$$1 : 6$$

$$VIII + IX + X = 52\%$$

The primitivity and disorganization of this personality manifest themselves in the subject's complete lack of objectivity (no F+ responses), the infantile, uncontrolled nature of her emotional reactions (5 CF−, 5 C) and her inability to analyze a stimulus and deal with it selectively unless aided in doing so by the introduction of discrete blocks of color. Where the blot is not separated by color, she can respond only with a whole interpretation. In addition, at all times, even when the situation becomes somewhat differentiated for her, she reacts impulsively and with an almost complete disregard of objectivity. She projects onto the circumstances whatever occurs to her at the moment in most arbitrary fashion (Card VIII, "orange dresser," Card X, "wearing a yellow dress"). Even her discrimination among the colored stimuli is weak and arbitrary, as indicated by the fact that, when presented with Card IX, she says "I told you this," confusing it with Card VIII solely on the basis of the fact that it too is an all-color blot.

The subject gives frequent expression to her sense of inadequacy and also tries feebly to justify her limitations. Thus there are the frequent statements: "I never saw it," "I never heard of it," "I don't know." Her weaknesses are also reflected in her perseverative tendencies and in her lapses into enumeration and description when she feels pressured (Card I).

Primitive, direct acting out of unresolved conflicts with authority are expressed through the C' responses and also suggested by the content of the responses on Cards VI and VII. The stress on dirt suggests feelings of being "bad," while dependency is reflected in the "leaf" interpretation on IV. In general the content of her responses fluctuates between such primitive concepts as "fire" and "water" on the one hand and pretentious intellectual strivings and adultlike interests as "maps" or "dresser" on the other.

This then is a child whose personality is minimally structured and whose development shows gross lags, being more like that of a three year old than of a child who is nearly eight. In view of the lack of objectivity and control that she shows, it can be assumed that her behavior will be disorganized and unacceptable, influenced little, if at all, by the demands of reality. Her efforts to relate to the environment, as well as a number of her other reactions, reflects her strong dependency on that environment, despite her inability to adjust to it.

This seven year old is suffering from postencephalitis. Her illness has crippled her in many areas. She has a serious speech impediment, cannot master first grade work, cannot get along with other children, and is constantly in difficulties. The parents have placed considerable pressure on her, demanding that she achieve and conform, and they are apparently unable to grasp the fact that her failure to comply with their demands is not just negativism on her part. They are overanxious to have her respond in normal, acceptable fashion, and their efforts to achieve this add greatly to her tension and confusion.

RECORD No. 35

Boy with Degenerative Disease of Central Nervous System, Age 8 Years 8 Months, I.Q. 90.

Card	Loc.	Det.	Content	P	Time	Response	Inquiry
I. 35″	W	F+	A	P	4″	1. Bat.	Body and big wings.
						(urged to give more)	
						2. Body.	(center) Body of the bat.
						3. Bump, two bumps.	(top center detail) On the bat.
II. 44″	D	F+	Hd		20″	These (points to top red), I don't know what they are.	
					32″	1. Foot.	(top red) Shaped that way.
III. 17″	W	M	H	P	6″	1. A man, two men holding a bucket.	Just look like men, got head, body, feet.
	D	F+	Clo	P		2. And a bow.	(center red) Look like it.
IV. 11″	D	F+	Hd	P	7″	1. Feet.	(usual) Big feet like a giant.
V. 12″	D	F+	Ad		4″	1. Ears.	(top detail) Big, like a bat.
	D	F+	Ad			2. Legs.	(lower center detail) Of a different bat.
	D	F+	Ad			3. Wings.	(usual) Spread out like wings.
VI. 32″					8″	I don't know.	
	d	F+	Ad		17″	1. Whiskers.	(little lines on top detail) (of what?) Cat.
	d	F+	Ad			2. Legs.	(side projections) Of a cat.
	d	F+	Ad			3. Another leg.	(small projections on top, side of large lower area) (?) Of cat.
VII. 18″	W	F+	H		2″	1. Two girls.	Shaped like girls.
						2. Hair.	On the girls.
						3. Body.	Of the girls.

RECORD No. 35—continued

VIII. 34"	D	F+	At	1. Ribs.	(usual center area) Looks like ribs.
	D	F−	Hd	2. Shoulder.	(gray) Comes out like it.
	D	F−	At	3. Appendix.	(lower center) Looks like it.
	(D	FM A P)		(Add. Oh, it looks like a fox [usual walking.])	
IX. 26"	D	F+	At	1. Backbone.	(midline) Goes up straight.
	S	Po	At	2. Neck.	(space above midline) That's where it comes.
X. 50"	D	F−	At	1. Ribs.	(top gray) Shaped that way.
	D	F−	At	2. Heart. I've got an encylcopedia.	(usual wishbone) Looks that way.
	D	F+	At	3. Backbone.	(top gray) Looks like it.
	D	F−	At	4. Bone that's in the middle.	(center blue) Just looks like it.

R   21 + 1

W	2⎫3	F+	14⎫19	A	1 + 1⎫7 + 1	P	4 + 1
W	1⎭	F−	5⎭	Ad	6⎭		
				H	2		
D	14 + 1	M	1	Hd	3		
		Po	1	At	8		
d	3⎫4	FM	0 + 1	Clo	1		
S	1⎭						

W	14%	F	90%	A	33%
D	67%	F+	74%		
d + S	19%				

$$M : C$$
$$1 : 0$$

$$Fm + FM : C' + c$$
$$0 : 0$$

$$VIII + IX + X = 43\%$$

Inability to integrate his perceptions and organize his concepts into meaningful wholes (especially Cards V, VI), poverty of associations and rigidity of thought processes are conspicuous in this case. Able to see parts of animals, the subject is unable to relate these parts to one another. Similarly, if he does perceive a whole figure, he is unable to break up the perception and form a new one (Cards, I, VII). It is mainly by selecting isolated aspects of a situation that the subject manages to maintain a certain amount of control and objectivity. However, with the introduction of emotional pressures, and also possibly as fatigue sets in, this control weakens (all the F− responses occur on Cards VIII, IX, X), perceptions become more inadequate (perseveration of body parts) and reasoning deviant (position response on Card IX, possibly on VIII).

The control this boy does achieve is bought at great cost to the total personality development. He either cannot or dare not indulge in fantasy activity of any kind and, aside from his formal pseudointellectual approach to his experiences, has no other way of dealing with them. In such a case, as tensions mount, it would seem inevitable that there would be a direct acting out of impulses since no other channels have been developed for dealing with them.

The subject's marked preoccupation with body parts points to his anxiety about himself and his "intactness." Again, he is able to struggle with this, not adequately but with some success, until confronted with emotionally charged circumstances. Then he strives for control by avoiding the strongly colored areas, and responding almost exclusively to the grays and browns.

Despite these efforts he becomes disorganized and ineffectual. Body concern takes on a morbid coloring. Nevertheless, he tries to perform as he feels he should, and attempts to justify his performance by bringing in recognized authority (Card X, "I've got an encyclopedia").

This, then, is a very anxious child who is trying to conform, but whose efforts in this direction are hampered by his anxiety and by the difficulties he has in integrating his perceptions. Only by avoiding emotional involvement can he maintain control and, even then, his reactions are not truly adequate. As soon as he is confronted with complex and affectively charged circumstances, his judgment becomes very poor. In all circumstances his responses tend to be stereotyped, and he lacks flexibility and resources. Nevertheless, he strives to conform, even though his efforts in this direction frequently serve to highlight his weaknesses. Thus, on Card I, when urged to give additional responses, he tries to meet this demand in the only way he can, by elaborating on what he has already produced. This is a method frequently employed by children who, for one reason or another, are limited in their capacity to associate to the blots, but who feel that they must comply with the examiner's request. In this case, a paucity of associations, in conjunction with the subject's serious disturbance in integration, his complete inability to maintain objectivity in emotional situations, his marked anxiety and his body preoccupation all point to the diagnosis of an organic disorder of the central nervous system.

This child is the older of two, his sister being about two years old. He was born while his father was in military service and did not see him until he was between four and five. During the father's absence, the mother built up the father in every way possible, talking to the boy about him, showing him pictures of the father, etc. When the father returned, the relationship between the parents proved to be most unsatisfactory and, about the time that the sister was born, the father deserted. Shortly after this the boy developed a most striking tic pattern. He would raise his arm and clench his fist as though he were going to strike at someone. At the same time his tongue would dart out violently. The whole picture was one suggesting severe aggression and hostility toward the environment. The boy was placed in therapy but his symptoms did not abate. It was after he had been seen in therapy for about a year that he was given a battery of psychological tests. These all pointed strongly to the presence of an organic disturbance, and neurologic examination confirmed this, indicating that the child was suffering from a deteriorative disease of the central nervous system. Death occurred within the year. The tic pattern he manifested undoubtedly did express his hostility, and his weakened control made it impossible for him to repress such expression of his feelings.

RECORD No. 36

Boy with Congenital Syphilis, Age 9 Years 1 Month, I.Q. 95

I. 23"	WS F+	Obj	1. Medal.	It got wings, and two things on top and open spaces and a point on bottom.
II. 35"	DrS F− (Descript.)	A	I don't know. 1. Butterfly. Red ink is on there and red spots and black spots.	(all red and spaces) That ain't no butterfly. Yes, a dead one. (points to spaces)
III. 25"	W F+ (Descript.)	H P	1. This is a man and this is a man. And the red is inkspots in the middle.	Got a nose and foot and shoes on.
IV. 18"	W FM	(A)	I don't know what this is. 1. Monster.	He's looking down trying to find people to eat. (asked if a monster was human or animal) Animal monster.
V. 7"	W F+	A P	1. Butterfly.	One thing in front and one in back.
VI. 12"	D F+ (Descript.)	A	1. Mosquito, a darning needle rather. And black ink.	(top detail) Cut this off and it looks like a darning needle.
VII. 27"	D F− (Descript.)	A	This is too hard to guess. 1. Mosquito, no a darning needle. And black ink.	(lower third) Long thing in middle.

RECORD No. 36—continued

VIII. 25″	D	F+	A	P	4″ 1. Some kind of a dog on this side and some kind of a dog on that side. And red and blue, and lighter red and lighter blue, etc.	(usual) Four legs and a head.
		Cn				
IX. 20″	D	F+	Pl		3″ 1. Tree.	(pink and midline) Long stick and round on top.
		Cn			And red and green and lighter red, etc.	
X. 49″	(Descript.)				10″ This is a real hard one. Green ink, and red ink, and blue ink, etc. (names color of every detail)	
33″	D	F+	A		1. And a turtle.	(side brown) It's got two legs and a head up here.

R   10

W	2		F+	7		A	7(1)		P	3
W	1	4	F−	2	9	H	1			
WS	1					Pl	1			
			FM	1		Obj	1			
D	5									
			(2 Cn)							
DrS	1									

W	40%		F	90%		A	70%
D	50%		F+	78%			
DRS	10%						

$$M : C$$
$$0 : 0$$

$$Fm + FM : C' + c$$
$$1 : 0$$

$$VIII + IX + X = 30\%$$

Rorschach productions in this case reveal a very limited, barren personality structure. This boy has no way of dealing with experiences except on a formal basis. There is no capacity for enriching his experiences and setting up warm and mutually satisfying interpersonal relationships. Similarly, there is only minimal capacity for fantasy and this is of a very immature order (no color, only 1 Fm, no M).

His naming and description of colors suggests that he is aware of emotional aspects of the environment and would like to do something about them, but is unable to achieve this except on a most infantile level (enumeration and description rather than interpretation of colors). In the face of emotional demands, he becomes disorganized in a way that strongly suggests that he is suffering from an organic disorder.

Another indication of his regressive tendencies is to be found in the mildly perseverative trend he shows ("mosquito" to "darning needle" in two instances).

That this boy finds many situations too much for him is manifested by his own statements. "I don't know" and "This is too hard" appear a number of times in the record. He apparently tries to compensate for his inadequacy with the prestige answer "medal" on Card I, but he ends up with the response "turtle" on Card X, a response revealing the feelings of insecurity and need for shelter.

Because of his very impoverished personality and his inability to appreciate what is involved in interpersonal and social situations, this boy's behavior is likely to be deviant and unacceptable, especially when he is under pressure. It was this behavior which first brought him to the attention of a psychiatrist. Thorough neurologic examination revealed the congenital syphilis.

CHAPTER XIV
Mental Retardation

CHILDREN with limited mental endowment naturally have special problems. The difficulties which they have in learning will often produce deviant concepts and formulations, with the result that their reactions are out of line and unacceptable. In similar fashion, the weakness of their understanding and intellectual control often makes for marked emotional instability. Superimposed on the problems resulting from their congenital weakness are the problems created by environmental demands.

The Rorschach records of mentally retarded children can serve two special functions: they can help establish the degree of emotional stability the subject has achieved and can indicate potentials that may not have been discovered on formal intelligence testing. In fact, the Rorschach can at times give definite indication that the subject actually is not really defective but simply so blocked or inhibited that he cannot use his assets fully and effectively.

In general it is the child with the I.Q. of about 65 to 80 who shows the superimposed emotional problems most keenly. The child with this mental level is partially aware of his inadequacies, feels that he is "different" and recognizes that those who are emotionally important to him are not satisfied with him. The frustration, aggression and tension induced by his limitations and the world's response to these limitations can generally be found in his Rorschach record, along with evidence of his weak organizational capacities, his poor reality testing and possible impulsiveness, lack of control and limited (or complete lack of) capacity for internalization and symbolization.

The four cases of mental retardation presented here were obtained from subjects with very different capacities and problems.

RECORD No. 37

Girl, Age 6 Years 3 Months, I.Q. 67

I. 48"	W	F−	A	1. Duck.	(points out parts in vague, confused manner)
II. 75"	W	F−	A	1. Dog.	(again no well organized concept) (asked to tell more about the dog) He bites me, cause I hate the dog, cause I don't want him to bite me. I'd run to my mother.
	D	F+	Clo	2. Shoe.	(top red) One shoe, looks like another shoe, looks like you walk in.
III. 65"	W	F+	A	1. A horse.	I see a horse with legs.
	D	F−	Clo	2. Hat.	(side red) Big thing on hat.
	D	F−	Clo	3. Dress.	(points uncertainly to lower black center)
IV. 74"	W	F−	Obj	1. Chair.	Big chair.
	D	F−	A	2. Duck.	Duck on the chair. (top half of blot)
V. 74"	W	F−	A	1. Horse.	Big horse.
	W	F−	A	2. Duck.	Just a duck.
VI 51"	W	F−	Pl	1. Chestnut tree.	Big tree.
VII. 30"	W	F−	A	1. Ducks.	(vague pointing)
VIII. 41"	W	F−	Clo	1. Hat.	Three hats (top gray and blue is one hat, lower center another hat, sides are third hat)
IX. 21"	W	F−	A	1. Duck.	A whole duck.
X.	W	F−	A	1. Duck.	Big duck.

R 15

W 10⎫
     ⎬11
W   1⎭

D 4

W 73%
D 27%

F+   2⎫
       ⎬15
F− 13⎭

F   100%
F+ 13%

A   9
Clo 4
Pl   1
Obj 1

A   60%

P 0

M : C
0 : 0

Fm + FM : C′ + c
    0 : 0

VIII + IX + X = 20%

This record is included simply because it shows the similarity between a six year old defective and the productions of an average three year old. Outstanding is the poor reality testing and the arbitrariness with which reality demands are met. There is a striking lack of objectivity, no personality resources and only minimal capacity for differentiation and discrimination.

This little girl is small, pert looking and verbally facile. The parents have therefore not realized the extent of her mental retardation and it was only when she went to school that her inadequacies became conspicuous.

RECORD No. 38

Girl, Age 8 Years 1 Month, I.Q. 59

Card		Response	Location	Determinant	Content	Inquiry
I. 32"	7"	1. Looks like a mouse. (urged to find more) I don't know.	W	F−	A	I said it was a duck, it's a duck.
II. 7"	3"	1. That looks like a chicken.	(Denial) (W	FM	A P)	I said a squirrel, a little elephant, two elephants tasting that—I don't see any chicken.
III. 10"	3"	1. Ducks.	W	F−	A	(usual men) Head, neck, body.
IV. 23"	15"	1. Man. I know what it is but I forgot.	W	F+	H	(what kind of a man?) Bad, awful.
V. 6"	3"	1. Squirrel.	D	F+	A	That (center detail) is the body, but that (wings) isn't the body.
VI. 10"	4"	1. Bird.	W	F−	A	They fly in Central Park. (is this one flying?) No.
VII. 11"	7"	1. Squirrel.	W	F+	(A)	Toys, looks like an animal. We make these in school.
VIII. 12"	3"	1. A midgie.	W	F−	A	(means a pigeon) Face, body.
IX. 12"	4"	1. A midgie.	W	F−	A	Face, body.
X. 10"	3"	1. A midgie.	W	F−	A	Face, body.

R   9 + 1

W   7⎫
W   1⎭ 8 + 1

F+   3⎫
F− ·6⎭ 9

A   8 (1) + 1   P   0 + 1
H   1

D   1

FM   0 + 1

W   89%
D   11%

F   100%
F+   33%

A   89%

M : C
0 : 0

Fm + FM : C′ + c
0 : 0

VIII + IX + X = 33%

This girl's poor mental endowment interferes with reality testing, and her general lack of resources (no movement or color answers) makes stable, mature, meaningful social and interpersonal relationships impossible. This girl shows only minimal capacity for differentiation and discrimination (89 per cent whole responses), and her understanding and judgment are exceptionally poor (33 per cent F+). In general the findings are comparable to those obtained from three and a half to four year olds. Since her mental age is 4 years 9 months, her personality development is not quite on a par with her intellectual level.

This girl is the older of two children. Developmental history is one of retardation in all areas, with late walking, late talking and late toilet training. In fact, the subject's speech is still most childish (note responses on Cards VIII, IX, X) and limited. She has been unable to adjust in school and can only get along with very young children. She cries easily, but is also easily distracted from her grief, as well as from any other activity. She becomes irritable when frustrated, but her anger does not last long and shows itself primarily through momentary sulking.

RECORD No. 39

Girl, Age 9 Years 1 Month, I.Q. 75

Card	Response	Loc.	Determ.	Content	Inquiry
I. 27"	7" 1. Like a bird or something. (urged to find something more)	W	F+	A	Wings, foots, body, like a New York thing. (means NRA emblem)
	2. Like a bear sitting on a tree.	D→W	FM−	A & Pl	(side is bear, but cannot point out adequately; rest is tree)
II. 22"	4" 1. Two bees.	D	F+	A	(top red) Have little feet, little ears, noses.
	2. And two dogs kissing. Two bees with two dogs kissing each other.	W	FM	A P	Because they're kissing.
III. 13"	3" 1. Two skinny men.	W	F+	H P	See head, and feet and back.
	2. And butterfly.	D	FC (Denial)	A P	(center red) Has wings and colors.
	3. And two dogs with the butterfly.				(denies dogs now)
IV. 20"	5" 1. This is like a monkey. Let me see. That's all I know.	W	F−	A	(center lower detail is feet, all rest is monkey)
V. 11"	1" 1. Bee, no, butterfly I mean.	W	F+	A P	Just looks like a butterfly.
	2. And a bee, a big bee.	W	F−	A	(denies then admits, can't really point out parts)
VI. 17"	Is this the right way? V9" 1. Two bears measuring themselves. That's all I know.	W	FMC'	A	(large lower section) Because they got hands and colors. (what colors?) Black.
VII. 29"	9" 1. Yeah, but they have no heads, sheeps like, play ring-around-arosy. (top two thirds)	D	FMC'	A	Sheeps because they got body and legs, this could be head, and they're white.

					Response	Inquiry
VIII. 18"	D	F+	A		6" 1. This is like a lion.	(usual) Got four feet.
	D	F+	Obj	P	2. Ship.	Has this and this, makes it go. (points to top gray and lower center)
IX. 11"	D	F+	A		3" 1. This is lobsters.	(orange) Got little things. (points to claw-like extensions)
					And that's all I know.	
X. 18"	D	F+	A		5" 1. Lobster.	Has these things. (side blue) (points to leglike extensions)
	D	F+	Obj		2. Wishbone.	(usual) Looks like it.
	D	FM	A		3. Fishes.	(top gray) Saying "I'll break your head if you bother me."
	D	F–	A		4. Crocodile.	(side brown) Got a mouth like that.
					And that's all I know.	

R   18

W	4⎫		F+	9⎫12		A	15		P	5
W	3⎬8		F−	3⎭		H	1			
D→W	1⎭					Obj	2			
			FM	3(1−)		Pl	0 + 1			
D	10		FMC'	2						

FC   1

W	44%		F	67%		A	83%
D	56%		F+	75%			

$$M : C$$
$$0 : \tfrac{1}{2}$$

$$Fm + FM : C' + c$$
$$5 : 1$$

$$VIII + IX + X = 39\%$$

The intellectual limitations of this girl are indicated by her lack of mature identification (no M) and her extremely stereotyped thinking (83 per cent A). The quality of the responses likewise shows marked immaturity and a lack of resource and richness.

Although she is intellectually limited, it is evident that this girl has some awareness of environmental demands and is capable of some control and conformity (1 FC). However, she withdraws from the environment (very low color sum), probably because she finds little satisfaction in her contacts with it and sees it as a frustrating force (2 FC' responses). Instead of releasing her feelings in an outgoing direction, she works them out in fantasy of very childish order (no M, 5 FM). On the whole, these fantasies are of a passive nature and indicate a strong need for acceptance (Card II, "two dogs kissing," "two bees kissing"; Card VII, "two sheep playing ring-around-arosy"). Her concern about her own effectiveness is suggested by her interpretation on Card VI, "two bears measuring themselves." What she fears finds expression on Card X, "Fish saying 'I'll break your head if you bother me.'" It is most probably this rejecting, punitive attitude that causes her to withdraw and at the same time to strive so desperately to control and conform.

While there is no doubt that this an an intellectually limited girl, her reactions to the Rorschach test raise some question as to the validity of the I.Q. That she is using her energy primarily to repress her impulses and achieve conformity is obvious. This repression is bound to have repercussions in the intellectual as well as in the emotional sphere. It she were less anxious to please and less inhibited, it is possible that she would function more effectively and vigorously, and attain a somewhat higher score.

This girl is the second of three children, all girls. The general mental level of the family appears to be in the dull normal to low average range. This girl's functioning is therefore somewhat below that of the other members of her family. She has been made to feel that she is inadequate, that she is stupid and unacceptable, and more or less in everybody's way. Even her younger sister is able to dominate her, and the older one definitely "pushes her around." She submits to this pushing in the hope that by accepting whatever the environment offers, she will be accepted. Overtly she is docile but given to telling tales which are clearly fantasy productions. These stories deal with her acceptance by other children, the invitations they extend to her and the parties they make for her. It was because of these tales, this acting out of her dreams and needs, that she was referred for psychiatric care.

RECORD No. 40

Boy, Age 9 Years 2 Months, I.Q. 65

I.
30" W F+ A P
(Looks around the room)
15" 1. Butterfly. (in questioning voice) (urged)
Don't see no more.
Just looks like a butterfly.

II.
14" W F− Pl
5"
9" 1. Flower.
Don't know.
Don't see no more.
Like a round circle.

III.
18" W F+ H P
     D F+ A P
     D Cm Light
3" 1. Man.
2. Butterfly.
3. Light.
And I don't know this. (points to lower center)
Got a head and hand and feet.
(center red) Got wings.
(side red) Red, climbing up like.

IV.
40" W FM− A(?)
     W F−   A
10" 1. Butterfly.
2. Cockroach.
It's not a butterfly, it's something climbing. (what?) I don't know.
Just looks like it.

V.
7" W F+ A P
3" 1. Butterfly.
That's all.
There he is, cause he looks like one.

VI.
32" D F− A
     D F− Obj
     D F+ H
5"
15" I never saw this before.
1. Pigeon.
2. Statue.
3. Man.
That's all.
(top detail) I don't know.
(top detail) I don't know. (of what?) Of Liberty.
(top detail) I don't know.

Card / Time	Loc.	Det.	Content	Response	Inquiry
VII. 13"	D	F+	H	4" 1. Indians.	(top two thirds) Because they got a feather in their head.
	D	F+	A	2. Butterfly.	(lower third) Got a bead and wings.
VIII. 20"	D	F−	A	4" 1. Cockroaches. That's all.	(usual animal) Got four legs.
IX. 28"	D	F−	A	4" I don't know. 7" 1. Cow.	(orange) He looks like one, but I don't know.
(Denial)					No butterfly there.
	D	F+	H	2. Butterfly. 3. Man.	(orange) Got a head and body.
X. 32"	D	F+	A	10" (makes a distressed sound) 22" That I don't even know. 27" I don't know. 1. Butterfly.	(usual wishbone) Got wings and a head.
	D	F+	Obj & H	2. Parachute. That's all.	(lower center detail) There's a man on it.

R   18

W   5⎫6   F+   10⎫16   A   10   P   4
W   1⎭   F−   6⎭   H   4 + 1
                                    Pl   1
D   12   FM   1−   Light 1
                                    Obj   2
                Cm   1

W   33%   F   89%   A   56%
D   67%   F+   63%

M   :   C
0   :   1½

Fm + FM   :   C′ + c
1   :   0

VIII + IX + X = 28%

The absence of resources in this subject (no M, only 1 FM, only 1 C) is conspicuous. This boy stays close to what is familiar and obvious (4 popular answers) and, when circumstances become difficult, he will fall back on these familiar concepts even when they are not appropriate (poor "butterfly" responses on IV and IX). His approach and his thinking are on a simple, concrete level, but even so he cannot exercise good judgment and control with any consistency (only 63 per cent F). There is apparently considerable awareness of his own inadequacies (many "I don't know" and similar statements). Despite his limitations, this boy tries to meet the demands that are placed on him, tries to respond to each stimulus with which he is confronted. Thus, even though he protests that he "never saw this before" he stays with the situation and finally comes through with an interpretation. His efforts at complying are especially well demonstrated by his effort to cover all aspects of Card III, and his final admission that he cannot understand the lower center detail of the blot. As the circumstances become more complex (on Cards VI, VIII, IX, X), he no longer makes such an effort, but simply deals with those aspects of the circumstance that he feels he can handle. In this way he manages to maintain some control and conformity.

This is an obese boy, the older of two brothers. He is a conforming, "good" child, the only complaint being his inability to learn. He has recently been placed in a class for children with retarded mental development.

CHAPTER XV

The Rorschach Test and Psychotherapy

PSYCHOTHERAPY WITH CHILDREN is a term that covers a wide range of activities, including play therapy, intensive psychoanalysis, support and guidance, and varying forms of treatment which seek to alter feelings and habit patterns either with or without providing insight into the nature and meaning of these patterns. The child in need of psychotherapy is obviously a child whose conflicts, insecurity, and anxiety interfere with his ability to resolve his problems constructively, and whose energy is therefore absorbed by self-defeating forms of behavior rather than devoted to the normal developmental processes. If his anxiety and conflict can be alleviated, more energy becomes available for the ongoing, unfolding activity that is part of childhood development.*

Almost every disturbed child, unless he is a very low grade defective or a seriously deteriorated "organic," finds some relief from his tensions and disturbances in a therapeutic relationship. However, the extent to which he can benefit, the goals that the therapist should set, can be more clearly and accurately defined if he has knowledge of the nature of the child's conflicts, their intensity, the extent to which they involve the total personality structure, and the assets and liabilities that are present as aids and hindrances in the relearning process he is undertaking with his patient. The Rorschach findings can definitely add to any information he has as the result of his preliminary conferences with the parents and the child. While his contacts with the child in the therapeutic relationship will eventually yield him this information, the Rorschach findings provide it in advance, and so help him avoid certain detours and blind alleys. With the evaluation and information provided by test results, the therapist can more easily determine the type of therapeutic relationship that will develop, how far he can go in working with a particular child, and what he can look forward to at the termination of treatment.

The universal problem in all therapy is to help the individual alter his feelings about and perception of himself, of others, and of the relationship that exists between himself and others. Important in this connection is the self that the individual does not permit to come into consciousness, the self against which all his defensive efforts are geared. Concomitantly, there

---

* One of the most important bits of evidence in this connection is the almost inevitable rise in I.Q. which follows as the result of even a limited experience in therapy.

is the self that the individual tries to present to the world, the self he feels he should be or tries to convince others he is. The self which does not come into awareness to any great extent or with any frequency is compounded of some of the reflected attitudes of others plus certain needs and fears that the individual child has experienced throughout the course of his life, while the second self is the result of training and identification. All the attitudes and habits that the child has developed are the outgrowth of these two concepts of himself and his need to maintain them in a certain relationship to one another.

What the individual's unconscious concept of himself is can be obtained from the Rorschach in a variety of ways (pp. 54 f.). His fantasies as reflected in his human movement interpretations; his unacceptable impulses which are ascribed to animals; the defenses he employs in keeping these fantasies and impulses out of awareness; the experiences and feelings he is defending against; the things he fears and the things he seeks, all give clues to the nature of his basic self-concept. The test findings must be used in inferential fashion in this connection, against the examiner's background of clinical experience. Handled in this manner they yield very accurate information about the "basic self."

The "self" that the child wishes to present to the world can also be determined in part from the nature of the defenses he employs, what he is defending against, and the aspects of his experiences that he emphasizes in his communications with others. In the sense that the same mechanisms are applied to keep certain aspects of the self out of awareness and also to make certain impressions on others, the two selves can be considered opposite sides of the same coin.

The gap that obtains between these two concepts of the self gives a measure of the "distance" the individual must travel in the course of therapy. In some cases the distance is so great and the individual's strength so limited that goals must necessarily remain limited and prognosis guarded. Where the distance between the two concepts of self is very small or non-existent, there is again a very poor prognosis for therapy.* The optimum distance that must obtain between these two concepts cannot be defined in exact numerical terms, certainly not at our present state of understanding and measurement, but clinically it is possible to recognize when the relationship is a profitable one for therapy and when it is not. There must, of course, be sufficient conflict and anxiety to motivate the individual to seek to change, but this must not be of such proportions as to make it impossible for him to make constructive efforts in such a direction.

In addition to evaluating the "distance" to be covered by therapy, the

* For example, the psychotic who has accepted his fantasies of himself and presents these to the environment as the self he wishes other to see is almost inaccessible to therapy as long as this fusion between his two concepts of himself holds.

test findings can give indication of the assets the child possesses which can be effectively mobilized in attempting to alter his concepts of himself and of the picture he wishes to present to others. Where there are good capacities for symbolic and fantasy experience, these can be used for role playing and problem solving. Where constriction is extreme, release of this will be undertaken slowly. Where anxiety is overwhelming, a strong supportive relationship may be emphasized initially, and so on.

Furthermore, the test results will indicate whether or not the child has the ability to make an emotional contact with others, as well as the level at which such a contact will be made and the ends to which it will be employed. The child who gives no color answers or perhaps only one color answer will be difficult to reach because he has turned away from the environment and is minimally responsive to emotional pressure from the outside. On the other hand, the child who has little or no capacity for internalizing his feelings may relate on a very dependent and demanding basis, but it will be difficult to move him from this level to a more self-sufficient one.

The test results can also shed light on the core problems with which the individual is struggling and the significant objects involved in these problems. That these are almost inevitably the parents goes without saying but, in each individual case, the nature of the subject's perception of these figures—father and mother—can provide the therapist with evidence regarding the exact nature of these problems and also with some indication of the type of relationship the child is likely to set up with him. Thus the child who has always tried to manipulate the parents is very likely to attempt the same operations with the therapist, and it is very important for the therapist to know this in advance. Again, there is the child who will use the therapist simply to satisfy his dependency needs. As long as the therapist fills this role, the relationship survives, while any effort at doing more than supportive therapy may seriously threaten, if not completely destroy, the relationship.

Knowing what the child's core problems are does not mean that the therapist will immediately attack them. The chances are that he will avoid them for a considerable time, certainly until he has cemented the relationship and the transference is a strong one. Nevertheless, knowing well in advance what the critical problems are, how the patient feels about these problems, and the significant figures associated with them, will enable the therapist to plan his approach to the child and his troubles in more meaningful fashion. He will have a map of the territory he will eventually invade, and will be better able to interpret everything the subject says and does, since he knows in advance what is responsible for the particular attitudes and habits the child has developed.

Finally, there is the difficult question that always comes up in connection with disturbances in children, namely, is this disturbance simply a passing manifestation, something to be ignored, or is it a symptom associated with a basic disturbance which therefore demands treatment? For example, there is the child who suddenly begins to wet the bed after having been dry for several years; or the child who suddenly presents eating problems where none previously existed. There are two ways in which the Rorschach can be helpful in this connection. If the personality picture portrayed through the test findings is a relatively stable, well integrated one (in terms of what can be expected for the child's age and ability), it is very likely that the present symptom is merely a passing manifestation, not an indication of deep underlying disturbance. On the other hand, if there is evidence of much anxiety and conflict, the immediate symptom is probably an expression of this disturbance and therefore requires professional attention.

The other way in which the Rorschach test can shed light on this question of the significance of a symptom is in its predictive value. A number of therapists have commented on the fact that the Rorschach findings frequently are more indicative of what is likely to happen in six months to a year's time than of the immediate adjustment. Thus, if the test points to relatively smooth, integrated functioning, the chances are that the immediate disturbance is of a temporary order, and will disappear in a short time; whereas if the picture that the test presents is a disturbed one, it is likely that the present maladjustment is a forerunner of a general maladjustment.

Despite the advances that have been made in the treatment of emotionally and mentally disturbed patients, therapy is still, to a large extent, in a "trial and error" stage. Anything which can serve to clarify its goals and direction is an invaluable tool. This the Rorschach has proved itself to be. With its aid better understanding of personality development and functioning can be obtained, and the nature of the therapeutic relationship and the end results in therapy can be estimated.

Selected Bibliography

1 AMES, L. B., LEARNED, J., METRAUX, R. W., AND WALKER, R. N.: Child Rorschach Responses. New York, Paul B. Hoeber, Inc., 1952.
2 BECK, S. J.: Rorschach's Test, Vol. I, II, III. New York, Grune & Stratton, 1944, 1945, 1952.
3 ——: The Rorschach test in problem children. Am. J. Orthopsychiat., 1: 501–509, 1931.
4 BELLAK, L.: The concept of projection: an experimental investigation and study of the concept. Psychiatry, 7: 353–370, 1944.
5 —— AND ABT, L.: Projective Psychology: Clinical Approaches to the Total Personality. New York, Knopf, 1950.
6 BENDER, L.: Childhood schizophrenia. Am. J. Orthopsychiat., 17: 40–56, 1947.
7 ——: Problems of children with organic brain disease. Am. J. Orthopsychiat., 20: 404–415, 1950.
8 BOCHNER, R. AND HALPERN, F.: The Clinical Application of the Rorschach Test, ed. 2. New York, Grune & Stratton, 1945.
9 DAVIDSON, H. AND KLOPFER, B.: Rorschach statistics: Part 2, normal children. Rorschach Res. Exch., 3: 37–43, 1938.
10 DAY, F., HARTOCH, A., AND SCHACHTEL, E.:A Rorschach study of a defective delinquent. J. Crim. Psychopathol., 2: 62–79, 1940.
11 DES LAURIERS, A. AND HALPERN, F.: Psychological tests in childhood schizophrenia. Am. J. Orthopsychiat., 17: 57–67, 1947.
12 FENICHEL, O.: The Psychoanalytic Theory of the Neuroses. New York, Norton, 1945.
13 FORD, M.: The application of the Rorschach test to young children. Univ. Minn. Child Welf. Monogr., No. 23, 1946.
14 FRANK, L.: Projective Methods. Springfield, Charles C Thomas, 1948.
15 FREUD, A.: The Ego and the Mechanisms of Defense. New York, International Universities Press, 1946.
16 FREUD, S.: A General Introduction to Psychoanalysis. New York, Boni and Liveright, 1920.
17 ——: New Introductory Lectures in Psychoanalysis. New York, Norton, 1933.
18 ——: The Problem of Anxiety. New York, Norton, 1936.
19 GAIR, M.: Rorschach characteristics of a group of very superior seven year old children. Rorschach Res. Exch., 8: 31–37, 1944.
20 GANN, E.: Reading Difficulty and Personality Organization. New York, Kings Crown Press, 1945.
21 GOLDFARB, W.: Personality traits in a group of enuretic children below age ten. Rorschach Res. Exch., 6: 28–38, 1942.
22 ——: Rorschach responses of institutional children. Rorschach Res. Exch., 8: 92–100, 1944.
23 ——: Effects of early institutional care on adolescent personality: Rorschach data. Am. J. Orthopsychiat., 14: 441–447, 1944.
24 ——: Psychological privation in infancy and subsequent adjustment. Am. J. Orthopsychiat., 15: 247–255, 1945.
25 ——: Rorschach test differences between family-reared, institution-reared and schizophrenic children. Am. J. Orthopsychiat., 19: 624–633, 1949.

[26] HALPERN, F.: An investigation into the nature and intensity of the anxiety experienced by three clinical groups of children at two different age levels and of the defenses they develop against their anxiety. Ann Arbor, Univ. Microfilms, No. 2763, 1951. *Also* Ph.D. thesis, New York University, School of Education, 1951.

[27] HERTZ, M. R.: The Rorschach ink-blot test: historical summary. Psychol. Bull., *32:* 33–66, 1935.

[28] ——: Evaluation of the Rorschach method and its application to normal childhood and adolescence. Charac. & Pers., 1941.

[29] —— AND MARGULIES, H.: Developmental changes as reflected in the Rorschach test responses. J. Genet. Psychol., *62:* 189–215, 1943.

[30] —— AND EBERT, E.: The mental procedure of six and eight year old children as revealed by the Rorschach ink-blot method. Rorschach Res. Exch., *8:* 10–30, 1944.

[31] HERTZMAN, M. AND MARGULIES, H.: Developmental changes in Rorschach test responses. J. Genet. Psychol., *62:* 189–216, 1943.

[32] KAY, L. W. AND VORHAUS, P. G.: Rorschach reactions in early childhood. Part 2: intellectual aspects of personality development. Rorschach Res. Exch., *7:* 71–77, 1943.

[33] KERR, M.: The Rorschach test applied to children. Brit. J. Psychol., *25:* 170–185, 1934.

[34] KLOPFER, B.: Personality diagnosis in early childhood: application of the Rorschach method at the preschool level. Psychological Bulletin, *36:* 662, 1939.

[35] ——: Personality differences between boys and girls in early childhood. Psychological Bulletin, *36:* 538, 1939.

[36] ——: Personality diagnosis in childhood. *Chapter in* LEWIS, N. D. C. AND PACELLA, B. I.: Modern Trends in Child Psychiatry. New York, International Universities Press, 1945.

[37] —— AND KELLEY, D.: The Rorschach Technique: A Manual for a Projective Method of Personality Study. New York, World Book Co., 1946.

[38] —— AND MARGULIES, H.: Rorschach reactions in early childhood. Rorschach Res. Exch., *5:* 1–23, 1941.

[39] KRUGMAN, J.: A clinical validation of the Rorschach with problem children. Rorschach Res. Exch., *6:* 61–70, 1942.

[40] KRUGMAN, M.: Rorschach examination in a child guidance clinic. Am. J. Orthopsychiat., *11:* 503–512, 1941.

[41] ——: Psychosomatic study of stuttering children: Rorschach study. Am. J. Orthopsychiat., *1:* 127–133, 1946.

[42] LOOSLI-USTERI, M.: Le test de Rorschach appliqué à differents groups d'enfants de 10–13 ans. Arch. de Psychol., *22:* 51–106, 1929.

[43] ——: Le Diagnostic Individuel chez l'Enfant au Moyen du Test de Rorschach. Paris, Hermann, 1937.

[44] LOPFE, A.: Über Rorschachschen Formendeuteversuche mit 10–13 jahringen Knaben. Ztschr. f. ang. Psychol., *26:* 202–233, 1926.

[45] MAHLER, M. S., ROSS, J. R., JR., AND DE FRIES, Z.: Clinical studies in benign and malignant cases of childhood psychosis (schizophrenic-like). Am. J. Orthopsychiat., *19:* 295–305, 1949.

[46] McFATE, M. Q. AND ORR, F. F.: Through adolescence with the Rorschach. Rorschach Res. Exch., *13:* 302–319, 1949.

[47] MEER, B. AND SINGER, J. L.: A note on the "father" and "mother" cards in the Rorschach inkblots. J. Consult. Psychol., *4:* 482–484, 1950.

[48] MELTZER, H.: Personality differences between stuttering and non-stuttering children as indicated by the Rorschach test. Psychol. Bull., *30:* 726–727, 1933.

⁴⁹ MURPHY, G.: Personality. New York, Harper & Bros., 1949.
⁵⁰ PAULSEN, A.: Rorschachs of school beginners. Rorschach Res. Exch., 5: 179–185, 1941.
⁵¹ PEARSON, G. H. J.: Emotional Disorders of Children. New York, Norton, 1949.
⁵² PIOTROWSKI, Z.: A comparison of congenitally defective children with schizophrenic children in regard to personality structure and intelligence type. Proc. Am. Ass. Ment. Def., 61: 78–90, 1937.
⁵³ ——: Rorschach records of children with a tic syndrome. Nerv. Child., 4: 342–352, 1945.
⁵⁴ ——: A Rorschach compendium, rev. ed. Psychiat. Quart., 24: 543–596, 1950.
⁵⁵ —— AND LEWIS, N. D. C.: A case of stationary schizophrenia beginning in early childhood with remarks on certain aspects of children's Rorschach records. Quart. J. Child Behav., 2: 115–139, 1950.
⁵⁶ RABIN, A. I. AND BECK, S. J.: Genetic aspects of some Rorschach factors. Am. J. Orthopsychiat., 20: 595–599, 1950.
⁵⁷ RAPAPORT, D.: Diagnostic Psychological testing, Vol. II. Chicago, Year Book Publishers, 1946.
⁵⁸ RICHARDS, T. W. The individual child's development as reflected by the Rorschach performance. Rorschach Res. Exch., 12: 57–64, 1948.
⁵⁹ RORSCHACH, H.: Psychodiagnostics. Bern, Hans Huber, 1942. New York, Grune & Stratton (distrib.), 1942.
⁶⁰ SCHACHTEL, A. H.: The Rorschach test with young children. Am. J. Orthopsychiat., 14: 1–9, 1944.
⁶¹ —— AND LEVI, M. B.: Character structure of day nursery children. Am. J. Orthopsychiat., 15: 213–222, 1945.
⁶² SCHACHTEL, E. G.: Contributions to an understanding of Rorschach's test. I. The dynamic perception and symbolism of form; II. On color and affect; III. Subjective definition of the Rorschach test situation. Psychiatry, 4: 76–96, 1941; 6: 393–409, 1943; 8: 410–448, 1945.
⁶³ SENDER, S. AND KLOPFER, B.: Application of the Rorschach test to child behavior problems as facilitated by a refinement of the scoring method. Rorschach Res. Exch., 1: 5–17, 1936.
⁶⁴ SIEGEL, M.: The diagnostic and prognostic validity of the Rorschach test in a child guidance clinic. Am. J. Orthopsychiat., 18: 119–133, 1948.
⁶⁵ STRAVIANOS, B.: An investigation of sex differences in children as revealed by the Rorschach method. Rorschach Res. Exch., 6: 168–175, 1942.
⁶⁶ SULLIVAN, H. S.: Conceptions of modern psychiatry. Washington, D. C., William Alanson White Psychiatric Foundation, 1947. (Reprinted from Psychiatry, 3: 1 and 8: 2.)
⁶⁷ THETFORD, W. N., MOLISH, H. B., AND BECK, S. J.: Developmental aspects of personality structure in normal children. J. Proj. Tech., 15: 58–78, 1951.
⁶⁸ TROUP, E.: A comparative study by means of the Rorschach method of personality development in twenty pairs of identical twins. Genet. Psychol. Monogr., 20: 461–556, 1938.
⁶⁹ VORHAUS, P. G.: Rorschach reactions in early childhood. III. Content and details in preschool records. Rorschach Res. Exch., 8: 71–91, 1944.
⁷⁰ ——: Non-reading as an expression of resistance. Rorschach Res. Exch., 10: 60–69, 1946.
⁷¹ ——: Rorschach configurations associated with reading disability. J. Proj. Tech., 16: 3–19, 1952.
⁷² WERNER, H.: Rorschach method applied to two clinical groups of mental defectives. Am. J. Ment. Deficiency, 49: 304–306, 1945.

Index

Adjustment, evaluation of, 5
Age patterns
  four and a half to six year olds, 3, 69 f.,
    78 f., 114 f.
  six to ten year olds, 3, 71 f., 79 f.
  two and a half to four year olds, 3, 67 f.,
    76 f.
Animal responses. *See* Content
Anxiety, 56 f.
Approach, 24
Architecture. *See* Content

Bender, L., 182, 189, 261
Bridges. *See* Content

Card turning, 43
Cards, 45 f.
CAT, 10
Caves. *See* Content
Color
  achromatic
    scoring, 19
    significance of, 32 f.
  chromatic
    scoring, 19
    significance of, 32 f
Constitutional factors, 1
Content
  scoring, 20
  significance of, 36 f.

De Fries, Z., 182, 262
Defense mechanisms, 59 f.
  deflection, 63
  denial, 61
  detachment, 61
  doing and undoing, 61
  flight, 62
  identification, 62
  projection, 62
  reaction formation, 61
  regression, 63
  repression, 59
  sublimation, 63
Denial. *See* Defense mechanisms
Detachment. *See* Defense mechanisms

Details
  large
    scoring, 17 f.
    significance of, 22
  small
    scoring, 18
    significance of, 23
Development
  phases in 1, 2 f.

Ego strength, 63
Emotionally disturbed child, 111 f.
Examiner, 52 f.
Experience balance
  scoring, 33
  significance of, 34
Explosions. *See* Content

Fire. *See* Content
Flight. *See* Defense mechanisms
Flowers. *See* Content
Form
  scoring, 18
  significance of, 24 f.

Gann, E., 113, 261
Geography. *See* Content
Goldfarb, W., 113, 261

House. *See* Content
Human responses. *See* Content

Identification, 55
  See also Defense mechanisms

Krugman, M., 113, 262

Leaf. *See* Content

Mahler, M. S., 182, 262
Map. *See* Content
Mental retardation, 249 f.
Movement
  scoring, 19
  significance of, 26 f.